The Ultimate Benefit Book

HOW TO RAISE
$50,000-PLUS
FOR YOUR ORGANIZATION

The Ultimate Benefit Book

HOW TO RAISE $50,000-PLUS FOR YOUR ORGANIZATION

Marilyn E. Brentlinger
Judith M. Weiss

OCTAVIA CLEVELAND, OHIO

Published by Octavia Press, 3546 Edison Road, Cleveland, Ohio 44121, 216-381-2853.

Design by Donna Lipson

Library of Congress Cataloging in Publication Data

Brentlinger, Marilyn E., 1925-
    The ultimate benefit book.

    Includes index.
    1. Fund raising.   I. Weiss, Judith M., 1950-
II. Title.
HG177.B74   1987   361.7′068′1   87-12171
ISBN 0-940601-01-X

To all the volunteers, staff professionals, underwriters and patrons whose contributions, in support of vital not-for-profit organizations, ultimately benefit the communities in which they live

Table of Contents

Discipline With Discretion • Role of the Board of Trustees

Acknowledgements

We wish to thank our many friends, new and old, in the benefit "business" who have so generously shared their experiences with us. Their names are listed below. Special gratitude is due to Dean R. Gladden, Mark A. Randol, barb Richardson, Bill Rudman, Richard S. Pollak and Audrey S. Watts for reading parts or all of the manuscript. Their corrections and comments helped to immeasurably improve the finished work. However, all errors, whether of omission or commission, are our own.

Mary T. Abbott
Marge Alge
Paul E. Altig
Phyllis Baker
Lin Bartel
Betsy Beckwith
Barbara Bornhorst
Albert I. Borowitz
Ralph Brody
Marilyn K. Brown
Gina Ciresi
Betty Cope
Anita Cosgrove
John P. Craig
Patricia Jansen Doyle
Chet Edwards
Cindy Einhouse
Richard W. Evans
Marianne Evett
Bonnie Femec
Shirley C. Fernberg
Robert F. Frankel
George Fraser
Jean Frazier
Barbara Y. Galvin
Wally Gbur
Robert E. Geuder
Elaine Gilbert
Rocco Gioia
Dean R. Gladden
Marcie Goodman
Nancy W. Goslee
Bobby Griesinger
Linda C. Griffith

Marietta Gullia
Elaine G. Hadden
Richard H. Hahn
Donna Hartley
Barbara Janowitz Ehrlich
David G. Kangesser
Judy Kauffman
J. Richard Kelso
R. Eric Kennedy
Nancy Bigler Kersey
Gerrie King
Mary Elizabeth Klein
Lena La Rose
Susan Levine
Teri Levine
Barbara Meals
Frederick G. Meissner, Jr.
Margaret Mitchell
Mark D. Mittleman
Lindsay Jordan Morgenthaler
Helen F. Moss
Janet Neary
Peg Neeson
Amy M. Nelson
Kevin O'Donnell
Polly Paffilas
Mary Papandreas
Joanne Parrino
Julie Paulus
Robert Pavey
Elsa Pavlik
Sue Peay
Charles M. Phillips
Robert S. Pile

Anthony J. Poderis
Richard S. Pollak
Mark A. Randol
barb Richardson
Cici Riley
Barbara S. Robinson
Bill Rudman
Sue Sackman
Larry J. Santon
Diann G. Scaravilli
Lynn Schmelzer
Mary Anne Schmitz
Sandra R. Schwartz
Marcia Shanafelt
Ben Shouse
Thomas G. Stafford
Julie A. Stahler
Carol Story
Karen K. Strang
Mary Strassmeyer
Holly Strawbridge
K.K. Sullivan
Andrea Taylor
Sarina Teta
Kathleen Teltsch
Peter Tomko
Martha Towns
Onetha Trammer
Susan Valentine
Jana Van Vliet
Audrey S. Watts
Margaret S. Wheeler
Suzie Wiley
Betty Zekan

Foreword

As one who has attended many a benefit — black-tie and otherwise — in my capacity as chairperson of the New York State Council on the Arts, I think that there is a definite place for them in the volunteer fund-raiser's arsenal. This does not mean that I believe it appropriate to spend enormous amounts on party decorations and refreshments, however. The philanthropic rule of thumb is that at least 70 percent of the proceeds of a fund-raising event should go to the charitable cause it is intended to support. All benefit planners should strive to match or surpass this percentage of net profit.

Those who share my belief that fund raising is a discipline as well as an art will welcome the publication of this book. Not only because, until *The Ultimate Benefit Book*, there has been no handy and complete reference on the "special-occasion" gala. But primarily because *The Ultimate Benefit Book* approaches benefits as a *business*, not as a hobby.

Generating the most income possible from these events is important for several reasons. First, there is the obvious consequence of a middling success on the volunteers' morale. Second, it's a necessity in this era of decreased government support of all not-for-profits. Finally, there's the matter of competition. With tax reform making individual and corporate patrons more choosy about their charitable "investments," those benefits that can guarantee a significant percent of one's ticket price will go straight into the organization's coffers are most likely to be supported.

I applaud this book's publication on another count. I have long been interested in the role of women in society. In 1966 I chaired New York's Statewide Conference on Women and later I was appointed special consultant to Governor Nelson Rockefeller on women's opportunities. I am happy to report that, in their eagerness to explore new horizons, most women I've met have not abandoned volunteerism — difficult as it may be to juggle this activity with a career and/or motherhood. And I'm delighted that a new generation of women (and — yes — a growing number of men!) who volunteer in their spare time or in their professional capacities will now be able to more readily acquire the management skills and savvy that previously came only from a lifetime of committed volunteerism.
Kitty Carlisle Hart

Introduction

"Doesn't everyone already know how to do benefits?" asked one of the virtuoso volunteers we interviewed when we began research for *The Ultimate Benefit Book*. "There are so many benefits already, are you sure you want to encourage more?" asked another.

We're well aware that in most big cities today there are more fund-raising dinners and special events than even the most enthusiastic patron could attend. We don't have to *encourage* groups to mount benefits — they are already doing so. In these uncertain economic times, more and more not-for-profit organizations are jumping on the benefit bandwagon, seeking to keep up with escalating operating costs, to replace government funds that have been cut back and to expand their bases of support. And organizations and volunteers entering this competitive arena for the first time need expert guidance and advice.

For a long time, benefits were run by an "old girl" network of full-time volunteers, with younger women learning the ropes by assisting their more experienced colleagues. Though this hierarchical training system still exists in many communities, volunteerism is no longer the career of choice for most young women. Instead, we're seeing more corporate and professional women and men giving their time to work on benefits — whether as "loaned executives" representing their companies or as individuals seeking the personal satisfaction that can only be found in community service. This diversity, we believe, is all to the good — but it does mean that the new volunteers may have a lot to learn quickly.

We have written *The Ultimate Benefit Book* in order to help volunteers and the boards of trustees and staff members of not-for-profit organizations learn, by instruction and by example, the artful business of mounting profitable benefits. We hope, likewise, to help them avoid some of the pitfalls that await the inexperienced. We cringe when we hear well-meaning volunteers say: "We don't expect to make much money on this benefit, but it's okay as long as we break even." Benefit committees need to have a clear sense of purpose, to generate profits as well as pleasure and to view publicity, not as an end in itself, but as a means to build long-term support for their organizations.

The impetus for this book grew out of a feature story published in Northern Ohio LIVE magazine, a monthly arts and entertainment publication based in Cleveland, Ohio. When we — Marilyn Brent-linger, with 25 years' experience as a benefit volunteer as well as a stint as staff development director of a not-for-profit organization, and Judith Weiss, free-lance writer, former development/public relations director and occasional benefit volunteer — first met in the spring of 1985, it was at the request of Diana Tittle, then editor of LIVE. We had gathered to discuss a story that we all agreed needed to be written. The idea was to look behind the glitter and glamour of benefits and examine the social and economic forces that drive them. Diana suggested that Judith follow one event from start to finish, observing how committees are formed, how decisions are made and, above all, how much of the money raised actually goes into the coffers of the deserving not-for-profit organization.

The event to be observed, she had decided, was The Ball at the Halle Building, a fund-raiser for the Great Lakes Theater Festival for which Marilyn was serving as chairperson. Because the occasion was to be the grand reopening of an historic building that had housed the late, lamented Halle Bros. department store, and because the volunteer committee had received extensive underwriting from the building's owner-developer, The Ball seemed the ideal event to serve as the story's vehicle.

Following Marilyn, her accomplished volunteer committee and their savvy corporate collaborators for six months proved to be an eye-opening experience for Judith (who had had some experience with benefits) and Diana (who had little behind-the-scenes knowledge of such events). By the time Diana left Northern Ohio LIVE to start Octavia Press, both she and Judith were convinced that the know-how required to organize a successful benefit ought to be codified in book form and that Marilyn's hard-won expertise in just such matters was worthy of dissemination and emulation. The next step was to persuade Marilyn to collaborate with Judith, a proposal she enthusiastically embraced.

We have chosen to draw the examples that illustrate various management points primarily from the Cleveland area; most of the outside experts interviewed live here, too. This was a matter of choice rather than convenience. Cleveland boasts an exceptionally lively, diverse and sophisticated benefit scene that is still dominated by hands-on volunteers. Of the 12 largest arts organizations (with annual operating budgets of $400,000 or more) in this part of the state, the Ohio Arts Council reports that nine raised a total of $1,031,762 through benefits held in fiscal 1984-85 (the latest year for which figures are available). In the years since then, two more of the 12 organizations on this list have begun annual benefits, and the one remaining institution is expected to enter the field soon. In addition to these groups (the only ones whose income from benefits the Ohio Arts Council tracks), dozens of smaller arts organizations, to say nothing of hospitals and other social-service agencies in our region, are raising significant sums through benefits.

In fact, our community has a national reputation for philanthropy. In 1914 Clevelanders created the first community trust; today The Cleveland Foundation annually awards grants in excess of $20 million. The Cleveland-area United Way, to cite another prominent example, consistently reports the highest per-capita giving for any major city in the country. To the best of our abilities we have condensed the savvy of the entire community on the subject of benefit fund raising into a single reference source of ideas, inspiration and proven strategies for success.

For her role in this endeavor, we wish to express special thanks to Diana Tittle, our editor and publisher. Her good influence is evident on every page of this manuscript, and her confidence in the merits of the project sustained us through the 18 months it took to complete the research and writing. Thanks are also due to Kitty Carlisle Hart for contributing the foreword. Our deepest gratitude and love belong to Paul S. Brentlinger and Robert Weiss, who provided much-appreciated support, both moral and otherwise; to David Brentlinger, who was the first to encourage his mother to share her expertise, and to Alexander Weiss, Judith's baby boy, who joined us midway through the project and injected a delightful dose of levity into our frequent editorial meetings.

Marilyn E. Brentlinger
Judith M. Weiss
Cleveland, Ohio
July 1987

To Benefit or Not?

So, you want to have a benefit. Welcome to the club! If you've ever worked on a benefit committee before, you know how much fun *and* hard work a successful benefit can be. If you've ever attended one, you've no doubt been caught up in the glamour and excitement of an important social event at the same time that you've felt the satisfaction of contributing to a worthy cause. And if you haven't done either—well, where have you been hiding?

Benefits are all around us; hardly a week goes by without the newspapers featuring previews and pictures of this or that organization's gala ball, auction or fashion show. With fewer federal dollars available since the beginning of the decade, more and more not-for-profit organizations are turning to benefits these days as a way to boost contributed income to help meet ever-rising expenses. Such events are popular because they give volunteers the opportunity to exercise their creativity while providing much-needed support for their favorite organizations.

Successful events don't just happen, however; they take months of planning, research, organization and endless detail work in order to run smoothly and achieve their goals. This has never been more true than it is today, when competition among benefits—for choice dates, new ideas, volunteers' time and patron support—is increasing.

In the Cleveland area, where the coauthors live, Ohio Arts Council chairperson Barbara Robinson has observed a dramatic rise in the number of these events since she was named to the board in 1983. "I know we're receiving invitations from many more types of organizations than we used to," says Robinson, an experienced benefit organizer and frequent benefit patron herself. "It seems we could go to a benefit a week during the season, and some weekends there are two—sometimes there are even two on the same evening."

The suppliers who work on area benefits confirm Robinson's impressions. David G. Kangesser, chairman of Coyne-Kangesser, Inc., owner of numerous downtown Cleveland parking garages, has developed a "sizeable new undertaking" in the last ten years, providing valet parking service to some three dozen benefits annually. And Robert S. Pile, chairman of Hough Caterers, for many years one of Cleveland's leading catering firms, believes the number of benefits he serves annually has doubled in the last five to six years. "The size of the parties is growing, too," Pile adds, "and there is a greater intensity about them as the prices go up."

Groups and agencies that have never done benefits before are scrambling to test this fund-raising tool. Society columnist Mary Strassmeyer of the Cleveland *Plain Dealer* guesstimates that in the past year she received press releases from no fewer than 30 "new" benefits.

A similar proliferation can be observed on a national level. The Philanthropic Advisory Service (PAS) of the Council of Better Business Bureaus published results in 1985 of a survey of the officers of nearly 500 major industrial, service and advertising firms concerning fund-raising dinners. Those responding to the survey (230 companies) reported attending, in the aggregate, 4,930 such dinners in 1984, or an average of 22 events per company. Some indicated that it's not unusual for their companies to receive up to 400 invitations a year to these events. In 1985 the *Los Angeles Times* counted more than 2,000 dinners and luncheons in support of charitable causes in its metropolitan area alone.

For all the swirl of activity on the benefit scene, most groups that mount such events still raise a relatively small portion of their total operating funds through this means. *But* that amount is increasing. Theatre Communications Group (TCG), a national service organization for not-for-profit professional theaters, found that while a sample study group of 45 member theaters had realized, in the aggregate, only 2.55 percent of their total budgets (taking into account both earned and contributed income) through benefits in 1985-86, the aggregate dollar amount raised by benefits had increased 16.7 percent over the previous year. "Of course, that 2 to 3 percent can mean the difference for some theaters between operating in the red or in the black," points out Barbara Janowitz Ehrlich, TCG director of management services.

Which brings us to the *raison d'etre* for this book: If benefits are playing an ever-more-critical role in the financial health of the country's social and cultural agencies, then it is vital that each and every benefit mounted be a financial as well as aesthetic success.

HERE'S TO YOUR SUCCESS

Whether you are:

• An experienced benefit chairperson looking for new ideas and ways to increase your profits and manage volunteers more effectively;

• A former lieutenant who's just been promoted to general and needs a handy reference manual to help plot your strategy;

- A newcomer who needs a road map through the maze of organizational details;
- A board member responsible for approving and backing a benefit committee's plans;
- A corporate executive or professional who'd like to share your expertise with a deserving organization for reasons of philanthropy, good will and enlightened self-interest; or
- A concerned staff member of an organization on whose behalf a benefit is being given—

The Ultimate Benefit Book is for YOU.

While there are several books available that give an encyclopedic overview of special-events fund raising, there is, to our knowledge, no book-length source of detailed information and advice on how to plan and execute a successful benefit, from the first brainstorming session to the final evaluation. To ensure that your event is as profitable as is possible, we have included step-by-step instructions, as well as:

- Examples of themes and programs you can adapt to create your own unique benefit concept;
- Hints from professional caterers and floral designers to help you turn your ideas into beautiful reality;
- Worksheets, timetables, job descriptions, checklists, charts and forms to help you organize your time and mobilize your team;
- Management advice and philosophy borne of coauthor Marilyn Brentlinger's 25 years' experience in chairing successful benefits, plus the collective wisdom of a number of other top benefit volunteers; and
- Marketing strategies for making profits of $50,000 or more.

Information in *The Ultimate Benefit Book* is arranged roughly in the order in which the benefit process unfolds:

I. To Benefit or Not? helps you determine whether or not a benefit is an appropriate strategy for your organization at this time and, if not, suggests steps you can take to get ready for one.

II. Creating a Concept deals with considerations of location, date and entertainment.

III. Watch Your Figures assists you in putting together a professional budget, with formulas for assessing sources of potential income, estimating expenses and pricing tickets.

IV. Department of Human Resources, Part I helps you assemble an effective volunteer committee and keep it motivated. Complete descriptions for each major responsibility enable you to choose the right person for each job.

V. Department of Human Resources, Part II deals with the potentially tricky relationships between volunteers, paid organization staff members and outside suppliers, along with some suggestions on how to learn to negotiate cooperation as well as price.

VI. Maximizing Profits describes how to secure all-important underwriting and maintain mutually beneficial relations with corporate sponsors, as well as how to mobilize a sales force to assure a sellout.

VII. A Sense of Occasion shows how to make the original benefit concept blossom into an exciting special occasion through creative use of theme, visuals, music, food and drink.

VIII. The Final Countdown helps pull you through the last hectic weeks before the benefit, with a time line of last-minute details to help you keep everything moving on schedule.

IX. It's a Wrap guides you through that post-benefit period of combined exhaustion and euphoria when you need to prepare final reports, thank all participants and put the event into perspective.

As you read this, you may already be deep in the planning stages of a benefit, in which case you'll probably want to go directly to the section that covers your most pressing concerns. We recommend a quick review of the principles outlined in this chapter, however, to reconfirm your goals and help put your responsibilities in perspective. If you are just getting started, this chapter will help you evaluate your resources and ideas, in order to come up with appropriate strategies and goals.

THE BENEFIT CONCEPT

A **benefit**, according to *Webster's Third New International Dictionary*, is:

> an entertainment or social event to raise funds for a person, public program, or cause (a **benefit** luncheon); *specif*: a theatrical performance whose proceeds are given to a particular actor or a designated cause.

This broad definition can apply to many types of fund-raising events, from bingo games for a neighborhood church's building fund to coast-to-coast televised extravaganzas such as the annual United Negro College Fund telethon. Specifically, we are referring to events that are sanctioned and sponsored by legitimately incorporated organizations designated not-for-profit and tax exempt under section 501 (c)(3) of the United States Internal Revenue Code.

Benefits to help a single person are rare these days, and when they do occur, they are more likely aimed at raising money for a sick child who needs an organ transplant than providing a pension for a single actor. Since it usually takes hundreds of people to put on a benefit, the cause has to be important to the whole community.

For the purposes of completeness, we have chosen to narrow our focus to a discussion of what we will call the "special-occasion" benefit: one that brings the "entertainment" and "social event" concepts from the above definition together in one package that is offered for a set, prepaid price that includes a specified amount as a tax-deductible contribution.

Examples of the special-occasion benefit include:

• A black- or white-tie dinner dance in an elegant location featuring big-name entertainment;

• A tribute luncheon honoring a national or community leader, complete with speeches and presentation of plaques by local celebrities and public officials;

• A fashion show staged around a brunch, lunch, cocktails or high tea;

• A cocktail party with hors d'oeuvres concocted by well-known gourmet chefs;

• A theatrical performance followed by supper or a dessert buffet with coffee and liqueurs;

• An auction of rare and precious antiques, art objects or exotic travel packages, following a dinner or reception for patrons;

• A preview party for major donors before a large-scale public event such as an auto race, opening night of the opera, dedication of a building, etc.

Throughout this book, we cite examples drawn from special-occasion benefits of which we have knowledge or personal experience. Two that we will refer to again and again are Fantasy and The Ball at the Halle Building. Both were chaired (co-chaired, in the case of Fantasy) by Marilyn within the year preceding the writing of this book; and both were highly profitable events. Not surprisingly, both were planned and executed according to the principles we shall expound in the course of our discussion. They also illustrate contrasting committee structures, planning processes and levels of sponsorship. We have described them in full in the appendix, along with 18 other successful Cleveland-area benefits, many of which we will also refer to later in the text. In order to appreciate fully the instructions for drafting a budget provided in Chapter III, it will be necessary to familiarize yourself with the write-ups of at least Fantasy and The Ball.

The types of benefits featured in the appendix are distinct from the mass-marketed fund-raiser — such as a rock concert or sporting event — that depends on large numbers of people showing up at the box office. At such events, the ticket price is usually only slightly higher than the normal cost of such events, and any refreshments or souvenirs are extra, just as they would be at a non-benefit. Our featured benefits also differ from such special events as craft fairs and chili cookoffs, which charge a nominal admission, if any, and earn money through the sale of food, merchandise, games, rides, etc.; from participation events such as golf tournaments and running marathons that raise money through entry fees or sponsorship of individual participants; or from telethons and radiothons, which use the media to entertain and exhort their audiences to phone in contributions.

The Cleveland area boasts several outstanding examples of such fund-raisers that have gained nationwide recognition:

The Garden Center of Greater Cleveland's White Elephant Sale grew from an unassuming single booth in 1933 to the status of "largest known rummage sale," in 1983, according to the *Guinness Book of World Records*. The two-day sale, formerly held biennially in Cleveland's downtown convention center, a building the size of seven football fields, required the efforts of 1,500 to 2,000 volunteers and netted an average $200,000 every other year for the garden center's operating budget. It's interesting to note that, after its last giant production in 1985, the organization decided that the event had become too big to manage effectively; as of 1987 the garden center is holding a series of smaller weekend sales and has initiated a preview party to give volunteers first pick of the merchandise for a modest admission price (admission to the main event is free to the general public).

The National Council of Jewish Women, Cleveland Section's Designer Dress Days is a 17-year-old event (variations on this theme are done by a number of NCJW sections in other cities) that in 1986 netted $163,000 to support 22 community service projects through the sale of gently used furs, jewelry and women's clothing. Some 250 volunteers, led by a 28-member steering committee, are active year-round gathering, storing and pricing donated apparel. The sale, held in the council's two-story office building, is free to the public and raises as much in five days as the organization's two storefront resale shops net in a year.

The longest-running orchestra radio marathon in the world is the **WCLV/Cleveland Orchestra Marathon**, which has raised more than $2.5 million in 18 consecutive years, including $220,000 in 1987 for the orchestra's sustaining fund. The Women's Committee of the Cleveland Orchestra works for six months to collect merchandise, gift certificates and donations of private musical performances and other unique services. So expert has WCLV vice president Robert Conrad become at conducting the on-air programs and games designed to stimulate participation that he is frequently invited to consult and appear on other cities' orchestra marathons.

The **WVIZ-Channel 25 Auction** is a highly successful example of the televised auctions held by many public TV stations around the country. The Cleveland station raised $643,115 in nine days on the air in 1987, the local auction's 20th consecutive year. While one full-time staff member is assigned to the auction year-round, the major volunteer effort takes place between January and May, when 600 Go-Getters collect 4,000 items ranging in value from $50 to more than $10,000 (new cars are offered along with artworks, antiques and furnishings at the high end of the scale). During auction week in April, some 1,200 volunteers come to the station to answer telephones, assist with the on-air display of merchandise and tally the auction results.

All these kinds of events, which can be big money-makers, are worth considering, depending on the resources and objectives of your organization. We have chosen, however, to concentrate on the special-occasion benefit because it can be the most profitable type of fund-raiser for the time and money invested. Another reason for limiting our discussion to this type of benefit is that none of the more general references on special-event fund raising goes into great depth on the principles of planning, organization and marketing that we outline here. Even if your organization chooses to sponsor a different type of special event, you should be able to adapt these specifics to your situation. Finally, if you are already in the midst of planning another type of fund-raising project, you may be able to earn extra revenue by incorporating a special-occasion preview party into your plans.

CRITERIA FOR SUCCESSFUL BENEFITS

Success has become the buzzword of the '80s. Everyone wants to be successful, whether he or she is running a business, raising children, learning to play tennis or giving a party. So naturally this is the term most frequently used by benefit committee members to describe their project after the fact. Unfortunately, so casually is the word bandied about that we're never sure whether the speaker feels the benefit was "successful" because the weather was lovely, or because there were a lot of people there who seemed to be having a good time or because, in addition to the above, it made money for the organization.

In our opinion, the only way to determine the degree of success a benefit attains is to establish clearly defined financial and promotional goals in advance. If we have one message to convey, it's that benefits are indeed a business. Unless you approach them in a businesslike manner, your charitable intentions may go out the window. Therefore, to further refine the definition of a benefit, our "special occasions" must also meet the following requirements:

1) They make significant amounts of money. Net profits (from ticket sales, contributions and other income, minus expenses) should be no less than $50,000 or 10 percent of the organization's annual fund-raising budget. An event that earns less than this is not worth the time, effort and expense of putting it on.

2) They have a high ticket-price structure, relative to the actual cost of food, entertainment and incidentals. These costs should be reduced by underwriting and by the donation of professional, managerial and clerical services by volunteers.

3) Tickets are presold, through personal solicitation by committee members. Walk-ins or box-office sales are not anticipated, except for those benefits that offer a large number of "performance only" tickets at a considerably lower price than the complete package.

4) They are deliberately targeted to a well-defined market segment that includes those individuals who can afford and are willing to pay a premium for an evening out in order to demonstrate a high level of support for a worthy cause.

5) They promote community involvement and continuing support for the sponsoring organization, not only through publicity surrounding the event, but through a planned campaign that includes follow-up contact with individuals introduced to the organization through the benefit.

6) They are carefully planned and executed, right down to the last detail, so that the event itself goes smoothly and nothing is left to chance. Those who attend have a satisfying experience, those who hear about it afterwards wish they had been there, and all concerned go away with a favorable impression of the sponsoring organization.

By narrowing our definition in this way, we don't mean to imply that every organization should undertake this type of benefit, nor that all should try to attract only those individuals who like to attend such affairs. Indeed, a special-occasion benefit may not be in keeping with an organization's spirit and purpose nor even appealing to the potential donor groups that organization may have. We'll discuss how to determine what's best for your organization in the following section.

In addition to achieving important, tangible results — funds and friends — a successful benefit can have other desirable consequences for your organization:

- It can boost morale throughout the organization, by helping to ease financial burdens and by making tangible the community's feelings of good will and appreciation.
- It can actively involve people in the organization and build friendships among committee members, trustees and management.
- It can help to establish mutually beneficial relationships with corporate sponsors.
- It can promote pride in your organization's good works throughout the community.
- The event itself can be a lot of fun.

KNOW YOUR OBJECTIVES

As the dictionary definition suggests, the primary reason to have a benefit is to raise funds for a public program or cause. The question you should be asking as you contemplate your benefit is: How much money can be raised, and can it be raised more easily some other way? Benefits are costly productions, in terms of volunteer and staff hours as well as actual dollars spent on food, entertainment, decorations, printing and mailing, etc. A net profit of 65 to 70 percent of total benefit income is considered healthy, though with sufficient underwriting the net can approach 100 percent. This kind of profit margin may sound attractive when compared to those in the business world, but when compared to other fund-raising methods, benefits are far from cost-effective.

By contrast, a direct solicitation campaign consisting of one or two mailings, with personal and telephone follow-up costs much less to produce and requires only a few hours of each volunteer's time, yet it can result in more individual donations and more money raised. Foundation grantsmanship is even more efficient, in the sense that a single well-researched proposal can result in the funding for a whole program. Therefore an organization that is just getting established or one that has a small, well-defined financial need would do well to develop its fund-raising capabilities along these lines before attempting a benefit.

An established organization with a well-rounded development program will have first sought to raise funds through annual campaigns to individuals and corporations, foundation and government grants, endowments and deferred giving, capital drives and perhaps other special projects such as gift shops or cookbook sales. Only later will it turn to benefits as a way of getting additional donations from its old supporters and reaching new donors who might not respond to any other appeal.

Making new friends for your organization is one of the best reasons we know to include benefits in your repertoire of fund-raising projects. No matter how loyal and generous your current supporters are, you must continually cultivate new ones to ensure the organization's future. That's why you should also incorporate an education and development plan into the benefit process. By this we mean taking time to introduce any benefit committee members new to your organization to your officers, facility and programs; including a brief statement of the organization's purpose in all press releases, programs and other publicity materials relating to the benefit; and making sure that the development department will be able to follow up on any new contacts made through the event. Again, you must set objectives and plan ahead in order to get the most for your efforts.

However, if increasing community awareness and cultivation of supporters is your only goal, there are less expensive, equally effective, ways to accomplish it. We feel that too many gala events sponsored by worthy organizations do not literally earn the right to be called benefits. We suspect that many well-meaning groups have "benefits" when all they really want to do is have a party. Perhaps they have somehow acquired the notion that a not-for-profit organization isn't entitled to spend any money in self-promotion or celebration of its accomplishments. Actually, we believe there are many perfectly good reasons — anniversaries, opening nights, dedications and retirements among them — to have a party for your supporters. Members and friends shouldn't object to paying a modest amount per person to cover expenses, and you can still ask for donations of food, flowers, etc. What you don't have to do is create something newer, bigger and more dazzling than anyone has ever seen before in order to justify a big donation, especially if your organization realizes hardly anything of the proceeds.

If your objective is to introduce new friends to the organization, consider instead a "cultivation event": an informal occasion to which your trustees invite newcomers to meet key personnel and to view your facilities and programs up close. For example, if you're involved with a theater company, you could build an event around an actual performance (on a night when the house isn't sold out), followed by dessert and a chance to talk with the director and actors. After your guests have enjoyed the show, they should be receptive to a pitch for subscriptions or donations on the spot. And, because you haven't exhausted everyone's resources in one big blowout, you can repeat the event the following month with a new set of prospects.

WHEN IS A BENEFIT NOT OF BENEFIT?

• When it doesn't make money—a substantial amount of money, as described above.

• When it fails to take advantage of the opportunity to secure new friends for the organization.

• When it diverts attention from and interferes with the ongoing work of the organization.

• When it diverts attention from and interferes with other major fund-raising programs of the organization. If people are pleased to help when asked, they quickly become annoyed when another member of the same group asks for another favor a short time later. Corporations in particular take a dim view of organizations in which the right hand doesn't seem to know what the left hand is doing.

• When volunteers and/or staff members fail to communicate effectively, complete their assignments competently or treat one another with respect and consideration, undermining confidence and unity in the organization.

• When it fails to attract enough underwriting to keep expenses to a minimum.

• When the event itself is marred by preventable mishaps or, worse yet, suffers embarrassingly poor attendance.

DECIDING WHAT'S RIGHT FOR YOUR ORGANIZATION

Most benefits originate with a monetary need or a creative concept or both. The former is a given with nearly all not-for-profit organizations; whether it's a question of closing the gap between the organization's earned income and expenses, building a new wing or funding a special program, there's always an urgent need to be met. The latter occurs naturally to active and involved volunteers. An idea doesn't have to be 100 percent original to be good, but it's never safe to assume that because the community fine arts association was able to raise $100,000 at its recent masked ball, the youth recreation center can earn as much with a similar party. You must scale your benefit, as well as your expectations, to the needs of your organization and the interests of its supporters.

Therefore the first task of any organization considering a

benefit is to establish an attainable financial goal, which is agreed upon by both board and benefit committee members. We will cover the process of developing a sound budget — the blueprint for achieving that goal — in detail in Chapter III. For now we only want to convince you that this is the single most important element in your plan. The financial goal should serve as a point of reference for every decision the benefit committee makes; everything you do should fall into place behind it. Make up your mind now that you're going to confront the budget issue and go public with your goal; then let it work for you.

Your financial goal will grow out of the organization's need, tempered by other considerations, of course — the most important being the resources the board and benefit committee volunteers can command and the organization's previous level of support in the community.

If your group has sponsored benefits before, start by analyzing the last one. What kind of event was it? What were the ticket prices? How many people attended and in what price categories? Was attendance more or less than was anticipated? Did all the board members attend; if not, why not? Perhaps they're simply not aware that this is a board responsibility. Is the president or executive committee prepared to convince the board to accept it? It's a bad sign when a board doesn't throw its full support behind a benefit. If you weren't personally involved last time, you would be well advised to familiarize yourself with the circumstances. You may have some fences to mend.

You will undoubtedly want to raise more money this time than the last time the organization gave a similar benefit, so your challenge is to figure out how to: a) Increase attendance; b) Raise the ticket prices and at least maintain the same attendance; c) Add a raffle, advertising program book or other source of income; or d) Reach out to a new constituency with a different kind of event. If you choose the latter, you will have to go through many of the same steps as a group that has never mounted a benefit before, so read on.

When you're putting together a first-time benefit, begin by evaluating all your organization's support groups, from the board of trustees on down. This will help you determine how large a benefit committee you can muster and what resources individual members may be able to contribute to the effort. It will also help you gauge potential attendance and decide what to charge for tickets.

How large is the board? Are trustees active, committed and aware of their financial obligations? In other words, can you count on all of them to come to a benefit and bring their friends? Are they influential members of the community, with contacts in business and government? If so, they should be able to help you secure underwriting, sell tables to corporations and attract important guests who will lend prestige to the party. How much money do they give annually and through what channels (annual operating fund, endowment, building fund, etc.)? Your development department should be able to provide this information. In your subjective judgment, could they afford to give more? If you don't firmly believe they could and should, then how can you expect them to bear the expense of a benefit and make other hefty contributions besides?

Ask the same questions about the organization's other donors and support groups (women's committee, advisory board, "friends," etc.). Finally, ask: Do the organization's supporters like to go to parties? If they aren't enthusiastic about the idea of a benefit, you can't expect others in the community to buy all the tickets. Some people would really rather support your organization in other ways, and you have nothing to gain by going against their preferences.

Now consider who you might choose to chair the event and who might fill out the remainder of the benefit's executive committee. We can't overemphasize the importance of people in making a benefit happen. A chairperson who is creative, dependable and most of all works well with people acts like a magnet to attract good committee workers and to draw out their best efforts. (It may be helpful at this point to consult the complete job description for a benefit chairperson outlined in Chapter IV.) Is there such a person already involved in your organization, preferably on your board of trustees? Do you know anyone else with the right qualifications whom you can win over to your cause? Do you know whether that person is reasonably free of other binding commitments for the six to 12 months that it will take to organize the benefit?

Does your organization already have volunteer support groups in place that could be tapped to work on the benefit committee? If so, you will save valuable time. There are hundreds of tasks to be done, from stuffing and addressing invitations to staffing the hospitality table during the event. Support groups provide not only a ready source of workers familiar with your organization and eager to help your cause, but have built-in lines of communication through which you can locate the right person for each job.

Will your desired chairperson be able to recruit a large number of friends with varied skills and contacts to supplement the talent that is already available in the organization? Generally speaking, the larger the benefit committee, the more people who will attend the event, because each member is expected to buy at least a pair of tickets and preferably a table that he or she will fill with friends. Obviously, you'll need a strong and well-organized chairperson to keep all those volunteers moving on the right track.

Now look at the agency or institution itself. What does it do? Who are its clients or patrons and how many of them are there? How long has it existed and does it have a good reputation in your community? Does it serve people from all walks of life, as a hospital or medical research association does, or does it appeal to special interests, as does an arts organization or conservation league? Is there a religious or ethnic affiliation? Does it have instant name recognition? In other words, who are the people who perceive it as an institution that in some way affects their own well-being and therefore deserves their support? Do these potential supporters include a substantial number of people who are in a position to buy tickets?

Now assess what other types of fund-raising campaigns the organization engages in. Could a benefit dilute the impact of these established campaigns? A benefit must either tie in with other fund-raising projects or avoid conflicting with them; otherwise potential donors become confused and annoyed by repeated solicitations.

All of these factors have to be weighed in order to determine how much you can accomplish with this benefit. A small board of an organization serving a limited constituency might be able to handle all the arrangements for an auction, for example, but they might not be able to secure enough auction items or sell enough tickets to justify the expense of holding it in the ballroom of a downtown hotel and serving a four-course dinner beforehand. If your first benefit is successful on a small scale, we promise you there will be opportunities to expand it in the future.

Should you decide, after due consideration of the above factors, that your potential benefit income is not high enough, your workers would be stretched too thin or the timing would not be right, there is no dishonor in abandoning the idea—at least until you've had time to regroup. Cleveland's public television station gave up having benefits at its broadcasting studios when they began to encroach upon evening shooting schedules and permanent sets. In addition, the station broadcasts three membership drives and, as noted above, an auction, which span 40 days of each year. "They bring in a hefty $3 million and, if programming is on target, they should be reaching all of those who care about supporting WVIZ-TV," station manager Betty Cope explains.

By now you should have a clear picture of your principal ticket buyers, namely the people closest to your organization. Now it's time to look at your benefit concept again: Will it appeal to their interests and match their ability to give? Don't try to mimic what another organization has done, assuming you'll attract the same crowd it does. Stick with pleasing the people who know your organization best and try to reach other like-minded folks who are out there waiting to be brought into the fold.

The kind of event you choose should be in keeping with the purpose and tone of your organization. This helps to reinforce your primary message, and it helps attract people who are genuinely interested in what you do. For example, many arts organizations favor black-tie benefits, which are perfectly appropriate to the glamorous nature of the performing arts. Established institutions with older patrons seem to do well with the traditional cocktail-dinner-dance format. Younger organizations with less affluent supporters may prefer to experiment with offbeat ideas, informal settings and lower ticket prices. Avoid events that seem wildly out of character for the organization; putting on a gourmet dinner to raise money for a hunger center would be in questionable taste.

PLANNING A FIRST-TIME EVENT

To demonstrate the kind of reasoning that goes into the decision to have a benefit, here is an example from our recent experience:

In 1985 Marilyn was asked to chair the first wine auction for the Cleveland Center for Economic Education (CCEE), an independent agency whose purpose is to train public school teachers in economics so that they can better help their students to understand how our country's economic system works. The center, which raised funds annually for the preceding ten years, had never before mounted a benefit. Feeling that the center lacked community recognition, the trustees decided that the publicity generated by a benefit would give the organization a shot in the arm.

Since they wanted to establish an annual event that could be identified as CCEE's own, they hit upon the idea of a wine auction and dinner. This type of event has proven successful for organizations in other states; none had been attempted in Ohio. Some organizations might have been daunted by this lack of precedent, but not the center's trustees.

By the time board president Robert Pavey, a partner in the Cleveland venture capital firm Morgenthaler Ventures, approached Marilyn to chair the event, he had already put the wheels in motion. A knowledgeable and respected local wine merchant, Pat O'Brien, had already agreed to serve as auctioneer. A dialogue had been

initiated with the state to obtain approval of the concept.
O'Brien possessed the right combination of charisma and
salesmanship that an auctioneer requires. Janet AuWerter, a
member of the center's administration, had agreed to serve as
liaison between the center staff and the benefit committee
and to coordinate promotion for the event. The board and these
principals were eager to enlist Marilyn's aid in organizing the
benefit.

Marilyn recognized that the wine auction would be a real
challenge. There was no existing volunteer support committee that
could be called on for help, and the board members did not in
general know one another socially. Though they clearly had the
interest in undertaking such a complicated project, they needed an
effective leader to take charge. Lacking experience in the benefit
arena, they had already set a modest goal of $10,000 to $15,000 net
profit. Marilyn convinced them that it wouldn't be worth her time
to participate unless a higher goal — $20,000 to $25,000, which she
felt was within reach — was established.

The go-ahead decision was made at a luncheon meeting
attended by the board president and two other board members, the
auctioneer, the staff liaison and Marilyn, as chairperson-designate.
This was a crucial step, in that the meeting resulted not only in
executive-level approval of the benefit's financial goal, leadership,
date and ticket-pricing structure, but also in the board's acceptance
of its responsibility for supporting the benefit. Now Marilyn could
go forward confidently with the actual management of the project.

From this point on, her job was a matter of working out the
details. Marilyn's strategy was to keep the cost of tickets reasonable
enough to attract people who were interested in the opportunity to
buy wines donated from private collections, but were not previous
donors to the center. The committee decided to hold the event at
the midtown University Club, which offered the advantages of
central location, secured free parking and a competent kitchen
staff. More important, the club's dining room was the proper size
to accommodate 30 tables of eight within perfect sight of the
podium, with ample space in adjoining rooms for wine tasting and
the display of silent and live auction items. Because the wine
auctions were the focus of the evening, there was no need to
find an exotic location or hire a big band — in fact, such costly
alternatives would only have detracted from the main event. Finally,
the committee recruited Sandy Earl, president of a newly established
wine distributorship, whose contacts were invaluable in securing
donations of wine.

Cleveland's First Wine Auction was a sellout — attracting 240 people at $60 each and bringing in good prices for all the wines offered. It surpassed its goal, raising $29,000.

In sum, our example illustrates several important management points:

1) Always check out the legal ramifications of any new idea you may want to try, particularly if it involves liquor or gambling.

2) Know the board's capabilities and limitations; proceed cautiously to build on the former and correct or compensate for the latter.

3) Set a reasonable financial goal: Be sure it's attainable but high enough to justify the time and effort involved.

4) Be sure to obtain board approval of your plans, especially your financial goal, before going ahead.

5) Recruit committee members who have the skills and contacts needed to carry out the plans.

6) Don't make the affair more elaborate and costly than you have to; focus on a single theme and let the purpose of the event guide your selection of place, time, menu, decor, etc.

SHOULD YOU USE A PAID CONSULTANT?

To an organization that is in need but unsure of its ability to raise money, hiring a special-events consultant to organize a benefit may seem like an easy solution. But be aware that a consultant's role doesn't include doing your work for you. You are still responsible for recruiting an adequate volunteer force, as well as overseeing the consultant's work to be sure it's done to your satisfaction. Nor can a consultant guarantee that you will meet your financial goal, because it remains the committee's responsibility to secure under-writing and sell tickets.

Usually a consultant is called in when an organization needs to raise money or to stage an event for public relations reasons, but has a small staff and/or lacks a strong volunteer leader who can attract the numbers of workers needed to put on a major benefit. Consultants' services may vary, but generally they work with a volunteer committee in both planning and organizing the benefit. Cleveland special-events consultant Marietta Gullia, a former volunteer benefit worker and founding president of Cleveland Ballet, describes her function as a "behind-the-scenes general chairperson, while the volunteers are out front." Gullia prefers to begin work with an organization at the earliest stages of planning a benefit, rather than coming in after the concept has been established and the volunteer chairperson appointed.

Like Gullia, any consultant will begin by assessing the strengths and weaknesses of the organization and helping to develop a strategy for the entire event. This includes setting goals, creating a benefit concept, choosing executive committee members, helping to recruit volunteer workers, compiling a mailing list and working out timetables and a budget. She can also identify potential underwriters, match volunteer solicitors to prospects and make introductions, if necessary. Likewise, the consultant can lead the committee to the most reliable and cooperative suppliers and assist in negotiating contracts.

At this point, the consultant may bow out and let the newly formed committee take over the detail work, so as to keep fees to a minimum. If the organization wishes to pay for continued service, however, the consultant remains involved as coordinator until about a month after the benefit. He or she may move temporarily into the organization's office space, particularly during the final weeks before the event. The consultant will continue to delegate tasks to volunteers, but should be willing to follow up and make sure all deadlines are met. Any clerical help engaged by the consultant will be his or her responsibility. He or she should prepare a final report and hand over all pertinent records to the organization before departing.

Making effective use of a consultant requires careful research and a lot of soul-searching on the part of both the organization and the consultant. If you are thinking of hiring one, make appointments with several to get a general picture of how they work, whether you like their ideas and whether you feel you'd be compatible. As you would with any potential employee, ask about the candidates' background and experience and check their references. An unhappy experience with a consultant will do nothing to inspire loyalty for your organization among its unpaid volunteers.

If the consultants you interview are interested in your project, they will submit proposals detailing the work to be done, the starting and ending dates of their contracts and, of course, their fees. The latter should be a flat rate based on the amount of time each expects to spend on your benefit. Be wary of anyone who offers services on a contingency basis or requests a percentage of benefit income; these practices are considered unethical by the National Society of Fund Raising Executives, a professional association that sets standards for the industry.

Once a reputable consultant has taken a look at your organization and heard your plans, he or she will tell you if it is in your mutual interest to work together. Generally, consultants will only consider benefits of a minimum size or dollar amount; their fees would be hard to justify for small projects. If a proposed benefit doesn't have the potential for success, in the consultant's opinion, he or she will discuss this honestly with you and suggest alternative courses of action. A consultant has his or her own standing in the community to think of and wants to be associated with successful events, just as you do.

On the other hand, if your organization and your concept have the potential for success, shouldn't you be able to pull off a benefit without paying a consultant's fee? Answering the nine questions at the end of this chapter will enable you to make an accurate assessment of your needs. In a sense, hiring a special-events consultant is tantamount to admitting there is no one in your organization capable of chairing a benefit (or, as is increasingly the case these days, no one in your organization who has enough time to devote to the top job).

It's also important to consider whether potential volunteers might object to serving gratis on a benefit committee while a consultant is being paid to run the show. Many volunteers would agree with Barbara Y. Galvin, past president of the Women's Committee of the Cleveland Orchestra, who notes:

> I would not be in favor of hiring a paid consultant to chair a benefit. We are all trying like crazy to raise money for various institutions—why cut into your profits?
> I can say this because we've always been able to find a capable, willing person. This may not be so in the future. Most organizations have a wealth of ability among their members. Willingness is another story. As the volunteer pool decreases, the same women are being asked to do everything, and they are getting tired and burned out.

Since time is a most precious commodity, it may be necessary for some organizations to hire temporary help to assist in putting on a benefit no matter how committed their supporters and staff. Even though staffers may be assigned to assist with specified tasks, they can rarely devote full time to the benefit. Especially during the last hectic weeks before the event, it is essential to have someone running "benefit central": available at all hours to answer phone calls, keep track of reservations and follow through on last-minute details. Ideally, there will be a committee member able and willing to assume this duty, but in practice this is not always possible.

A good solution would be to hire a temporary secretary who would take over the more routine functions such as typing or word-processing reservation lists, writing letters, making phone calls and taking minutes of meetings, freeing the committee members for more sensitive tasks such as securing donations and selling tickets. If there is any extra space in the organization's offices, provide this person with a desk, phone, typewriter and access to the copying machine. The cost will be less than hiring a consultant, and the benefit committee will retain greater control.

CHECKLIST: ARE YOU READY TO BEGIN?

In summary, we believe you should have satisfactory answers to the following questions before proceeding with your benefit. If the answer to any one of them is "no" or "not sure," we recommend you rein in your enthusiasm until you have remedied the problem.

1) Do you have a potential chairperson who is qualified and willing to work hard for your cause? The chairperson is the key to success in any benefit. A strong leader does more than plot strategy and execute details; he or she inspires loyalty, keeps morale high and brings out the best in every committee worker.

2) Do you have volunteer supporters who are organized and ready to help? If so, get them involved in the early stages of planning to determine how they can best work with you. If not, allot extra time to assemble and educate a work force.

3) Do you have an active, dedicated and supportive board? If so, you should have no trouble getting them behind a well-prepared plan. If not, their apathy could undermine your best efforts and leave you feeling unappreciated. Be sure they have the where-withal—personal funds and contacts for underwriting and donated services and supplies—to back you up.

4) Is there enough time for the chairperson and committee to do a thorough job? Allow a minimum of six months, preferably 12, to plan and organize a benefit.

5) Do you have adequate staff support? You will need at least the approval of the executive director and the active involvement of the development and public relations staff, as well as some clerical assistance. Be sure everyone's areas of responsibility and lines of reporting are clearly understood and accepted.

6) Does your organization have an up-to-date mailing list? Computerized lists are best, because they can be printed out quickly, in several different formats, at nominal cost. If your organization doesn't have a readily accessible list, allow two to three months to compile one from scratch.

7) Will this benefit be the organization's only request for funds at this time? Competition within your own organization looks bad to outsiders and may create conflict within. Also, be aware that your organization may be prohibited from competing with major community fund-raising campaigns such as United Way if it is a beneficiary of such funds.

8) Is your organization well recognized in the community? This includes your trustees and staff, as well as the services it performs. People give to people they know and trust. If no one knows your organization, you will first have to lay the groundwork through effective PR about the organization itself.

9) Do you have the potential sponsors and ticket buyers to make a substantial net profit? Remember, if it doesn't make money, it's not a benefit!

When you can honestly answer "yes" to all these questions, you are ready to begin creating a concept.

Creating a Concept

As we noted, the benefit process usually begins when an organization identifies a monetary need that is not being met or when someone comes up with an idea for a benefit that excites the imaginations of the organization's supporters. Then it is the board's responsibility to see that the proposed event will: a) conform to the objectives and image of the organization; b) enhance rather than conflict with the organization's other activities; c) fit into the organization's calendar; and d) achieve its financial goals. Since it's seldom possible for all the members of a board to get involved in the detail work of mounting a benefit, the responsibility for executing the benefit is usually delegated to a capable chairperson, who in turn recruits a committee of key workers.

Before handing over the reins of a benefit, the board or its executive committee must approve not only the concept, but also the date, location and proposed budget. This crucial step ensures that the board understands, accepts and supports the benefit committee's effort and stands ready to help in any way possible.

Obviously, in order to choose a competent chairperson and evaluate the benefit plan, the board must have one or more members who are knowledgeable about benefits in general. This book can be a useful reference for the board president or board member serving as benefit liaison who needs a thorough understanding of the process in order to work effectively with the chairperson and committee who will represent the board in mounting the benefit.

Large organizations that have benefits on a regular basis often appoint a standing board committee whose purpose it is to coordinate and oversee all fund-raising events. In some organizations, a women's committee or another support group may take responsibility for establishing a procedure for benefits, as well as for mounting the events. It is a good idea to have a standing committee in place to provide long-range planning and continuity, to give experienced advice to the temporary benefit committees that plan each event and to review each benefit concept before it is presented to the full board.

WHAT COMES FIRST?

At the start of the benefit planning process, theoretically everything is possible. This can be a very creative period, offering the opportunity to toss around all kinds of suggestions and come up with an ideal plan that answers this basic marketing question: "What does our prospective patron want?" It can be a frustrating time, as well, because pinning down the various elements of that plan is a complex procedure. Each variable—financial goal, ticket prices, date, location, entertainment and chairperson—has a bearing on all the others, and most of them depend as much on factors outside your control as on the needs and objectives of your organization. You'll need to keep your options open and be prepared to accept restrictions imposed from both inside and out. Not until you have settled all these points, however, can you begin to formulate a budget and a detailed blueprint for achieving the desired bottom line.

HOW BIG A TICKET?

Typically, a specific financial goal is dictated by the organization's development needs or by the amount raised by a previous, similar benefit. To create an event capable of meeting that goal, you must judiciously balance the remaining variables discussed below.

You won't be able to set fixed ticket prices until the budget is drawn up, expenses have been itemized and you have a clearer sense of the income the benefit must produce to meet its financial goal. But you should at least start with an idea of how much you can charge for tickets and what kind of package you'll need to offer in order to sell them at that price.

Let's say you want to charge a minimum of $100 per person. If you know that some of your organization's supporters have paid this much to attend other benefits, they should be willing to pay as much for yours, as long as you offer a similar caliber of food, entertainment and atmosphere. If, on the other hand, you believe they can't or won't spend more than $50 per person, then scale down the ambition of the benefit—plan a luncheon or cocktail party instead of a dinner dance—to reduce expenses so that you can still make a substantial profit. If you plan to make most of your profit through an auction or gambling, you can set a lower ticket price and cut back accordingly on the food—but don't stint on the liquor when you want to stimulate spending.

If at all possible, try to line up major underwriting while you are still in the process of creating your concept. Most frequently, this underwriting comes from a company seeking increased visibility for a grand opening, which immediately determines your choice of location and date, not to mention relieving you of many expenses right from the start. A knowledgeable and enthusiastic underwriter can help set the tone of the event and provide valuable guidance.

SAVE THE DATE

Choosing a date can be tricky at best; the idea is to schedule your event on a day when the greatest number of your potential supporters have nothing better to do. Obviously, the more civic, cultural and social activities in your city, the harder it will be to find an opening. Fridays, Saturdays and Sundays are most desirable; it's hard for most people to get dressed up and stay out late on a weeknight. Avoid all major religious holidays. You are fortunate if your organization has an historical claim on a particular weekend in the community calendar by virtue of hosting a popular benefit annually on that date. You can't guarantee that other events (e.g., the World Series, political rallies, other organizations' benefits) won't be scheduled at the same time, but if your previous benefits have been successful, others may be reluctant to compete with your event.

Sometimes a date will be dictated by another event in your organization's calendar, such as an opening night or anniversary. Even if the occasion seems tailor-made for a benefit, you must be aware of the competition. If there are already other activities that your potential patrons are likely to attend scheduled around that time, you will only frustrate everyone by introducing a conflict.

If you have decided on a particular location or kind of entertainment for your benefit, your choice of dates may depend upon availability of that place or those performers. If you have received an offer of a location and major underwriting from a co-sponsor, you'd be hard pressed to refuse almost any date offered.

ALL DRESSED UP WITH SOMEPLACE TO GO

The choice of a location can dramatically affect the concept of a benefit. Obviously, the larger the facility, the more tickets you can sell and the more income you can generate; but there's no point in paying for space you can't fill with paying guests. Not only do the size and layout of the place determine the number of people you can accommodate, but the presence or absence of certain amenities can restrict your choice of activities, food, decor and so on. Every place has its own character, which can work to your advantage or disadvantage. Nothing is impossible if you're willing to spend enough money: You can redecorate, rewire, move walls, bring the outdoors in or the indoors out. But the challenge for any benefit committee is to overcome the liabilities of the chosen facility and still stay within a strict budget.

Since all benefits have certain basic requirements, keep the following considerations in mind as you shop around for a site:

Location. Ideally, you want a place that is centrally located for the majority of your patrons. Is it easy to get to and easy to find? Will patrons feel safe in the neighborhood? Is the facility reasonably attractive?

Capacity. Is the facility big enough to accommodate the number of guests you expect and the kind of activities planned? Managers of hotels, clubs and party rooms can tell you exactly how many they can serve, depending on the configuration of seating. If the facility isn't normally used for parties, you can calculate an occupancy figure based on the size of your tables and the amount of space needed around each for chairs and serving. A good caterer or equipment rental company can help you with this calculation (see the PEOPLE MOVING section in Chapter VII.) Don't try to squeeze in more than the maximum number, as your guests' discomfort will be long remembered. As Thomas G. Stafford, president of Cleveland's Great Lakes Theater Festival, a summer Equity company, observes: "Two common failings of benefits are over-crowding (the urge to get all the profit possible is difficult to suppress), which makes food and bar service inadequate, and noise levels, which can be a function of bad acoustics, the music and/or crowd size."

Accessibility. Are entrances and exits clearly marked and easy to secure? Is the building fully accessible to the handicapped? Are there freight elevators and loading docks for delivery of equipment? Is there an escalator or grand staircase offering a panoramic view of the festivities?

Parking. It should be ample, secure and preferably free; negotiate this as part of your agreement to use the building. Check out what other events will be taking place on the premises and in the vicinity the same day that might compete for spaces.

Kitchen facilities. Some caterers can work without an on-site kitchen, but obviously it's easier if there's a good-sized, fully equipped one available. If there is none, look for sources of running water and electricity, including a 220-volt line for cooking equipment.

Restrooms. Remember that your patrons will be eating and drinking for several hours. Are the restrooms conveniently located, clean, decently appointed and in working order? Are there sufficient stalls and wash basins so that patrons won't have to stand in line?

Electricity. In old buildings especially, wiring can be inadequate and outlets few. Try to anticipate how much power you'll need and where you'll need it for stage lighting, amplifiers, projectors, air conditioners, coffeepots, etc. If the building seems dimly lit, it may be a clue that the wiring won't be up to carrying the extra load. Consult an electrician, if in doubt.

Acoustics. If patrons in the back of the room can't hear the program, they'll begin to talk and soon no one will be able to hear. On the other hand, if the music is uncomfortably loud, some patrons may leave. Spaces with high ceilings or tile walls simply don't adapt well to certain types of entertainment. Consult a sound technician to find out what will work in the building under consideration.

Dance floor. You can rent one, but sometimes the sections don't fit together well and the uneven surface can be hazardous. If dancing is to be your main entertainment, why not find a place that has a built-in dance floor? The same applies to a stage, if your featured performers need one.

Liquor license. You may not have to apply separately for a temporary license if the hall already has one. Check this out with the hall manager or your state board of liquor control.

Sight lines. If there's to be a stage show or auction, will everyone be able to see it? Look out for pillars or other obstructions that can't be moved.

Image. Is the building well maintained? Are curtains, carpets and upholstery a decent color and not threadbare? If it's a hotel, restaurant or club, is it known for its good food and service? New or old, is it a place that people will perceive as exciting?

Sometimes the best parties are held in the unlikeliest places, such as warehouses, factories or unfinished buildings. That may be because it takes a certain audacity to transform an otherwise utilitarian facility into an environment that guests will enjoy while dressed in their best clothes. For many years, patrons of the Northern Ohio Opera Association, a not-for-profit organization that sponsored the Metropolitan Opera's once-annual spring tour to Cleveland, flocked to pre-performance dinners in the Pavilion, a temporary restaurant that was installed in the cavernous basement of the city's Public Auditorium. Even though the building was more suited to trade shows and conventions than to grand opera, decorating motifs usually inspired by one of the operas being performed made the Pavilion the place to be seen during "Met Week."

THE PICK OF PARTY ROOMS

Hotel ballrooms, restaurants and clubs are in many ways the easiest facilities to work with and the best choices when you're short on planning time. They come fully decorated and equipped to handle crowds; they should have adequate parking, restrooms, cloakrooms and kitchens; they are usually outfitted with public-address systems and other audio-visual equipment. Since they accommodate all kinds of gatherings, they should be able to offer a selection of floor plans, any one of which can be set up quickly without help from committee members. Such service may prove frustrating, as it sometimes leaves little room for the committee to be creative. If you want to do something special with the decor, you may not have time in which to do it because of back-to-back bookings of your room. You may have barely enough time to put place cards and centerpieces on the tables before the doors open to your patrons. Another drawback: The more familiar the hotel or club, the harder your job will be to convince potential patrons that an event held there will be something out of the ordinary. On the other hand, people know they can expect a certain level of comfort in such a place, which is more than can be said for some unusual locations.

New buildings offer jaded party-goers a refreshing change of scene and may attract some patrons purely out of curiosity. But they can be a nightmare for the benefit committee. The chief worry is whether the new facility will, in fact, be ready on time for the benefit serving as its grand opening. Not even the building's owners have complete control over construction schedules. It's wise to have a contingency plan in case the building is completely unusable on the appointed day, since it's difficult to postpone the benefit once tickets have been sold and almost impossible after the food and flower orders have been confirmed. If it is necessary to move to a different location, the owner/co-sponsor should pick up the tab. Of course, it may not be possible to find another facility on short notice. If you are really worried, quietly pay a deposit to reserve one.

More likely the building will have a roof, four walls and an (hastily issued) occupancy permit, but not such amenities as carpeting, light fixtures and stall doors in the bathrooms. The problems here could be more than aesthetic; you may encounter everything from poor acoustics to dangerously low visibility. Even if the building is in "move-in" condition, there will probably be bugs in the heating/cooling system or an electrical failure somewhere down the line. The committee would do well to assume such problems will occur and come up with a contingency plan; it's easier in the end than being caught unprepared.

Often a new building that announces its opening with a benefit wasn't designed for a party in the first place. It may have neither kitchen nor dining room nor enough restrooms. You'll need to hire a caterer with the right equipment to handle this situation and recruit as committee members designers who can create an attractive, comfortable environment from scratch.

Private homes are inherently appealing, because they represent hospitality and individual taste rather than institutional function-alism. Night of 100 Stars, which took place in late August 1986 for the benefit of the United Negro College Fund, was the first major fashion show ever held at a private home in Cleveland. The "100 stars" of the title represented the benefit guests themselves, since attendance was limited to that number (at $100 per ticket). The guests wore white or silver to match the glittery decor of George and Jean Fraser's home and enjoyed a theater-style (stand-up) dinner of broiled baby lamb chops, veal roulades, salmon *creme fraiche* with caviar and other delicacies before viewing a $250,000 collec-tion of furs by designer Carolina Herrera presented by Saks Fifth Avenue. As George Fraser, who was at the time director of marketing for United Way Services of Cleveland, observes: "The warmth and friendliness of a house provides a party atmosphere. Generally, people have interesting conversation pieces like artworks that stimulate socializing and add to the overall ambience."

At-home parties can be time- and cost-effective for a benefit committee, too; you won't have to pay rent, and in many cases the host and hostess will also assume responsibility for cleaning, rearranging furniture, ordering the flowers and hiring the caterer or preparing the meal themselves. The drawbacks are potential theft or damage to the hosts' house and furnishings from spilled food and cigarette burns. (As with a corporate underwriter, you need to establish in advance just what is expected of the hosts, what the committee will do and who is liable for any loss, injury or damage.)

The other problem is to figure out how to accommodate enough patrons to make the benefit profitable. Most people with large homes who entertain frequently know how many they can serve comfortably. If there is any question, an experienced caterer can help a hostess size up her house and yard. Not too many homes can accommodate more than 100 people, but there are several ways to work around that fact when planning a big event.

The first and most obvious is to let the party spill outdoors. This is charming as long as the weather cooperates, but you can never, repeat, *never*, count on it. The experiences of 100 Stars' planners are instructive. According to Saks' Cleveland fashion director, Cynthia Petrus, she and Fraser spent most of the summer working out the logistics of setting up a tent on the Frasers' sloping, tree-studded lawn, only to discover the afternoon of the show that the portable runway had to be taken apart and repositioned because the tent was installed a few feet off line. Before the guests arrived, rain forced the cooks to move their equipment into the only available shelter, a garage that had already been set up as the models' dressing room for the fashion show.

Fraser, who remained the genial host in spite of the frantic maneuvers going on around him, offers the following pointers as a result of this experience:

> In planning any outdoor event, always expect the worst possible weather. Make sure there is adequate tenting for all guests and activities (including rain curtains in case of unusual winds) and a covered area leading from one site to another. Be prepared to handle adversity with cool, calm and wit. It will help everyone enjoy the evening!

A "progressive" dinner is another way to increase the number of guests that can be accommodated by a private-home benefit. At a progressive dinner, each participating household is responsible for providing one course, and guests move from one to the other for a complete meal. This type of party resists a strict timetable because of the travel involved and the possibility of patrons getting lost between stops. There's also the problem of inertia—once guests remove their coats and start having a good time, they may be reluctant to move on. You might arrange to have a costumed reveler—say, a Pied Piper or a drum majorette—lead patrons to the next stop at the appointed time. Progressive parties seem to work best when the participating households are within walking distance of one another. For most people, three houses are about the limit for one evening; after that they tend to get tired or lose interest.

A nice variation on this idea is to use two houses next door to one another with a single, unfenced yard in between. You can serve different courses in each home or duplicate the menu in both. And, if you really want to be informal, you can close off a street for a block party.

The greatest number of patrons can be accommodated by serving complete dinners in several houses at the same time. Even more can be served in shifts or open house-style—that is, with guests coming and going at will and helping themselves from a buffet table. With this plan, you're limited only by how many hosts you can find.

Do establish some ground rules, however, so that there is consistency in the quality and type of food served. You don't want some patrons to feel cheated when they compare notes with others who were at different homes. Again, there are a couple of ways to go about this: You can have a single menu and theme throughout or suggest an umbrella theme and let hosts and hostesses come up with their own variations. Cleveland Ballet's popular International Night was based on the latter principle. Each of the ten to 20 participating households was the scene of a different party featuring the cuisine of a foreign country, giving patrons their choice of food and hosts. Dessert was served in a central location so that all participants could socialize at the end of the evening, if they chose. Another option would be to offer three different types of meals — say, a picnic, a buffet and a formal dinner — at three different price levels.

Any public building that is large enough and has the bare necessities of parking, plumbing, heating and electricity, can be a candidate for a benefit, if you use a little imagination. Here are a few suggestions:

Historic or monumental architecture such as city halls or courthouses can be fascinating to benefit-goers. They also tend to be cavernous and resonant, so take care to center activities around focal points and consult an acoustician on ways to keep the sound levels manageable. Music and speeches may not work in certain areas.

The disadvantage of using public buildings lies in the complexity of securing permission to use them. City governments aren't necessarily as public relations-oriented as corporations. If you have an in with someone in the current administration, start with that person. If not, just call the most likely sounding department and keep following referrals until you find the person who can respond to your request. Also bear in mind this advice from the former chairperson of Cleveland's Mayor's Awards for Volunteerism, Lynn Schmelzer:

> When working with city hall, the most important issue to resolve at the very beginning is who talks to whom — and I don't mean politically. I am referring to the chain of command. On the volunteer side, there should be only the chairperson and possibly the co-chair who talks to the city hall representative, who is the *one* person designated to handle all the details of your project. Too many people talking to too many people confuses everything. Any project connected with the city, its mayor or its city hall takes time and patience, but is well worth it.

Museums of all kinds make wonderful benefit sites — they usually offer plenty of space and good lighting and the decor is all around you. You don't have to strain to come up with an original theme — just work with what is already there. Benefit planners and patrons alike find their fantasies unleashed in such places.

Cleveland has two that are particularly favored — the Cleveland Museum of Natural History and the Crawford Auto-Aviation Museum of the Western Reserve Historical Society, where you can dine among dinosaurs or vintage cars, respectively — and most cities have similar cultural facilities. Planetariums and botanical-garden greenhouses have great atmosphere, too, though they may not have as much open space for tables.

Theaters and concert halls are obviously suited to benefits that involve a stage show; but consider also using their grand lobbies, green rooms and even their stages for other types of parties. The biennial Cleveland Orchestra Ball is sometimes held in the orchestra's elegant art deco home, Severance Hall. Dancing is on the stage and dinner is served on the concourses outside each seating level, in the green room and in the boxes. While this is a visually interesting arrangement, it does pose special logistical problems. Food service is very difficult to manage on multiple levels, and planners can't fit in as many tables as in a single large room. People-watching is fun from the different vantage points, but traversing the space to talk to someone is another matter. Getting onto the stage is also tricky; planners may have to build a special gangplank and provide escorts to make sure guests negotiate it safely. The thrill of dancing on a real stage and the elegance of the setting make the effort worthwhile, however.

Stores and shopping malls are constantly on the lookout for special promotional activities; grand openings aren't their only excuse to sponsor benefits. They will also underwrite fashion shows and open their doors to special events after hours. After all, for many people malls have become major entertainment centers, as appropriate for an evening of fun as for a day of shopping. Stores and malls hardly lend themselves to quiet, dignified, exclusive parties, but they work well for audience participation-type events such as casinos and previews of all kinds of sales. You can also do a variation of the progressive dinner party, offering a different course on every floor or in every participating shop, to the accompaniment of different entertainers.

It takes careful planning to keep people from wandering off in such a large area. Patrons will cluster around live entertainment, buffet tables and bars, but it's also wise to have good security to discourage straying. You'll also need security guards and a well-conceived registration system at the doors, because somehow malls and stores seem to invite gate-crashers.

Outdoor locations can pose the biggest problems, for two major reasons: The first is, obviously, the weather. No matter what your climate, you can't predict the temperature and the probability of precipitation six months to a year in advance, when you have to set the date for your benefit. So you must always go to elaborate (and usually expensive) lengths to keep patrons dry and comfortable. (See the discussion of Night of 100 Stars, under *Private homes* above.) The second reason is that many outdoor spots lack running water, electricity, telephones, paved walkways and so on. Unless you're planning a party around a campfire, you cannot run a benefit without these amenities.

Marilyn once worked on a series of designers' showhouses for the Brevard Symphony Orchestra in Florida. The first year a remodeled old home was featured. Unfortunately, the redecorating scheme didn't include replacement of faulty wiring, so flashlights came in handy when the power went out during a special showing. The second year several townhouses in a new development located far out on a dark country road were showcased. Since the water had not yet been hooked up, the beautifully decorated bathrooms couldn't be used (though they were clearly marked "Out of Order," some visitors either didn't read the signs or didn't believe them.) At times there were lines outside the outdoor facilities — hardly a classy sight at a preview showing. Needless to say, this is the type of experience that gives benefit planners gray hair. Why did the Florida volunteers do it? Because the developer underwrote most of the expenses.

The best outdoor locations are those featuring permanent structures big enough to shelter the expected number of patrons, with adequate electricity, lighting, a public-address system, rest-rooms and telephones: i.e., zoos, theme parks or country clubs. Such outdoor sites obviously have their own built-in atmosphere, which no one ever tires of, as well as nearby parking lots, main-tenance crews and sometimes even their own cooking facilities and transportation systems such as zoo trains. Parks, beaches and nature preserves may be somewhat more rustic, but they usually boast parking and sources of electricity and running water.

If you need to provide shelter, tents can be rented in all shapes and sizes, and some come nicely appointed with floors and elec-trical outlets. Be sure to specify in your rental contract the number of outlets you'll need or, if it happens to be less expensive, that you will provide your own electrician.

Betsy Beckwith, administrative assistant of Shaker Lakes Regional Nature Center, an outdoor educational facility on Cleveland's East Side, uses the following checklist when contracting for tent rental for benefits:

Size: Determined by location, number of guests, number seated at each table, dance floor (if needed), size of band and band platform.

Type: Clear or opaque, color, number and placement of openings, number of canopies.

Lighting: Where, how much, power source, outlets for band and cooking tent.

Astroturf: "To have or have not."

Timing: "Insurance and security must be in place from the moment tents are installed until they are removed. Two days before the event is ideal; that gives you time to correct errors of omission or commission.

"And, it goes without saying," Beckwith concludes, "get a written quote on everything."

LET US ENTERTAIN YOU

Every so often, someone suggests a "stay-at-home" benefit as a cost-saving alternative to a long evening of milling around in stuffy clothes and tight shoes, in the belief that most people would prefer just to send in their checks and spend the evening in front of the TV. In fact, most not-for-profit organizations already offer their supporters this option: It's called a membership or sustaining-fund drive. The reason these same organizations also have special-occasion benefits is that many people *like* to get out into the social spotlight, to meet the top brass of the sponsoring organization, to see and be seen.

One of the most clever twists on the stay-at-home benefit we've seen was the Artfilled Brunch, "the benefit that comes to you," created by the Cleveland Center for Contemporary Art, a gallery and educational organization devoted to presenting and documenting trends in contemporary art. Anita Cosgrove, president of the center, explains that the brunch (actually, a selection of four different home-delivered menus named for contemporary artists, including a children's meal delivered in an Andy Warhol-Campbell Soup paint can) wasn't intended to be a major benefit, but rather a "breather" offered to a loyal constituency that might be "benefitted out."

Cosgrove cites several logistical advantages to the portable-meal benefit: It can be quickly implemented, just by engaging a caterer, planning the menus and printing the invitations; its overhead is low and it requires fewer volunteers than a traditional benefit. Expenses, however, ran high for the four-color invitation/brochure and the elaborate brunches, which were accompanied by fresh flowers, fine-art posters and publications and, in the case of the brunch bearing that artist's name, even a Jim Dine "signature" robe. Cosgrove feels that the event was a public-relations success, if not a financial one, since it fell short of its modest $10,000 net-profit goal. She believes that the idea has potential to become more profitable if marketed more aggressively and offered annually so that it builds a following.

The example of "benefit alternatives" to the contrary, conviviality is the essential benefit entertainment, we believe. All the various amusements — the fashion shows, tea dances, art auctions and so on — are basically excuses to bring people together. That's not to imply that the choice of entertainment doesn't matter; quite the contrary. If yours were the only major benefit in town for the entire season (which was a common occurrence in many communities 15 to 20 years ago), you could get away with simply hiring a dance band year after year: The social prestige of the event would be enough of a draw. But with plenty of competition today (both from other benefits and from the high-quality entertainment available in most cities), you need to offer something new and different that will make *your* benefit irresistible.

After food and drink, entertainment will no doubt be the next major expense item. Because benefit patrons expect something special in return for the high price of their tickets, you may need to consider bringing in big-name performers from out of town. One way to keep this expense in line is to find out what performers are scheduled to play in nearby cities around the time you want to have your benefit. If you can offer them an extra gig while they're in your area, they may be willing to lower their fees. Of course, you will have to be flexible about accepting their available dates.

Whatever your choice of entertainment, it will determine other costs you may not have foreseen, such as sound and lighting systems, stagehands' wages, props, printed programs, etc. Co-chair barb Richardson, who negotiated the contract to employ Le Masquerade, a New York troupe of exotically costumed mimes and dancers, for the Cleveland Play House's Fantasy benefit, offers this hard-earned advice:

> Don't be afraid to express any questions and constantly be alert to hidden costs.
>
> For example: Although we had been assured many times that Le Masquerade would bring its own sound system, it was not until three weeks before the benefit that we discovered exactly what the performers would be bringing. In a telephone conversation Cleveland Play House technical director Jim Irwin found out the "sound system"

SAMPLE PERFORMER'S CONTRACT

Name of event: _____

Date: _____

Place: _____

Type of function _____

Start time: Cocktail hour _____ Dinner hour _____ After dinner _____

Package description

_____ Entertainers   Price _____

_____ Sound and lighting system   Price _____

_____ Special effects _____   Price _____

_____ Party favors _____   Price _____

_____ Specialty performers _____   Price _____

_____ Other _____   Price _____

SUBTOTAL _____

Special instructions _____

_____

_____ will start performing at

_____ and will remain at function for a total of _____ hours. If, by mutual agreement, the services of the entertainers are required past the allotted time, there will be an overtime charge of _____ per hour or any part thereof. (Mutual agreement is with permission of _____.)

Please make arrangements to have light food or snacks provided for entertainers. I will _____ Will not _____

Please make arrangements for local hotel accommodations and transportation. I will _____ Will not _____

Terms of payment _____

_____

(Entertainers' agent)   Accepted by (signature)

Subtotal price _____   _____

Overtime _____   Organization

Other _____   _____

Other _____   Address

Total price _____   _____

Less deposit _____   _____

Total due _____   Telephone

consisted of three "boom boxes."

Since the Play House complex [where the benefit was to be held] has high ceilings and hard surfaces, we had been nervous about echoes, but this news made us spastic! Jim used his connections and we were lucky to be able to hire at the last minute a sound company to install mufflers, baffles, filters, etc., to help balance the innate echoes and distortion.

It was an unexpected, unwanted, unbudgeted expense [of $2,500], but crucial to making the sound level that evening bearable.

My advice is: NEVER take for granted a public building's sound system. Check it out beforehand and if it doesn't work, brace yourself for providing your own!

Also, how do 40 wardrobe trunks and 20 performers get to and from your airport? We hired a Greyhound bus. How do they get back and forth from their hotel to the theater for a rehearsal and performances? We ended up using shuttle buses and after the benefit several of the committee [members] carpooled them back to their hotel. What do they want to be fed during the performance? We ordered deli trays at $90 a crack. What are their space requirements for wardrobe storage and costume changes? What are their temperature, sound and electrical requirements? Be careful they don't blow a fuse. Do not agree to a late-afternoon arrival or "walk-through" [on the day of the event]. It's too nerve-racking and much too confusing.

What are your arrangements for a "no-show" or weather delay? Does your committee have a Plan B? (We considered putting a hold on a local band, just in case.) What are the entertainers' charges for overtime? Or their policy of mingling with the committee for a nightcap? When are they paid?

If those were not considerations enough, be forewarned that your choice of entertainment may also have an effect on the number of patrons you can accommodate: You can seat more people in the same amount of space auditorium-style (that is, in rows facing a stage) than you can around dining tables. If you have strolling entertainers, you will need more of them to work a large or broken-up space than a compact space with good sight lines.

SHALL WE DANCE?

There are five basic entertainment formats for a special-occasion benefit. Adapt them creatively — as did the Cleveland area benefits featured in the appendix of this book — and your guests will swear they've never been to a more memorable event!

The classic dinner dance. Otherwise known as the "charity ball," this is the archetypal special-occasion benefit. (After all, how many occasions do we have these days to get dressed in black tie for an evening of ballroom dancing?) The formula for such an evening is simple: Provide a glamorous setting, a formal (sit-down) dinner, plenty of drinks and the best band you can find. Variations on this include the tea dance, held in the late afternoon with cocktails and hors d'oeuvres, and the masked ball, with guests coming in costume.

The obvious place to have such a party is a hotel ballroom, but as this can get to be routine, many benefit committees prefer to find a more unusual location. You can have a dance in almost any kind of building or tent, as long as you have a proper dance floor and good acoustics. And you can combine dancing with other activities, if you so choose. A dinner dance works well as part of a grand opening, because patrons need something to do after they've had a good look at the new building, and upbeat dance music adds to everyone's enjoyment of a fine meal. Some people don't dance, of course, so it's a good idea to provide a more-or-less quiet retreat from which non-dancers can watch the action. It's also important to gear the style of music to the age range of the expected guests; unless your patrons are baby boomers or younger, don't let the decibel level get so high that it impedes conversation.

Different treatments of the dinner dance concept are illustrated by the following benefits described in the appendix:

> April in Paris
> Country Cookout at Hickory Lane Farm
> The Ball at the Halle Building
> Fantasy
> A Festival in Venice

The preview party is similar to a grand opening in that it gives patrons a chance to be among the first to see something — usually an exhibition — before it opens to the public. When items in the exhibition are for sale, patrons get the first crack at buying them. Examining the displays is therefore the main event; music, drinks and food provide a background for socializing. Our examples are:

> Holiday Festival
> 11th Annual Western Reserve Antiques Show

Performance. For arts organizations especially, a gala performance is the obvious choice of entertainment, which can be arranged in either of two different formats. The first resembles the classic dinner dance, except that a performer (usually a comedian, improvisational troupe or popular singer) has been substituted for the dance band. Usually the audience remains seated at the dinner table, nightclub-style. The performance is created expressly for the special-occasion benefit, and only those who buy the package get to see it.

The other performance format features a concert or play given in an auditorium. Tickets to the performance alone — which can range from classical music anpd drama to comedy and pop, rock, jazz or folk — are available to the general public, while the special-occasion package includes choice seats and a private party or dinner, often with the star as special guest, after the performance.

There are a couple of potential problems with performance benefits, however. One is that as soon as the lights go down, all socializing ceases — or it should, anyway — and that can be frustrating for benefit patrons who have come to enjoy the evening with friends. The other is the possibility of a poor performance by a guest star. This isn't always the sponsoring organization's fault, but it still leaves a bad taste in everyone's mouth. Certain well-known entertainers have become *persona non grata* in Cleveland by indulging in what they thought were funny jokes about the city during benefit performances. Planners should take care to find out which stars can be counted on to be gracious guests as well as first-class entertainers.

Examples of performance-centered benefits include:

Light of Day
Puttin' on the Ritz
Red, White and Bravo!
Una Notte Sensazionale

Sports events such as tennis matches, auto races and polo matches can also serve as the entertainment for a benefit, with less risk of the problems just noted. See:

Vestax Cleveland Polo Classic

Fashion shows are favored more by women than by men. Traditionally, they are held during the day and usually accompanied by a luncheon, but with more and more women working, that schedule may prove counterproductive. No matter what the scheduling obstacles, it's unlikely that benefit committees will abandon this format because of the retail underwriting that is usually involved. Our examples are:

Dazzle
A Sterling Spectacular

Testimonials or roasts. While we have our reservations about the latter—they must tread a very fine line between good humor and bad taste—we endorse the former as possibly the most profitable kind of benefit. Testimonials are a very simple and straightforward way to make money for a good cause. Expenses are minimal. The only prerequisite for success is that the honoree must be a person whom everyone genuinely likes as well as respects for his or her philanthropic work. The wider and more varied this person's community activities, the better, because then you can attract patrons from many organizations besides your own. The main entertainment at a testimonial consists of speeches, not necessarily by the honoree. And they needn't all be tedious recitations of his or her good works; sometimes an excellent speaker on a subject of interest to the guest of honor is a better choice.

Our words of praise notwithstanding, it should be noted that the testimonial dinner is rapidly becoming an overworked and unwelcome concept in many areas, particularly from the point of view of the corporations that are continually asked to support this type of event (see the CORPORATE CONCERNS section in Chapter VI). Our example:

32nd Annual Humanitarian Award Dinner

Audience participation. If you believe that the abovementioned formats won't strike a responsive chord with your organization's supporters, you may want to consider building your benefit around entertainment in which they can take a more active part. Because these events are sometimes more specialized or trendy than the others, they may appeal to a narrower or younger constituency. Within this category there are several options from which to choose.

Auctions are a form of entertainment that doubles as an income-generator. When an auction is the only entertainment offered, however, it can make for a long evening. In order to hold patrons' interest, you'll need excellent merchandise, preferably items and services that aren't available for purchase anywhere else, such as fabulous trips to exotic locales led by celebrity guides, with meals and lodging in private wine cellars, palaces and so on. A catalogue that benefit patrons receive a week or two before the event, so that they can come ready to bid, is a necessity, as is a large committee to handle acquisitions, catalogue production and the transporting, storing and pricing of items. You'll also need an experienced auctioneer with clear diction, excellent timing and salesmanship, a well-tuned audio-visual system and a good team of spotters.

Auctions that offer something for everyone can indeed be difficult to sit through, because for every item that interests you, there are a dozen that don't. Auctions that specialize in antiques, art or wine tend to attract serious collectors who are less interested in socializing, but may enjoy the proceedings more. Perhaps the most appealing auction is a short one that is not the benefit's sole entertainment.

Scheherazade
Zippity Zoo Doo

Casino gambling is an activity that most people find conducive to socializing, but be forewarned that there are those who take it very seriously, even when only play money is involved. Once seated at their favorite game, they won't budge to give others a turn. Like dancing, though, gambling can be amusing to watch even if you don't do it well yourself. If you decide on this kind of event, you'll need to hire professional dealers to run the tables, but you can ease up on the usual house rules to give your patrons better odds, which should encourage them to bet more. To increase the excitement, use celebrities as croupiers and cashiers. You'll also need to provide something for patrons to "buy" with their play-money winnings, supplemented by cash if desired; these items should, naturally, be donated. Save a few special items or packages for a play-money auction at the end of the evening.

Food and wine events are a favorite of those for whom an outstanding meal is the best possible entertainment. In this case, ignore the general dictum about serving middle-of-the-road fare; patrons will come expecting something extraordinary. Food events can be produced with amateur or celebrity chefs or restaurants providing the repast and can be set up as bazaars, progressive dinners or giant buffets. Variations on this theme include chocolate extravaganzas, grand desserts, chili cookoffs, madrigal feasts and so on, indefinitely. If you settle on a wine or beer tasting, make sure it's informative as well as fun by enlisting an expert to conduct it.

Shirley C. Fernberg, the volunteer caterer in charge of recruiting more than 20 gourmet chefs to prepare dinner hors d'oeuvres and serve them at trailside at the Shaker Lakes Regional Nature Center benefit, Le Papillon (described in detail in the appendix), shares the following tips for making the experience a rewarding one for the "artists":

Each chef naturally wants a table in the "best" location. I had them select their tables in a drawing, which was done as they arrived. This assured their early arrival. We permitted individual decoration of the tables, but no advertising—no restaurant napkins, matches or other items. Professionals and amateur chefs alike received equal accolades in the program.

The chefs want to walk around and sample, too. It's easy to accommodate their desires by having more than one shift or allowing two people to serve at each table.

Probably the most important factor in maintaining enthusiasm is to have a knowledgeable gourmet in charge of working with the chefs.

Our other examples of food and wine events are:

Cleveland's Second Annual Wine Auction
Ribaffaire '86

Tournaments are audience-participation events geared to serious game-players who want to show off their abilities. They can range from the athletic, such as tennis or golf, to the sedentary, such as bridge or Monopoly. Usually they raise money through both an entrance fee for participants (which may be paid by corporate or other sponsors) and through ticket sales to the participants' relatives and friends. These matches, too, can be more attractive when they involve celebrity players, announcers or referees and unusual prizes. They should be professionally run, as well, although there can also be competition for duffer categories such as best costume, most unusual technique and so on. When tournaments are used as special-occasion benefits, there is as much emphasis on the subsequent awards banquet, at which all the spectators join all the players, as on the game itself.

Murder mystery dinners and weekends are great fun for amateur sleuths and are equally attractive to younger and older patrons. They involve a staged murder (or series of murders) that guests are invited to solve by observing the behavior and verbal clues of everyone around them. As benefit entertainment goes, they are exceptional for getting patrons to mingle, and they actually work best when the guests aren't familiar with one another; then no one can be sure who's a character in the drama and who's an innocent bystander. The essential elements for a mystery event are an intricate plot, preferably one tailored to the location and the organization hosting the benefit, and professional actors to take the principal roles. Commercial troupes that mount these productions at restaurants and resort hotels are springing up in most cities; if you check around, you may discover a published mystery writer in your community who could create a well-crafted story for your group as an in-kind contribution. Volunteers who have a theatrical flair may also play bit parts, and clues may be planted on certain patrons as one of the perks of buying a higher-priced ticket. The plot itself will dictate your choices of scenery, props and menu items, which may be as simple or elaborate as the budget for your production allows.

Obviously, endless variations on these basic formats are possible. Many organizations try to find a type of event that no one else is doing and then repeat it annually—a sound strategy as long as the event stays fresh. As soon as it gets too formulaic, patrons may begin to lose interest.

A word of caution, however: You can get carried away with innovations to the point of losing those elements that have lasting appeal. When patrons spend a high price for their tickets, they want to be sure they're going to have a good time, so they expect any new diversions to be cloaked in familiar comforts. In other words, they want the food and liquor to be of good quality and in plentiful supply, the entertainment in good taste and the environment conducive to enjoying it all—not too hot or too cold, too noisy or too dull, too hurried or too slow. It's a delicate balancing act; the object is to provide novelty within predictable limits.

WHO'S IN CHARGE?

It isn't strictly necessary to identify a chairperson before creating the concept for a benefit. Often the general outline of the event has been decided by the time the board appoints a chairperson, particularly if a standing committee on benefits has been involved. The person who first comes up with a benefit idea and does the groundwork of negotiating for the site or entertainment may seem like the obvious choice for chairperson; after all, the one who thought of it in the first place ought to have the clearest picture of how the event should take shape. But this isn't necessarily the best way to go.

The chairperson's job is so complex and sensitive that we have devoted an entire section of Chapter IV to describing it. While creativity is desirable, we believe strong leadership skills and sound financial acumen are more important in a chairperson. It is worth going to considerable lengths to secure a person with such skills, even if you have to go outside your own ranks to do so. Only a strong chairperson can supervise the various subcommittees, juggle overlapping time lines and coordinate the myriad details that go into a benefit while keeping the budget on target so that the organization can achieve its financial goals.

As former chairperson of Cleveland Ballet's benefit advisory committee, Teri Levine selected and worked with numerous volunteer leaders on a variety of events. Here are the qualities she looks for in a benefit chairperson:

1. Scope of community involvement.
2. Connections.
3. Pizzazzzzz!!!
4. Financial and time leverage.
5. Sincere desire.
6. Organizational skills.
7. Ability to attract some of her own committee workers.

An experienced chairperson will be able to size up your plan and suggest improvements. If your desired chairperson doesn't feel as much enthusiasm for the benefit concept as the person who thought it up, give him or her a chance to come up with some alternatives. A good chairperson will be too honest (and too busy!) to take on an assignment unless he or she believes it has potential.

THE BENEFIT NOTEBOOK: YOUR TRAVELING DESK

As with any complex project involving the efforts of many people, a benefit generates mountains of paperwork and information that can elude you just when you need it most. We recommend a notebook as the most convenient system for organizing this data. Its advantages over file folders or a shoebox are that, once organized, a notebook is easy to add information to, keeps all important papers in one place and is handy to carry around, so that the information you need is always at your fingertips. Marilyn, who's always involved in several benefits at once, keeps separate notebooks for each one in her car. Traveling from one meeting to the next, she has only to pull out the appropriate notebook to be instantly organized and ready to address the subject at hand.

By the time a benefit is over, a notebook holds the complete record of the planning process. It is the ideal tool for the benefit chairperson and subcommittee chairs to pass on to the corresponding chairs of the organization's next benefit. The development officer should keep a duplicate set of notebook materials for the organization's records. Some benefit committees make it a policy to file the chairperson's notebook in the organization's offices as soon after the benefit as possible, so that it's available for reference. Many benefit chairpersons are relieved to get the materials out of the way once the event is over. But it's a good idea for the chairperson to hold onto a duplicate set, because she'll undoubtedly want to retrieve phone numbers, adapt letters and so on, when she goes to work on her next benefit.

A benefit chairperson's first move on accepting the job should be to purchase a large, sturdy three-ring binder and two packages of divider pages with pockets. A three-hole punch will also come in handy. Paste a pocket-sized calendar on the inside front cover with your benefit date and important intermediate deadlines marked for easy reference when setting days for meetings.

By setting up the necessary categories at the outset, you'll immediately see what support materials you need to obtain and where you should file all documents for easy retrieval. For most benefits, you'll use at least these headings:

Benefit committee list enumerating everyone who participates in any capacity, with all names correctly spelled and addresses and office and home phone numbers listed. It's helpful to divide the list according to subcommittee assignments.

Board of trustees. You'll need their names, addresses and phone numbers handy, too, so that you can personally contact each of them and ask their support for various phases of the benefit, such as attending the kickoff party (see the similharly titled section in Chapter VI for a complete discussion of this marketing tool), reserving tables, helping solicit prospects for underwriting, etc. Put the rosters of the organization's support groups in this section, too.

Budget. This document should be kept near the front of the book, where you can consult it easily. Keep every revision in sequence so you can see how your planning has evolved. Comparing your first draft to your final income statement can be instructive.

Time lines. You'll have a general time line and probably a few specialized ones for such responsibilities as printing or decorating.

Minutes. You may want to keep minutes of all meetings in one section or have separate divisions for each subcommittee.

Table hosts and hostesses (see Chapter VI for a description of their role). As you'll want to print the names from this list on the invitation, accuracy here is a must.

Underwriting. Here's where to keep copies of solicitation form letters; names, addresses and phone numbers of corporate and individual prospects; records of all follow-up calls and results.

Correspondence, written and received.

Public relations. Copies of all press materials, media lists, PSAs, clippings.

Printed materials. It's important to keep typed copies of any text you give the printer to use later in proofreading; otherwise you may not catch omissions or typos. You'll also want to save examples of each printed piece here.

Other headings as needed. You may want a separate division for each subcommittee's records; for licenses and permits; menus and catering contracts; floor plans and so on.

Subcommittee chairs can adapt this model to fit their activities.

PLOTTING A TIME LINE

With all the myriad details and intermediate deadlines a benefit committee must juggle, a general time line is essential to keep the entire committee moving ahead on schedule. It can also be helpful in recruiting volunteers, since it shows clearly when workers will be needed for each different task. Every subcommittee chairperson and professional staff member involved in the benefit should have a copy of an overall time line, which the benefit chairperson should draft as soon as the date is set, working backwards from the event.

To speed that job, we have provided in this chapter a sample time line that notes the most important tasks to be accomplished in planning most benefits, as well as some that apply only to those incorporating auctions or exhibitions. The chairperson will undoubtedly think of many additional tasks particular to his or her own event. It would be wise to figure out intermediate deadlines for some of the more complicated jobs. Each subcommittee chairperson should also develop a more detailed time line for his or her committee's responsibilities, which should be reviewed with the benefit chairperson as well as the subcommittee members.

Next to each task listed on our adaptable time line are spaces in which to fill in the beginning date, due date or meeting date, whichever is appropriate. In some cases you may want to write in a period of time (e.g., "3/25-4/8" for researching major expenses) or a deadline ("by 5/1" for applying for a particular license or permit). We have indicated the person usually responsible for each job by title (for a full job description of each executive committee position, see Chapter IV), but, of course, feel free to assign tasks to someone else if it makes more sense. Where subcommittee chairs are listed as responsible, they may want to delegate the task to other volunteers on their committees or to a staff member. We do recommend that you identify the person responsible for every task by name and that the appropriate subcommittee head discuss the assignment, including the deadline, with that person.

The closer you get to your benefit date, the more arrangements you have to coordinate. For an even more detailed look at those last busy days, see Chapter VIII.

BENEFIT TIME LINE

Name of event: _____

Date: _____

DATE	TASK	PERSON(S) RESPONSIBLE

Six to 12 months (or more) before

_____ Board of trustees establishes benefit financial goal.   _____

_____ Standing committee on benefits researches possible dates, locations and chairperson; locates co-sponsor, if possible.

_____ Standing committee on benefits meets with co-sponsor and support group representatives, if any, to determine chairperson and suggest benefit concept.   _____

_____ Benefit chairperson assumes responsibility; appoints subcommittee chairpersons who make up benefit executive committee.   _____

_____ Board executive committee approves benefit executive committee's concept proposal.   _____

_____ Benefit chairperson meets with co-sponsor to designate responsibilities and allocate expenses.   _____

_____ Benefit chairperson meets with organization's executive director and staff liaison to determine nature, extent and timing of staff support.   _____

_____ Benefit executive committee researches major expenses (caterers, entertainment, etc.)   _____

_____ Chairperson and subcommittee chairs meet to finalize date, location, entertainment, theme, type of meal, ticket prices, etc.   _____

_____ Chairperson drafts proposed budget with assistance from development director and subcommittee chairs.   _____

_____ Benefit chairperson presents all plans in budget form for approval by board executive committee.   _____

_____ Subcommittee chairs appoint committee members.   _____

_____ Benefit chairperson compiles committee list with correctly spelled names, addresses and phone numbers (business and home) of all members.   _____

_____ PR chairperson compiles and distributes preliminary fact sheet to all committee members.   _____

————— Benefit chairperson begins to organize notebook. —————

————— Addressing/mailing committee compiles new benefit mailing list, if needed (allow three months); or revises, updates and expands existing list (two months). —————

————— Chairperson schedules regular meetings of executive committee, ideally every two weeks in same location, from now until date of benefit. —————

————— Subcommittee chairs schedule meetings of their committees as needed; benefit chairperson attends if possible. —————

————— Benefit chairperson makes regular progress reports to appropriate staff members and board president. —————

————— Chairperson, printing coordinator and PR chairperson meet with graphic designer to develop concept for all printed pieces. —————

————— Addressing/mailing chairperson checks currency of bulk mailing permit, postal rates and regulations. —————

————— Auction, raffle or casino committee (if any) begins to collect donated items for prizes. —————

Five to six months before

————— Benefit chairperson or executive director signs contracts with caterer, hall, entertainers, etc. —————

————— Building manager or caterer and food/beverage chairperson rough out floor plan. —————

————— Designated staff or committee members apply for liquor license, occupancy permit, insurance rider, etc. —————

————— Underwriting subcommittee develops prospect list with help of development officer; secures cash, in-kind donations and corporate tables to meet budgeted goals. —————

————— Printing coordinator supervises copywriting and design of kickoff party invitations, if needed and "save the date" cards, if used. —————

————— Benefit executive committee approves final design and copy for abovementioned pieces. —————

————— Addressing/mailing committee hand-addresses and mails kickoff party invitations. —————

————— PR committee issues personal invitations to media to kickoff; updates fact sheet for distribution at party. —————

_____ Addressing/mailing committee labels and mails save the date cards. _____

_____ Chairperson phones kickoff party invitees who haven't responded if needed to increase attendance. _____

_____ Benefit executive committee hosts kickoff party. Have sign-up sheet for table hosts and hostesses; make list of those attending for later follow-up. _____

_____ PR committee sends press releases announcing details of event to reporters not present at kickoff party. _____

Two to five months before

_____ Food/beverage chairperson meets with caterer to finalize menu and floor plan. _____

_____ Designated committee or staff member meets with city fire marshal, if necessary, to have floor plan approved. _____

_____ Patron/sponsor subcommittee sends personalized solicitation letters to upper-level ticket prospects. _____

_____ Printing coordinator supervises copywriting and design of invitations, response cards and envelopes. _____

_____ Auction catalogue editor (if any) compiles copy. _____

_____ Benefit executive committee approves design and copy for invitations, reply cards and envelopes. _____

_____ Printing coordinator supervises production of invitations, reply cards, envelopes. _____

_____ Addressing/mailing committee hand-addresses, stuffs and sorts invitations. _____

_____ Entire benefit committee convenes for one general meeting; chairperson briefs members on overall plans and progress of ticket sales. _____

_____ Printing coordinator supervises copywriting and design of benefit program. _____

Eight weeks before

_____ Addressing/mailing committee mails all invitations. _____

_____ Reservations/seating committee updates reservations list daily and begins assigning tables per request; transfers checks promptly to treasurer for deposit. _____

_____ Reservations/seating committee begins telephone _____

follow-up of table hostesses whose reservations are not yet in.

Two to six weeks before

_____ Executive committee approves decorating subcommittee's final plan. _____

_____ Dress rehearsal (optional): set table, taste complete meal and wine, correct any problems with food, crowding, centerpiece, etc. _____

_____ Technical rehearsal: entertainment coordinator and technicians check existing lighting and sound system; adjust if necessary. _____

_____ Deadline for underwriters', upper-level patrons' names in program. Executive committee approves program layout and copy. _____

_____ Personnel manager arranges for security, emergency medical service, maintenance, restroom attendants and clean-up before, during and after event. _____

_____ Personnel manager arranges for parking; reviews traffic control plans with police department. _____

_____ Chairperson sets date for wrapup meeting after benefit; distributes evaluation forms to subcommittee chairs; begins addressing envelopes for thank-you notes to underwriters, participating staff members, subcommittee chairs. _____

One week before

_____ Benefit executive committee meets to review schedule for remainder of week (see timeline in Chapter VIII). _____

Day after

_____ Decorating committee takes down decorations; returns borrowed items. _____

_____ Chairperson, subcommittee chairs write thank-you notes. _____

Two to three weeks after

_____ Chairperson hosts thank-you party/wrapup meeting for executive committee members and co-sponsors. _____

_____ Chairperson presents check to board, submits final report and passes notebook to development officer. _____

Watch Your Figures

Once the board has approved the major elements of the benefit plan—financial goal, ticket prices, date, location, entertainment—and has appointed a chairperson, the benefit committee takes over. Now it's up to the chairperson to draft a budget in consultation with the organization's development director and/or treasurer. Although this document will be revised many times along the way, it is important to have one from the beginning. The budget shows the benefit committee where it is going and what it has to do to get there.

It's easy to get so caught up in creating the benefit of your dreams that you lose sight of the hard realities involved in making a profit. We've all been taught since childhood to be generous about entertaining our friends, to provide the best of everything and to put our guests' pleasure before our own. We may hope to be repaid in kind, but we would never bring up the subject of money in our private social interactions. So it's difficult to turn around and put finances first when planning a social event for a public cause.

There's also a tendency to want to compete for the title of "benefit of the year," which may lead benefit committees to spend too much money on glitter and glamour, without thought for the bottom line. Perhaps those groups who say that they "don't care how much we make, as long as we break even" are really saying they're not willing to commit themselves to the hard-nosed discipline of a budget. They may think it's easier this way but, in the end, they are doing their cause a disservice because they have no way to ensure that the organization will reap the rewards of their efforts.

Here are the reasons why a good budget is indispensible:

1) It forces you to think through the entire project in advance. While your benefit is still in the conceptual stage, you need to put your creative ideas to a methodical test. When you begin to compare estimated expenses with projected income (based on previous levels of support, the capacity of your chosen location, the attractiveness of your theme and entertainment, ticket prices, etc.), you may well discover that the numbers don't justify your initial enthusiasm. You may conclude the whole idea is unworkable and go on to some other project. But, more likely, you'll play with the numbers until you come up with a combination that makes more sense. Perhaps you'll move to a bigger facility or add a second seating time so that you can accommodate more people. You may decide to throw in a raffle, auction, advertising book or other fund-raising device. However you manage to adjust the projected income statement in your favor, you will begin to anticipate contingencies.

2) **It helps you keep expenses in line.** It's easy to let your imagination run away with you, especially when planning decorations. There is no limit to what you can spend to dress up a room, unless you have something in writing to hold you back. To stay within a predetermined cost per plate, you may choose chicken Kiev instead of Chateaubriand or shorten cocktail time by half an hour to reduce the amount of liquor consumed. If you can't negotiate the musicians' rate within your limit, you will perhaps hire a smaller combo or use a local group instead of flying in Lester Lanin's orchestra. If you don't have a donor for your printing, you'll design a simple, one-color invitation instead of a five-color job. Once you establish that you have only so much to work with, you will think twice about exceeding that amount; if you decide the additional expense is necessary, you must find a way to make up for it somewhere else in the budget — either by increasing income or by decreasing another expense.

3) **It establishes committee accountability.** Every subcommittee chairperson should have a copy of the budget, so that he or she knows how his or her area of responsibility fits into the overall scheme. However, after the budget is approved, only one person, usually the benefit treasurer in consultation with the chairperson, should be authorized to approve expenses and sign checks. This prevents spur-of-the-moment purchases, such as when the hospitality chairperson decides it would be nice to send an orchid corsage to each table hostess.

4) **It helps you to identify items that could be underwritten.** Major corporate sponsors often prefer to underwrite a specific line item, rather than make a contribution to general expenses. Also, when you list your expenses, you'll see items at various price levels that could be suggested to underwriters as attractive packages. They may even be able to donate in-kind services or supplies, such as printing, decorations or transportation for out-of-town guests. Your projected attendance figures will also help convince potential donors that their gifts will be seen and appreciated by a large number of influential people.

5) **It challenges you to work harder to achieve your income projections.** Once you've written them down, you're committed —

and you'll feel like a failure if you fall short. Therefore, if you find ticket sales lagging behind your projections four weeks before the event, you'll mobilize your sales committee to get reservations in. If, on the other hand, it becomes apparent that, for some unforeseen reason, people are going to stay away in droves, you'll still have time to make alterations in your plans.

6) It shows the board, the organization's administration and potential underwriters that you're serious and well organized. These people deal with budgets all the time, so by preparing one, you are automatically talking their language. In order to gain their crucial support, you will need to demonstrate that you know what you're doing. A well-conceived budget lets them see exactly what this affair will do for the organization and, by implication, why they ought to do their part to ensure its success. If you can show the board's executive committee that you need 50 patrons at $500 per person in order to achieve your financial goal, the board members should be the first to buy those tickets.

HOW TO DRAFT YOUR BUDGET

Let's assume you have just agreed to chair a benefit for your organization, having satisfied yourself that the date is reasonable (there are no competing events around that time and you've been recruited far enough in advance — six to 12 months — to allow adequate planning time), the location is exciting, the entertainment is smashing, your board is enthusiastic and the community is supportive of your cause. In short, you have every reason to believe this event will be a sellout. It's time to draft your budget.

In this chapter you will find a blank budget sheet that you can photocopy and fill in. Use a pencil! Better yet, make several copies so that you can revise and compare versions as often as necessary. Each line item on the sheet is numbered to correspond with the textual instruction by the same number in this chapter; the instructions explain how to calculate the figures. We have listed only the most common expense items; under "Miscellaneous" in the instructions we suggest other expenses or contingencies you may encounter. Read this enumeration carefully to be sure you haven't forgotten anything.

Though it's obviously difficult to talk about budgets without using working numbers, we realize any figures we cite will probably be obsolete by the time this book is published. We know, too, that the prices of all supplies and services — even the price ranges of benefit tickets — vary widely from one region of the country to another and from big cities to smaller communities. So, in order to

BUDGET WORKSHEET NO. _____

Name of event: _____

Date: _____

INCOME

1) Ticket sales
    a) # _____ x $ _____ $ _____
    b) _____ x _____   _____
    c) _____ x _____   _____
    d) _____ x _____   _____
2) Corporate tables
    a) _____ x _____   _____
    b) _____ x _____   _____
3) Underwriting
    a) Corporate   _____
    b) Individuals   _____
4) Other   _____

    TOTAL INCOME $ _____

EXPENSES

  5) Facility rental $ _____
  6) Food   _____
  7) Liquor   _____
  8) Wine   _____
  9) Entertainment   _____
10) Sound & lighting systems   _____
11) Decorations   _____
12) Printing   _____
13) Postage & mailing list   _____
14) Special guests   _____
15) Licenses & permits   _____
16) Piano rental & tuning   _____
17) Equipment rental   _____
18) Kickoff party   _____
19) Security & maintenance   _____
20) Valet parking/limos   _____
21) Promotion & photography   _____
22) Contingency   _____
23) Secretary (optional)   _____
24) Miscellaneous   _____
    _____
    _____

    TOTAL EXPENSES $ _____

    NET PROFIT (goal) $ _____

give you concrete examples to work with, we have reproduced the working budgets from two Cleveland benefits, Fantasy and The Ball at the Halle Building, following the blank budget sheet. The next section will walk you through the entire budgeting process, comparing and contrasting the income and expense strategies of these two events and suggesting other alternatives to consider. Keep in mind that the total expenses you'll incur and the range of ticket prices you can easily sell will depend to a large extent on what is customary in your area.

FILLING IN THE BLANKS

A certain amount of research is necessary before you can actually begin filling in numbers on the budget worksheet. You can start on either the income or the expense side, depending on how much information you have. If you are an experienced benefit planner and your organization has a track record of successful benefits, you may feel confident enough to project income first (based on your judgment of this event's potential) and estimate expenses (after calling a few reliable suppliers for "ballpark figures" on major items) to get your first working draft. This was the method Marilyn used in planning Fantasy and The Ball at the Halle Building.

If you are a first-time benefit chairperson, you may find it easier to research the major expense items first and then figure out how much you have to charge to cover these costs. (The disadvantage of this method is that it may compel you to set your ticket prices too high.) The formula is as follows: Add up the expenses, using actual quotes for as many items as possible and estimating the rest. (You may be in for a shock when you find out how expensive a benefit can be!) Add to this total your fund-raising goal. *The sum must equal your income.* Divide this figure into ticket sales, underwriting and other income sources, according to the guidelines provided in the PROJECTING YOUR INCOME section of this chapter.

Once the board has arrived at a decision on the basic benefit plan, you should have the following information to work with (though any of these elements may still be subject to change):

Financial goal. Though you may feel it is either too optimistic to be achieved or not optimistic enough to challenge the benefit committee sufficiently, start with the figure the board dictates and revise it up or down after you have filled in all the income and expense lines.

Maximum attendance. This is determined by the size of the facility where the benefit is to take place and is probably governed

THE BALL DRAFT BUDGET

INCOME

Ticket sales	$161,250	
Underwriting		
Forest City (in-kind)	45,000	
Others	15,000	
Mini-auction	20,000	
TOTAL INCOME		$241,250

EXPENSES*

Food and liquor (in-kind)	45,000	
Entertainment (2 groups)	14,000	
Sound & lighting	1,500	
Decorations	4,000	
Printing	3,000	
Postage & mailing	1,500	
Special guests	800	
Piano rental & tuning	400	
Dance floor & stage	800	
Kickoff party	1,258	
Limos & hotel	3,125	
Contingency	1,500	
TOTAL EXPENSES		76,883
NET PROFIT		$164,367

*Facility rental, security, maintenance, parking, promotion and some printing costs were provided by the co-sponsor, so they do not appear in the budget.

FANTASY DRAFT BUDGET

INCOME

Ticket sales	$157,500	
Underwriting	20,000	
TOTAL INCOME		$177,500

EXPENSES

Food (700 dinners x $32)	22,400	
Gratuity	750	
Dinner wine	1,000	
Liquor, bartenders & setups	2,500	
Entertainment	20,000	
Decorating (fog machines)	2,000	
Design & printing	4,000	
Postage & computer labels	1,200	
Equipment rental (cylinders)	2,000	
Kickoff party	1,500	
Security & maintenance	1,000	
Promotion & photography	500	
Play House Club (major patrons)	1,000	
Guests	1,360	
Miscellaneous	2,000	
TOTAL EXPENSES		63,210
NET PROFIT		$114,290

by fire codes (as in "Occupancy of these premises by more than X number of people is unlawful"). You may be able to accommodate more people if they come in shifts. Don't pack people to the walls, however; leave sufficient room for registration tables, bars, buffet tables and/or dining tables, a stage or dance floor, waiters' stations, fire lanes, etc.

Entertainment. Many budgetary decisions, as well as logistics, depend on whether your main entertainment consists of a high-priced performance, an income-producing activity such as an auction or some combination of the two. If you choose the former, it will be a major expense item requiring you to set ticket prices high enough to cover all costs. If you go for the latter, you'll start with an income goal for the auction plus ticket sales and adjust all necessary expenses to stay well under that total. If you wish to incorporate both, keep in mind the relative importance of each activity in terms of time allotted to it during the benefit as compared to its income-producing potential.

PRICING DECISIONS

Everybody knows there's a limit to what people will pay to attend a benefit, but nobody seems to know what that limit is. Perhaps that's why we so frequently hear it expressed as a question: "Do they really expect people to pay *that much* for a ticket?" (This is the corollary to that perennial complaint: "How many benefits can you be expected to go to in one year, anyway?") The answer is, of course, that people will spend the money on something they feel is worthwhile. But how do you determine what other people consider worthwhile?

You have already established approximate ticket prices along with the decision on what type of benefit to have. Actual pricing decisions, just like those in business, will be reached through a combination of thorough research, shrewd judgment and unquenchable optimism. Just about everyone is likely to have a strong opinion about how much to charge for tickets, so discuss this issue in committee in order to achieve consensus. Then be sure to have your decision approved by the board of trustees, whose responsibility it is to buy tickets and to help you sell them to their friends.

Begin with statistics from a similar benefit given previously by the same organization, if possible. Look at the names of attendees as well as the number, if you have this data (standing benefit committees and/or development departments should keep these records). Assuming that approximately the same number of people will buy tickets at the same levels (not always a safe assumption, by the way), you can use this list to set higher goals (because you're going to do things better and get even better results!). You should recognize the names of many of the patrons and have some sense of their level of support for your organization and others in your area. Figure out who could be persuaded to buy tickets at a higher price; don't forget people you know whose names aren't on the list.

You wouldn't charge *less* than last time unless there was so much price resistance that the benefit didn't do well. (A certain amount of grumbling is to be expected; it won't hurt you as long as people buy the tickets.) Before you decide to charge more than last time, however, look around at what other organizations in your area are doing. If they are holding the line on ticket prices at a certain level, do you want to be the first to cross it? If you feel you can justify the increase, go ahead. If other benefits are charging more, could you be underselling your organization and missing a chance to make a greater profit? Your answer will depend on your judgment of your supporters' loyalty, willingness and ability to absorb the increase. More than likely, you'll cross your fingers and mark up the prices about 10 percent. With a bigger increase than that, you'd risk unpleasant repercussions.

If the organization has never had this type of benefit before, do not assume that patrons will pay as much for your first-time effort as they will for an established benefit. Look at your own supporters' giving patterns in other areas such as annual funds and capital campaigns. If they are not in the habit of giving generously and regularly to your organization, ask yourself whether it's because they can't afford to or because they haven't been asked in the right way. In either case, your job is to build support; don't set prices so high that you create resistance.

These guidelines work well in a community in which benefits are common and many people are accustomed to spending high prices for this type of entertainment. In areas where the habit of giving in this way isn't well established, you may be breaking new ground. Do you have to keep ticket prices low out of fear that no one will come if you ask for more? Not necessarily, if you proceed cautiously. If you can't judge your supporters' potential by what they presently give to the organization and other local not-for-profits, think about how they do spend their money and free time. Do they head for the nearest big city to shop, have dinner and take in a show? Do they drive 100 miles to see football games at the state university? Do they buy boats, recreational vehicles, expensive "home-entertainment centers?" If so, you can be sure they don't mind spending money to have a good time; they might even appreciate the convenience of attending a high-quality event closer to home and doing some good for the community while they're at it.

To get an idea of what you can charge in your area, estimate how much it would cost to have a complete dinner with drinks at the best restaurant in town, followed by a professionally produced play or concert or dancing to a big-name band. Now go ahead and for starters tack on a 50 to 65 percent premium—remember, it's for a "special occasion" and a contribution to your cause. Then plan to work with your caterer and other suppliers to keep expenses well below their retail value, as explained in the COST CONTAINMENT section of this chapter.

FINDING YOUR LEVELS

Benefit tickets are commonly broken into three or four price levels, as follows:

Base price. This is the lowest ticket price you offer for the complete package, usually cocktails and hors d'oeuvres, a full meal, dessert and entertainment. This price must cover the cost per person of the entire package, as well as include a substantial contribution to the organization. At the present time, a base price of $100 to $150 per person is common for dinner dances in Cleveland. In New York, Washington, D.C., Dallas and Los Angeles, a base price as high as $500 or even $1,000 per person is not uncommon, while in small towns $35 to $50 might be more acceptable. Experience has shown that approximately half of your patrons will buy tickets at the base level; the other half will be divided among the upper two or three levels, provided you work hard to sell those higher-priced tickets.

Mid-level. This includes the same package as above, plus a listing in the printed program and perhaps another perk such as valet parking that doesn't add much to the benefit's cost but justifies a larger contribution. This level is usually priced to appeal to corporations. With mid-level tickets at $250 each, for example, a company can buy a table of eight for a round $2,000. Individuals who attend many different organizations' benefits tend also to buy the middle-level tickets and may not support those organizations in any other way throughout the year.

Top level. Barbara Robinson, chairperson of the Ohio Arts Council, points out that major organizations can usually count on a small group of supporters who aren't price conscious to buy the highest-priced benefit tickets. By that she means people who are devoted to a particular organization and have the means to give large annual contributions can usually be counted on to support their organization's benefits at the highest level suggested. "There is always a question," Robinson notes, "how much high ticket prices detract from donors' regular annual gifts. No one has any conclusions yet, but the most sophisticated organizations are beginning to track this by computer."

Since the highest-priced ticket (usually $500 to $1,000 per person in our area) reflects a munificent gift, the perks you offer with this package should make the donor feel truly special (see PERKS THAT WORK in Chapter VII). They must still be provided at minimal cost to the committee, however. A commemorative gift is fine if it is donated, but if it has to be purchased, it may cancel out the additional income. Something personal, such as a private reception with the celebrity entertainers at someone's home, might be a better inducement to give at this level. Alternatively, you could offer a service, such as limousine transportation to and from the party, which some top-level patrons will decline and some will be willing to share with fellow patrons.

Partial package or "night owls." Some events break down into components in such a way that you can offer a much lower ticket price (say $25 to $50 per person) for part of the package — entertainment alone, for example. Inviting people to come in for drinks and dancing after the rest of the patrons have finished dinner is another common night-owl package. This ticket level is used mainly to attract new supporters, as it usually doesn't add much in the way of income.

PROJECTING INCOME

Now let's go through our examples to see how Marilyn put together the budgets for Fantasy and The Ball. As we go, we'll explain how you can adapt her calculations to fit your own situation.

1. Ticket sales. Both Fantasy and The Ball offered the same basic package at all ticket levels: cocktails, dinner, dancing and entertainment. The capacity for Fantasy, held to benefit the Cleveland Play House, was 750, but Marilyn's original projection was based on 700 tickets, the difference being allocated to complimentary tickets for various staff members and media guests. She used a formula drawn from observation of many previous benefits: half the tickets at the base price and the other half divided between the upper two levels, with the majority at the mid-level:

    a) 50 x $500 = $25,000
    b) 300 x $250 = $75,000
    c) 350 x $150 = $52,500

In addition, there was a super-category of $1,000 tickets, which she knew would attract only a few, very special patrons: The committee had five particular individuals in mind (at this level, it's not unusual to find singles, hence the odd number).

d) 5 x $1,000 = $5,000

To estimate the number of people who will buy your top-price tickets, you must again look to your organization's supporters, as well as others in the community who might be persuaded to join them. The program from your organization's previous benefit should have a listing of all those who paid the top prices. Are they all still living in town? Do they regularly participate in the organization's other activities? If so, it's reasonable to assume they'll return at the highest level — provided you extend them the courtesy of a personal invitation. (Never take any of your patrons for granted, especially your most loyal. A handwritten message on the invitation or, better yet, a personal note from someone on the patron committee is *de rigueur*. [See Chapter VI for further details on sales tactics.])

Note that ticket income is calculated on an individual basis, even though we recommend that you sell tickets by tables of eight or ten (see Chapter VI). The reasons for this are simple: First, you will receive checks from individuals, who need to be acknowledged separately for their own tax purposes and for the accuracy of your donor files. Second, this permits friends sitting at the same table to buy tickets at different price levels, according to their degree of commitment to your organization. It is much more difficult to try to establish the same price for everyone sitting at one table.

2) Corporate tables. The exception is corporations, which often buy an entire table with a single check and offer the individual tickets to their executives or guests at their discretion. You may find it helpful to set a goal of a certain number of corporate tables, in which case you can enter them on a separate line in your budget. Those corporations that haven't filled out their tables by a few days before the event should be asked if you may resell those tickets or fill the empty places with media or other special guests.

As it turned out, the Fantasy committee sold two corporate tables at $4,000 each and 16 at $2,000 each or the equivalent of 16 tickets at $500 and 128 tickets at $250, which brought the actual individual attendance figures very close to Marilyn's initial projection for mid- and top-level sales.

The procedure for The Ball at the Halle Building to benefit Great Lakes Theater Festival was similar. Here there was space for

1,000 people, but the corporate co-sponsor, Cleveland-based real estate developers Forest City Enterprises, reserved 25 tables of eight (200 tickets) for their own executives and guests. Since they were underwriting the cost of the building, food, drink and numerous incidentals, the benefit committee was happy to work with this arrangement. With 800 tickets to sell, Marilyn projected the following breakdown:

a) $70 \times \$500 = \$35,000$
b) $280 \times \$250 = \$70,000$
c) $450 \times \$125 = \$56,250$

The top line is a good example of that optimism we mentioned. Early in the summer before the November ball, with 39 reservations already in at the $500 level, Marilyn revised her original count from 40 to 70. As it happened, her first estimate was accurate; the final tally showed 39 patrons at this level.

Now let's say you want to offer a late-night option, as well. Perhaps your plans include a stage show following dinner in an auditorium that can seat an additional 300 people. If you charge $30 per person for this option, the potential income is:

d) $300 \times \$30 = \$9,000$

As you can see, the "night owls" are not going to generate much income, but neither will they cost much, since you need provide them only after-dinner drinks and dessert. Your purposes in offering this option are to cultivate patrons who, you hope, will remain loyal to your organization and contribute more in future years and to make it possible for friends of the organization who can't afford the higher-priced tickets to participate.

In planning The Ball, the committee decided against having a night-owl category on two counts: First, representatives of the Backstagers, a Great Lakes Theater Festival volunteer group consisting of young professionals (the type of patron this price level is designed to attract) complained that late comers to a previous benefit had been made to feel like second-class citizens. As one Backstager commented: "When you come into the room where everyone has been seated at dinner, there's no place for you to sit or put down your drink, so you have to stand out in the hall. After you go to the expense of buying your ticket, hiring a babysitter, renting a tux and getting all dressed up, you don't want to be treated that way."

The second reason was simple economics. Underwriter Mark Randol, president of Forest City Commercial Management and an experienced marketer, put it to the committee simply: "When your building will hold only so many people, you lose money by letting tickets go too cheaply. It's true that you leave some people out this way, but our purpose in giving a benefit is not to entertain the whole community. Our purpose is to raise money so that the Theater Festival can keep its regular ticket prices affordable."

You are not obligated to use the same three or four ticket levels discussed above. The idea is to offer prospective patrons a choice of giving levels so that they can find one with which they feel comfortable, but not so many as to complicate the decision. Always include a category considerably higher than the base price, however. This is where your real profit lies.

3) Underwriting. In order to make your benefit truly profitable, don't settle for less than 65 to 70 percent underwriting of your total expenses. Ideally, your goal should be to secure underwriting for 90 percent or more of expenses. *(3a) Corporate underwriting* may come in the form of in-kind donations (goods and services), and you should enter such donations under both income and expenses, as they are an important part of the financial picture. Cleveland Ballet's benefit advisory committee manual cites "future comparative study" as another reason to record the dollar value of in-kind donations. The manual similarly includes in-house expenses incurred directly by the benefit such as staff time or long-distance phone calls as part of the budget, though these expenses aren't paid directly by the benefit committee.

Outright cash contributions are also highly desirable. With the help of your organization's development department, make a list of potentially supportive businesses and the amount you believe each might give. Go through your expense list again to get ideas for in-kind contributions. The total is your goal for corporate underwriting.

In planning the Fantasy budget, Marilyn estimated only $20,000 worth of underwriting because, she felt, there wasn't enough lead time to secure major donors and because the Cleveland Play House was conducting another fund-raising campaign during the same period that would impede the committee's efforts to secure smaller donations; indeed, the amount achieved fell $5,000 short of that goal. Major corporate underwriters want to be mentioned in early publicity about the benefit and identified on the invitation; they tend to lose interest once those opportunities are past.

In order to reflect Forest City's underwriting of The Ball, Marilyn estimated its contribution at $45,000 and listed that figure as a donation from Forest City, which cancelled out the corresponding line items under expenses for food, liquor, facility rental, security and parking.

As helpful as that kind of co-sponsorship can be, it doesn't preclude your soliciting other contributions. In fact, corporate underwriters like to see their peers also participate once they've taken the lead in supporting a cause. So Marilyn sought another $15,000 in underwriting, of which $5,000 was promised early on by the May Company, one of the area's leading department stores.

(3b) Individual underwriting will come mainly from those friends of your organization who can't attend the party or prefer not to. Always include a line on the invitation response card for outright contributions. About 1 percent of your mailing list will take advantage of this option. Often people will give the tax-deductible amount of the ticket they would have bought, figuring that you won't have to provide them with a meal. Thus, if you send 5,000 invitations (providing your mailing list is drawn mainly from past supporters of your organization) and your base tax-deductible contribution is $100, you can expect approximately 50 responses with an average gift of $100:

b) 50 x $100 = $5,000

4) Other income. This can come from any device you employ to raise additional funds, for example:

Auction. This is such a popular attraction that many benefits use the auction as the main form of entertainment and fund raising. The amount you can make depends upon the quality of items you can get donated, as well as how attractively and informatively you present them. Remember, though, that people expect to get bargains at an auction, even when the purchase price is going to a good cause. You should be able to raise at least 70 to 75 percent of the total retail value of the items offered. The long-running WVIZ-Channel 25 auction in Cleveland collects about 85 percent of its total item value, which is considered an above-average return.

When Marilyn calculated her budget for The Ball, she felt sure the benefit had the potential to meet the theater festival's $120,000 net goal in ticket sales alone. In order to take maximum advantage of the occasion and add an extra cushion of profit, she decided to add a mini-auction to the evening's entertainment. Since the main entertainment that evening was to be dancing, the auction had to be brief, so she instructed the Backstagers committee assigned to run the auction to put together five or six extremely attractive packages valued around $4,000 apiece, for a total value of $20,000.

Raffle. The amount you can raise through a raffle is simply the number of tickets sold times the price of the ticket. It's not advisable to go out and buy a raffle prize; with only a limited number of potential ticket-buyers at the benefit, you can't make enough profit unless the prize is donated. Some people may even object to being solicited again for a raffle ticket, having already paid a high price to come to the benefit itself. Raffle tickets priced over $10 usually require preselling, as well as an exceptionally valuable prize. But note that it is illegal, under Title 18, Section 1302, of the United States Code, to solicit or send lottery (raffle) tickets by mail.

Reverse raffle. Instead of selling as many tickets as you can and pulling out two or three prize winners, with a reverse raffle you sell a limited number of tickets and draw them all. The last one left is the big winner. Since there's a greater element of suspense here, a reverse raffle can be more fun than a regular raffle. It also takes more time, so it must be presented with strong visuals to keep people's attention from wandering. Offer small prizes at intervals to keep participants involved. Apply the same pricing considerations here as to a regular raffle.

Advertising book. There are many variations on this device, including the benefit program, calendar or other printed piece containing tasteful institutional advertising, which is given as a souvenir to benefit patrons. Companies tend to regard such advertising as a straight contribution, but it gives them the opportunity to take the money out of a different pocket (i.e., their advertising and promotion budgets instead of their corporate contributions budget). At any rate, there's no way to calculate the cost of the ad in terms of circulation, as a magazine does, so you can charge as much as the traffic will bear and, assuming the printing and paper are donated, take close to 100 percent profit.

Gambling. Both races and casinos can provide exciting, income-producing entertainment for benefits. Before planning such a diversion, however, check with your state attorney general's office so that you set it up in a manner consistent with the law. Races can involve anything from horses to autos to sailboats. If you don't have a commercial racetrack in your area, you may be able to use a school athletic field or even watch an out-of-town event such as the Kentucky Derby on large-screen television. To calculate income from racetrack gambling, set a minimum bet, say, $10, if there are several heats, or $100, if there is only one; assume that everyone who attends will place at least one bet and some will place several. Winners receive donated prizes instead of cash, so all proceeds go to the organization.

At a casino, guests receive a small amount of play money with their benefit tickets to get started at the gaming tables; they may buy more with cash as the evening rolls on. You will need to rent equipment and pay professional dealers and possibly croupiers (Las Vegas habitues can get ruffled if you deviate from standard operating procedure). The amount you'll make depends to a large extent on how effectively you simulate a professionally run casino, with live music, plenty of drinks and strolling attendants coming around frequently to sell more play money (most states don't allow you to play with cash) to be redeemed for donated gift items.

Cash bar. In general, we don't recommend this option. With the high ticket prices most benefits charge these days, patrons have a right to expect that their drinks will be included. It may be acceptable, however, to set up a cash bar for late-night or entertainment-only guests who have paid a much lower price, providing you give those patrons who bought the full package bar tickets or some other form of identification. The object here is mainly to cover the expense of the liquor and set-ups, though you might clear $1,000 to $2,000.

The formulas given above are meant only as guidelines; there are no absolutes. The accuracy of your income projections will depend on your knowledge of the market (your organization's supporters and others in town who like to attend benefits), the event's appeal to that market and especially your committee's ability to sell the concept to potential underwriters and patrons.

COST CONTAINMENT

Now that you've had the fun of counting all the money you hope to make from your benefit, it's time to face reality. The chairperson can't personally research all the expenses of a benefit; her committee will spend a lot of time scouting out suppliers, comparison shopping and bargaining before arriving at the best possible prices for everything needed. But you should start out with at least a rough idea of what everything will cost. You will have to take into account most, if not all, of the following items:

5) **Facility rental.** There may or may not be a rental fee, depending upon the location you choose. A hotel or restaurant may not charge for the space used if you guarantee the purchase of a certain number of meals. If you use your organization's own building or one provided by a corporate co-sponsor, you shouldn't have to pay for the space; however, you may be expected to pay maintenance and security people at their usual overtime rates.

6) Food. Unless you are committed to using a particular hotel, restaurant or club, you should contact three or four caterers to find out what kind of meals they can provide at what cost per plate. Deciding how high to go can be difficult. We think a middle-of-the-road approach works best. People don't expect gourmet food at a benefit—in fact, when you serve anything too unusual, you run the risk of offending your more conservative, meat-and-potato patrons—but they do expect the style and substance of the meal to be worthy of the ticket price. The story is told of a local benefit that backfired by taking the economy idea too far—when a truck pulled up to the picnic site to deliver McDonald's "Happy Meals," some guests were not amused!

The cost of dinner for Fantasy was $32 per person plus $1.50 per person for set-ups, based on an estimated 700 persons; for The Ball it was $30 per person for 1,000 persons, inclusive. Different caterers were used for each event. Beef tenderloin was the entree chosen in both cases; the committees seemed to feel that it would please the majority of patrons and that anything less would be insufficient to justify the $100-plus ticket prices. The Fantasy budget shows that a separate gratuity of $750 was negotiated.

When comparing caterers' bids, be sure to find out whether they include charges for tables and chairs, linens, dishes, corkage or wine service and adequate kitchen and serving help. Also inquire about gratuities and overtime. Find out whether the caterer has on hand all the equipment and table settings it will need for the number of people you expect. You don't want to be charged extra for anything special the caterer may buy and keep for its own future use.

7) Liquor. This line is for the cocktail hour and after-dinner drinks, if you decide to have them. Depending upon your location and the laws of your state, you may need a special liquor license for your party (see point 14). Your caterer should be able to provide bartenders, servers and set-ups and can advise you on how much liquor to purchase. You'll have to decide whether you want premium brands or generic gin or something in between. We suggest you choose recognizable name brands to which no one can object.

As we said before, we don't recommend cash bars. You can control the cost of liquor, however, by keeping the cocktail period to an hour and a half. It's important to provide a non-alcoholic option besides the soda which is available for mixers. On a warm evening especially, a choice of punch or iced tea will be appreciated. Serving ice cream for dessert is an effective way to curb after-dinner drinking; somehow liquor isn't so appealing after tasting something cold and sweet.

8) Wine. If you wish to serve wine with dinner, you may wish to purchase it separately or, if your state liquor laws permit, have it donated. Your caterer or a knowledgeable wine merchant can help you select good, moderately priced vintages that will complement your menu. Offer both a red and a white if you are serving meat; some people won't drink red. If your entree is chicken or fish, you may serve white only. Your wine merchant or caterer can tell you how many cases you need; be sure to tell him or her if drinks will be served before and/or after dinner, so he or she can factor that in. (The standard red and white wines offered at the bar should be included in the line item for liquor.)

Dinner wine for Fantasy cost just under $1,000. Presumably it cost considerably more for The Ball, since the sponsors and members of the benefit executive committee held a blind tasting to choose their offerings; naturally they all preferred the more expensive bottles. This method of selection is fine as long as you have a very generous co-sponsor, but we don't recommend it for the average benefit.

Champagne is the traditional drink for celebrations and toasting, but it can cause special problems if it is to be served at the end of the meal during which other wine has been served. Usually it requires removing the regular wine glass and replacing it with a tulip or flat champagne glass, which can cause delays as well as add to the meal's cost. This ceremony is expected at a wedding, but at a benefit most people would just as soon get on with the dancing. If you must have champagne, why not offer it at the bar, instead?

9) Entertainment. Get a contract guaranteeing both the date and the agreed-upon fee as soon as you hire your entertainers. The contract should also specify how many hours the performers will work and whether or not you have to cover their travel costs, lodging and meals. Be sure to find out whether they will bring their own sound system, lighting and props; and if so, ask what kind of equipment they have, how big a space it was designed for, how much electricity it requires, etc. You may need to provide supplemental equipment and/or power (see point 10).

Fantasy used Le Masquerade, a troupe of fabulously costumed dancers who performed on individual pedestals dispersed throughout the crowd. Because the benefit was held in several connected lobbies of differing shapes and sizes, 19 performers were needed. At $1,000 each (plus a disc jockey), this represented a rather high entertainment cost for a party of its size, but since the benefit concept was entirely based on Le Masquerade's novel performing style, the committee couldn't skimp here. In general, $12,000 to

$15,000 should cover the main entertainment for a special-occasion benefit. Because Le Masquerade performed before, during and after dinner, no additional entertainment was needed.

The Ball secured the 18-piece Gene Donati Orchestra of Washington, D.C. for $12,000. The committee also hired a harpist and a woodwind quintet to play informally during the cocktail hour, which was held on a different level of the building than the ballroom. A brass quartet was hired to play a fanfare announcing the dinner hour; this proved to be a needless expense as it didn't help in this case to get people moving to their tables so that dinner could be served on time. The total cost of these additional entertainers was less than $2,000.

Since you are probably paying dearly for your main entertainment, you shouldn't spend too much on extras. If your organization and hall permit the use of nonunion entertainment, you can locate performers through music schools and colleges. Do audition them first to make sure their skills and repertoire are appropriate and do expect to pay a reasonable rate. Give them an exact performance time and hold to it so you won't have to pay them for waiting around.

10) Sound and lighting systems. Whatever your entertainment, for heaven's sake, make sure people can see and hear it properly. Insufficient lighting, too-loud music or inaudible dialogue can cause people to lose interest, resume their dinner-table conversations and disturb others. Even if your entertainers are bringing their own equipment, it's a good idea to have independent sound and lighting experts check out the facility and advise you on whether you need additional equipment.

The Ball budgeted $1,500 to set up a microphone for the auction, speakers for the band and special theatrical lighting — a figure that held true.

If you are considering an outdoor affair or one at a facility that lacks a public-address system, be sure to include the cost of installing one. A PA system is a necessity in case of emergency as well as for the entertainment. Nothing turns off patrons as quickly as being unable to hear or see what's going on.

11) Decorations. Whether your needs are simply for centerpieces or the complete transformation of a bare or empty space, you should consult a design professional, both for advice on creating an appropriate visual effect with minimum labor and materials and for help with identifying economical sources of supplies. Ideally, you'll recruit such a person for your committee, thus avoiding a fee. Sometimes a department store will contribute the services of a display artist. You should be able to borrow most of the necessary props, platforms and hangings from committee members, sympathetic retailers and community theater groups. Don't neglect to consider special lighting, as it can contribute much to the overall decor.

If you want fresh floral centerpieces, try to talk your florist into providing them for the cost of materials. Even so, be prepared to spend at least $25 to $30 per table to get a distinctive effect. Balloons are a popular alternative, but they are not necessarily less expensive.

12) Printing. Standard printing expenses include the design and production of invitations, response cards, acknowledgements or tickets, programs, table assignment cards, direction or display signs and any supplementary mailing pieces such as "save the date" cards or invitations to the kickoff party. Some committees incur the minor expense of having special stationery imprinted with the benefit logo, which lends a certain polish to all official correspondence, especially solicitations.

The amount you spend on invitations and programs can vary widely according to the size of the piece and weight of its paper, the number of ink colors used and so on. The Ball's invitation was a formal wedding-type announcement, printed in black on white stock with a printed tissue insert. Though partially underwritten, it still cost $2,000 for 8,000 copies. The Fantasy invitation was totally underwritten by a company that has its own print shop. Even so, its cost of $7,500 (nearly $1 apiece for a five-color job) was a bit extravagant for a benefit. It's hard for committees to resist the appeal of a great-looking invitation, but, remember, this is not your primary selling tool. It makes better economic sense to save as much as possible on printing without sacrificing a professional appearance.

We strongly recommend using a professional graphic designer to prepare all your printed pieces; he or she will know how to project the image you want in the most economical way. Of course, you should try to get this service donated, but even if you can't, it's worth spending a little money on it, because professional guidance can save you headaches in the long run — printers' specifications can be confusing to the uninitiated, and mistakes are costly, if not impossible, to correct.

13) Postage and mailing list. Use bulk mail whenever you send out 200 or more printed pieces. You must use first-class postage, however, on any pieces that include handwritten notes — which is why some patron committees prefer to send separate first-class letters to top-level ticket prospects rather than including personal solicitations in the general mailing. Postal rates change frequently, so check with your post office before figuring your postage costs.

If your organization uses a computer mailing house, you will have to pay for any lists and labels you have printed, with possibly an extra charge for updating; if it has an in-house computer you should only have to pay for the supplies.

14) Special guests. The subject of nonpaying guests is a touchy one. Usually there is a limited number of places available, so giving away tickets cuts into profits. Nevertheless, all benefit committees should allow for a certain number of complimentary tickets for staff members, media representatives and VIPs. State and local elected officials—governor, mayor, senators and representatives—should all receive invitations, unless your organization routinely invites them to other events during the year. If one or two politicians show up, they'll add a degree of importance to the event, as well as giving you an opportunity to educate them about your organization. Officials of philanthropic foundations should also be cultivated in this way. Insert a figure of $1,000 to $2,000 here.

15) Licenses and permits. Unless you are using a restaurant or hotel that has a liquor license, you may need a special one for the occasion. Check with your state's board of liquor control to find out when and how to apply for one; usually you have to send in a fee with your application several weeks in advance. You may also need an occupancy permit. Check with your organization's attorneys or the manager of the building in which the benefit will take place to find out what other regulations may apply (ignorance being no excuse). Your party can be closed down at the last minute if you don't adhere to all local regulations.

You'll also need to find out whether the event will be covered by insurance, either the organization's or that of the building owners. You may need a special policy or rider to cover your guests, their property and any equipment or decorations you may have installed.

16) Piano rental and tuning. Your entertainers' contract should specify whether they will need a piano, if it isn't obvious. Don't neglect to tune it the day of the event, after it's in place. This line item can come to several hundred dollars, as piano movers have their own union. Sometimes a music store will donate the use of a piano, in exchange for a credit in the program.

17) Equipment rental. You may have to rent anything from stages, platforms, dance floors or casino-style gaming tables to tents and porta-johns to outfit your facility for the party. To determine what equipment you'll need, walk through the site and imagine what will happen from the moment your guests arrive at the door.

Will they find protection from rain, a place to hang coats, a properly prepared surface to dance on, a dais for the head table, telephones, restrooms and so on? If these amenities aren't already in place, you will surely want to provide them.

18) Kickoff party. While it isn't necessary to have one, a kickoff party helps to build excitement for the event and gives ticket sales a push at an early date. A kickoff party should be short and simple; it's like an aperitif to whet your appetite for the main course that's being prepared. The only program necessary is an announcement of plans for the benefit itself.

The kickoff party is often held at a committee member's home, with food prepared by volunteers or the hostess picking up the tab, in order to keep expenses down. The Ball held its kickoff party at a downtown club at a cost of $1,258. The main costs were for reserving the room, drinks and a string trio for background music — since this kickoff party was held at cocktail hour, potato chips and pretzels were the only food served.

19) Security and maintenance. Everybody is concerned about security these days. It's unfortunate that we have to think about the possibility of theft or even worse disruptions at a charitable event, but there's no getting around it. People will feel more comfortable if they see a few uniformed security guards around the entrances, parking lot and cloakrooms (though too many uniforms may produce the reverse effect, causing guests to think the neighborhood is more dangerous than it really is). Likewise you'll want to have maintenance people on hand in case of power failure, equipment breakdown or broken drinking glasses that need cleaning up. You may even want restroom attendants to keep the facilities immaculate. The caterer's crew should remove all their debris without extra charge, but you will probably have to pay for some building cleanup, too. Hire the same security and maintenance forces that normally work the building, as they know the layout best. Your peace of mind is definitely worth the investment.

20) Valet parking/limos. These services are frequently offered as perks for high-level patrons and special guests. If parking is very inconvenient, you may have to provide it for everyone. Be sure to use a bonded parking service — hiring students may seem like a good idea until one of them scratches a patron's fancy sports car and you discover your insurance doesn't cover the damage. If you really want to go all out, dress your parkers in tuxes, but, please, have someone donate their rental. Parking attendants should be instructed not to expect or accept tips.

21) Promotion and photography. Good press coverage is

essential to the image-building goals of a benefit. Your public relations efforts needn't be expensive; you can prepare brief press releases and fact sheets to be mailed to society and feature editors or writers for the cost of photocopying and postage and follow up with phone calls. Taking an interested reporter or editor to lunch is a nice touch, and committee members are usually willing to do this at their own expense. A few days before the event, disseminate press kits containing updated fact sheets, committee and guest lists and a floor plan so your media guests can find the patrons they want to interview or photograph. You may want to charge the cost of their tickets to the promotion budget.

After your committee has put in months of work on the benefit, you'll want good pictures for your organization's records and personal needs. Sometimes benefit committees overlook the need for photography at the event itself, counting on the press to provide pictures, which is usually cause for disappointment. If you want good photos for future publicity (including your organization's annual report), hire a professional who specializes in weddings and parties. You will pay an hourly rate plus the cost of any prints ordered; the photographer may give you a better price if you guarantee that committee members will order a certain number of extra prints. Don't ask a guest who happens to be a good photographer to document your event; he or she will either be too busy working to enjoy the party or too busy having fun to do a good job. Volunteers may want to bring their own pocket cameras for snapshots, but you won't end up with anything publishable.

22) Contingency. Even though you think you've covered all the bases, there are always surprises. A contingency fund will also cover you in case one or more of your expense items exceeds your original estimate. Don't be too generous in estimating this item, lest someone gets the idea there's extra money available and spend it on something unnecessary. Include just enough to cover emergencies — no more than 5 percent of the total budget.

23) Secretary. Some benefit committees find it expedient to hire a temporary assistant who can handle routine correspondence, telephone calls, typing or word processing and record keeping during part or all of the benefit planning period (see the job description in Chapter IV). This is especially helpful when the event planned is large and complex and when both volunteers and staff have limited time available for the project. Obviously, the benefit's projected net income must be high (usually over $100,000) to justify the expense. Resist the temptation to hire an inexperienced person who's willing to work for low wages and look instead for someone with judgment, maturity and at least some knowledge of civic affairs. A retired person may offer the qualifications you seek without demanding a competitive salary. Perhaps a corporate underwriter could be persuaded to loan a secretary to the benefit committee on a part-time basis or a secretarial school could arrange an internship for a highly motivated student.

24) Miscellaneous. This includes last-minute items such as perfumed soap for the ladies room, some means of hostess identification such as flowers or name tags, parking passes for workers prepping the facility or anything we haven't mentioned so far that may be specific to your event, such as auction paddles and props, dry ice for special effects, etc. Often favors or commemorative gifts are presented at the end of the evening, and this expense should also be included here. In general, we don't think you should spend anything on a giveaway, but if you get something donated (perfume samples from a department store are almost a cliche by now), you may want to dress it up in a fancy wrapper.

CHECKING AND BALANCING

Now that you've totalled up the costs of everything you'll need to create the perfect party, you'll almost surely need to make some adjustments. Reexamine each item on the expense list to determine whether it is indeed legitimate and necessary *for this particular event.* But don't get too caught up in minutiae at the beginning—if you do, it tends to stifle committee members' creativity.

Start with your major expenses, namely food, drink and entertainment. These items establish a direction for the entire budget process. You can't eliminate any of these categories, but look for ways to trim their costs without sacrificing quality. If the main attraction is previewing a new building, and you believe that people will buy tickets just to tour it, you may not need to hire a big-name entertainer. If you're planning an auction or casino, a 20-piece orchestra would be superfluous; a small combo can provide just enough background music to promote a lively mood. If you want to reduce the cost of food, perhaps you could enlist several recognized gourmet cooks to provide the hors d'oeuvres or dessert.

Next, look at the expense categories that offer the most leeway, namely decorations, printing and rental. Instead of fresh flowers, could you use nonperishable centerpieces that could later be sold or recycled? Could your invitations be designed in a more economical size or printed on a stock that your printer won't have to special order? Can you find a place to move your outdoor event indoors if it storms in order to avoid having to set up a tent "just in case?" Instead of erecting an awning from the building entrance to the curb in case of rain, could you use a few golf umbrellas to keep guests dry as they alight from their cars?

When it comes to the minor expenses, however, don't be tempted to eliminate any that are necessary to produce the special effects you want your benefit to have. For example, proper sound and lighting systems are essential; without them all the money you spend on entertainment may be wasted. Adequate security and maintenance can assure that the event will run smoothly and prevent disasters that could spoil everybody's good time.

Above all, don't cut corners so obviously that any aspect of the benefit appears cheap or homemade. Your working committee should include people with expertise in many areas, including design and production, marketing, promotion and accounting. Benefits are too competitive these days and people in general are too sophisticated to accept anything less than professional polish, especially at the prices these special occasions command.

No matter how you economize, benefits are by their very nature costly productions. Underwriting is the key to making any benefit profitable. As noted above, you should attempt to find underwriting for 90 percent of your expenses. To find out how to attain that ideal, please turn to Chapter VI.

Department of Human Resources, Part I

Though it takes the effort of many individuals to mount a major benefit, a strong and well-organized chairperson is the key to success. Like the chief executive officer of a corporation, the chairperson is responsible to the board for achieving the benefit's financial and public relations goals. Since she cannot handle every detail personally, this means recruiting the best available workers, inspiring them with a personal vision of the completed project and providing them with that elusive balance of direction, support, supervision and freedom they need to get the job done.

THE BENEFIT CEO

Unlike a corporate CEO, however, a benefit chairperson can't motivate volunteer workers with big salaries and lavish perks. And while he or she can certainly fire incompetent or unruly volunteers, such an action does not pose a serious threat to their livelihoods. Volunteers work strictly on the honor system, so the issues of productivity and quality control must be handled with the utmost tact. They will give tirelessly of themselves as long as they believe their work is truly worthwhile and appreciated, but there's no way to force them to do jobs they don't consider necessary nor to cooperate with a boss they don't like. For, notwithstanding a benefit's hierarchical committee structure, a volunteer's relationship to the chairperson is essentially a matter of personal loyalty.

Traditionally, benefits have most frequently been run by women. The reasons for this are self-evident; for many years women with true executive ability were discouraged from seeking high-level corporate positions, but welcomed as volunteers by not-for-profit organizations, where they could achieve comparable status and make no less significant contributions to their communities. Perhaps, too, women have become more adept at the gentler art of leadership by persuasion and praise, which is much more effective with volunteers than the economic incentives used in the traditionally male business world. The very nature of benefit work requires that at the top levels it be virtually a full-time occupation, which used to mean that only women who didn't have paying jobs could devote themselves to it.

The demands of leadership are capsulized by R. Eric Kennedy, a young attorney who recently chaired his first benefit, the Vestax

Cleveland Polo Classic:

> It is impossible to maintain a full-time job and at the same time personally see to every detail of a fund-raising event. A tremendous amount of delegation and organization is called for. Even so, there is no getting around the fact that if you are going to chair a fund-raising event, your week is going to involve a great time commitment away from your work, family and social and personal recreation. If a person is not willing to make the sacrifice, then he should not get involved at the start.

As Kennedy's volunteer activity indicates, we are now seeing both working men and women increasingly serving on benefit committees, even as the number of women who pursue volunteerism as a full-time career diminishes. They may serve as "loaned executives," spending some of their working hours helping not-for-profit organizations with accounting, marketing or fund raising; or they may become involved as underwriters, integrating the image-building power of the benefit into their company's overall marketing scheme. They may be recently transferred employees who are interested in making friends and learning about their new community. Or they may be there simply because planning a benefit provides an element of fun, creativity and satisfaction that they need to keep their nine-to-five routines fresh and exciting.

As long as most of the experienced benefit volunteers we know still happen to be women, however, we will use the feminine pronoun throughout the remainder of this book.

And experience is definitely required. Just as a corporate board of directors would not hire a CEO straight out of business school, a not-for-profit's board of trustees should not turn over the sensitive, complex fund-raising responsibilities of a benefit to an untried volunteer. If possible, choose someone who has either chaired successful benefits in the past or has served in an important supporting role such as subcommittee chairperson. Ideally, the candidate will have a proven ability to manage *people* as well as planning and finances.

It's only fair to admit, though, that some benefit planners become complacent after a certain number of successes, tending to do things the same way time after time. A volunteer who has never before had full charge of a benefit, but has had a chance to assist with many different events, may prove to be more innovative. And occasionally an inspired entrepreneurial type like R. Eric Kennedy will emerge — someone whose lack of experience has yet to teach him or her the phrase, "It can't be done."

The chairperson's responsibilities fall into two major areas: finance and personnel. Under finance, she must develop and administer a budget that will achieve the organization's fund-raising goal, secure underwriting, monitor expenses and ticket sales and write a final report to the board of trustees accounting for expenses and net profit. It's not necessary to be a math whiz; anyone can prepare a budget with a pocket calculator, a bit of research and the instructions given in Chapter III. In order to secure underwriting, the benefit CEO must know personally many potential donors, both private individuals and businesspeople in a position to make decisions involving hundreds or thousands of dollars. Furthermore, she must have no qualms about calling upon these people, politely and persistently, for their support. In order to sell tickets, she should be known as a person who gives delightful parties and have many friends who like to attend affairs of this sort. (More than likely, she will have bought tickets to many of *their* benefits, so she can expect them to return the favor.) She must also be able to motivate and monitor the progress of her sales force, consisting of the benefit committee itself and the table hosts and hostesses (see Chapter VI). If the budget is sound, and she manages it successfully, presenting the final report should be a pleasant duty.

She won't be able to accomplish all this single-handedly, of course. Here is where her leadership abilities will come to the fore. The chairperson's other major responsibility is to recruit and manage a large volunteer committee who will work with paid staff members of the organization and the corporate co-sponsors, if any, to plan and execute every detail of the benefit. In order to find the best-qualified people and persuade them to give their time for the project, she must have the sort of personality that attracts a following. She needs a wide network of contacts, including people in business, government and various professions, as well as colleagues on the volunteer circuit. She should be equally poised, articulate, enthusiastic and businesslike whether chairing a meeting of her committee, speaking before a large group or soliciting a contribution from a potential underwriter. Charm is essential; she must meet people easily and project genuine warmth and interest in others.

She must be creative, energetic and self-confident. A flair for drama and a streak of humor are highly desirable traits, as these elements should turn up in the benefit plan. She should be able to generate ideas in such a way that others are encouraged to build on them. She needs to be firm, but tactful, in controlling the budget, keeping her executive committee members focused on the task at hand and making sure they complete their assignments on time. Above all, she should make every member of the benefit committee feel that his or her contribution is absolutely crucial to the success of the event because, in fact, it is.

An effective chairperson, we must add, needs certain attributes beyond the purely organizational. Such a paragon will never lack for projects of one kind or another, but in order to do justice to the benefit, she must be willing to make it her sole priority at the proper time. She also needs to command a certain amount of discretionary income, because she will need to assume many incidental expenses, including taking people out to lunch, hosting coffees, cocktail parties and thank-you luncheons for committee members. She will inevitably run up her phone bill and put hundreds of miles on her car. And she's expected to take at least one table at the benefit itself, preferably at the highest ticket price, to which she will invite important guests.

ARE TWO (OR MORE) HEADS BETTER THAN ONE?

The ideal number of chairpersons depends upon the circumstances of a particular benefit and the personalities of the players involved. If a single chairperson can be found who has all the characteristics described above, that individual should be able to handle the responsibility by herself. The advantages of having a single chairperson are that she can make decisions faster, respond immediately to any questions or problems and interact more smoothly with staff and volunteers. Whenever two or more people have to agree on a decision, time may be lost and confusion more likely to occur.

On the other hand, it's increasingly difficult to find a single person who has enough free time to take on the total responsibility even if she possesses all the requisite skills. When two or three (any more would be unwieldy) co-chairs have complementary strengths, respect one another's abilities and feel comfortable with each other's styles, a leadership team can be greater than the sum of its parts. The Fantasy committee was chaired by three equal partners who functioned as a three-person executive committee and divided the duties according to their areas of expertise: barb Richardson, a trustee of the sponsoring organization (Cleveland Play House), served as board liaison and entertainment chairperson; Barbara Meals handled the menu, invitations and hospitality; and Marilyn was responsible for finances, including the budget, underwriting and ticket sales. Each co-chair worked independently with the subcommittee chairs under her jurisdiction, though all three kept in constant touch with one another by phone and in-person meetings. When there was disagreement, they settled the matter by an informal vote. Having three people in charge proved fortuitous when a death in the family of one co-chairperson forced her to be absent during the last weeks before the event; the other two were able to step in and cover for her. Had this befallen a solo chairperson, the committee might have been at a loss as to how to proceed.

Still, it is helpful to have one person who is ultimately in charge. Marilyn personally prefers to divide the duties between a chairperson and one or two vice-chairpersons. The difference between this designation and equal co-chairs is subtle but important: In most cases, the benefit leaders will get together to discuss important issues, but when time is of the essence, the chairperson has the authority to make decisions and move forward without calling a special meeting, saving her time and frustration.

THE CHAIN OF COMMAND

While all volunteers are equal in theory, in practice most people feel more comfortable with a hierarchy of authority and clear lines of reporting. Whenever representatives of a corporate co-sponsor and/or paid staff members of an organization work alongside volunteers on a benefit committee, it is absolutely crucial to establish a chain of command in advance, since, in this case, you're actually dealing with three separate hierarchies. Whenever there are two or more co-chairs, an organizational chart should also be drawn in order to avoid duplicated efforts or, worse, neglected areas of responsibility.

As soon as a chairperson accepts the leadership of a benefit, she should begin to organize her executive committee, creating subcommittees to handle complex jobs and delegating certain other tasks to individual executive committee members. Choosing the right person for each subcommittee chair assignment requires as much care as the selection of the general chairperson. It's important to find someone with the appropriate skills and experience and the requisite time and resources — otherwise, the general chairperson may end up having to do the work of individual committee members in addition to coordinating the project.

Once the subcommittee chairs have been chosen, they will in turn recruit friends and associates to fill out their teams. The chairperson should make a point of getting to know each volunteer and showing appreciation for his or her efforts. It stands to reason that subcommittee members will owe their first loyalty to the friend who asked them to serve, but they will all look to the benefit chairperson for leadership. The chairperson should also stand ready to suggest reinforcements and to assist subcommittee chairs with any of their assignments. As Cici Riley, co-chair of Cleveland Metroparks Zoo's annual Zippity Zoo Doo in 1986, points out: "The chairperson ultimately has full responsibility for the success or failure of the event. She must be ready at a second's notice to step in and fill all the gaps."

THE JOB DESCRIPTION

In the appendix we give job descriptions for the most common executive committee assignments. While we have tried to make each as complete as possible, none is meant to be definitive. Every benefit committee will have a different structure, depending on the nature of the event and the particular mix of skills of the volunteers working on it. Except where otherwise noted, the first task of each executive committee member is to recruit her subcommittee members (after referring to the recommendations in the "Composition of Committee" section at the end of each job description).

The purpose of having job descriptions is to help everyone understand from the outset exactly where her job will fit into the overall structure and what her specific responsibilities will be. Volunteer committees rarely provide this information up front, assuming, perhaps, that experienced volunteers already know what to do or that such formality interferes with the camaraderie of planning a benefit. But we think people who work without pay deserve at least the same consideration as paid employees—that is, knowing what is expected of them. In the long run, it could prevent confusion that could undermine cooperation and damage the benefit itself.

While it isn't necessary to hand out a written job description, a chairperson should certainly tell a prospective volunteer as much as possible about the position. This way the recruit can decide for herself whether or not she has the time and inclination to take on that particular job. It's tempting to try to convince a friend to join a committee by promising that it will be a lot of fun and not too much work, but what purpose is served by raising unrealistic expectations? If a prospective volunteer can't fit the job into her schedule, it's better to know beforehand, rather than having her simply drop the ball halfway through the project. Besides, when a conscientious volunteer declines a big assignment, she almost always offers to help in some other way.

HOW MANY VOLUNTEERS DO YOU NEED?

Since every benefit is unique, we can offer no set formulas for staffing a benefit committee. Each chairperson will have to determine, with the aid of her executive committee, how many workers are needed to complete each task. On some subcommittees, such as addressing/mailing, you can go by the numbers. If you're planning to mail 8,000 invitations, and one person can hand-address 40 in an hour, then 200 person-hours will be needed to complete the project (not including stuffing, sorting and bundling time). If shifts are eight hours long, then you'll need 25 volunteers for this task alone.

On other subcommittees such as underwriting, the number of members may be determined not so much by the size of the financial goal as by the skills of the recruits. One person might have contacts at five companies, while another knows only one corporate prospect; but the possibility of landing that one donation will be reason enough for adding the latter volunteer to the committee as well as the former. Still other subcommittees, such as decorating, may decide to divide responsibilities into components, assigning one volunteer to lighting, another to centerpieces and so on.

As a rule of thumb, however, the more individuals you can meaningfully involve, the more successful your benefit is likely to be. For major benefits with goals of $50,000 or more, this usually means at least 50 to 100 committee members, including active volunteer workers, board patrons, table hostesses and representatives of the co-sponsor. If a large-scale auction is part of the plan, at least twice as many volunteers are needed.

There's a certain paradox here: Usually the progress made by a committee is in inverse proportion to the number of persons sitting on it. The opposite is true for benefits. One explanation is that prospective patrons like to see who else is involved before making their own decisions to participate. The first thing most people do when they receive a benefit invitation is to scan the committee list to see who will be at the party. The names of prominent civic leaders, media personalities and other VIPs constitute an endorsement; they lend an image of glamour and importance to the event. The sheer impressiveness of a star-studded list conveys the message that "everybody who is anybody" will be at this event—so don't be left out!

Another good reason to have a large committee is simply that *every member is expected to buy a pair of tickets and preferably to reserve an entire table.* That's right, committee members do not come gratis, but as paying customers. Hosting a table is a big responsibility in itself, as it means selling eight to ten tickets. It is hard for some volunteers to come to grips with this important principle; they feel that their effort should count as their contribution. Unfortunately, it doesn't work out that way. Usually the number of places is limited, so giving away tickets would cut into the organization's profits. The net effect would actually be to diminish the results of the volunteers' work. If other volunteers protest that they can't ask their friends to pay for a party that they're giving, they should be gently reminded that the event is for the benefit of their organization, not of its members.

We're not suggesting, however, that you create busywork to justify having a larger committee than you need. Don't ask 20 people to come in the afternoon of the benefit to place centerpieces on the tables when two can do the job. Everyone's time is precious, and anyone you involve should have a meaningful task to accomplish.

WHY VOLUNTEERS VOLUNTEER

If mounting a benefit looks a lot like planning a wedding (for a bride and groom with enormous families!), it is also very much a business. But for what other business do men and women work without pay for a year only to turn around and give their profits to someone else? Because most benefit workers are not paid for their time, keeping them happy is the key to productivity. There has to be a sense of value received for their efforts or they will soon stop making them. That value received is personal satisfaction.

Knowing what motivates volunteers will help you recruit them, stimulate their creativity, assign them to tasks they will do well and enjoy and ensure that they receive the personal satisfaction that will keep them working loyally for your cause. Some of the reasons people volunteer are:

• Because they want to help an organization — to improve its programs and services, to balance its budget, to get out of debt, to build a new edifice or start an exciting new project.

• Because they strongly believe in what the organization stands for.

• Because they want to help improve the quality of life in the community in which they live.

• Because they enjoy a sense of pride of ownership that comes from personal involvement in an organization.

• Because they want to meet new people.

• Because they want to become better informed about what's going on in their community.

• Because they believe their businesses will improve as a result of the contacts and good will their participation generates.

• Because they have time to spare and talents to share (this is particularly true of retired persons or women who don't work outside the home). Benefit committees provide a good outlet for unused energies, the satisfaction of meeting a challenge and the opportunity to socialize with people of compatible interests.

• Because they want to develop or exercise skills that aren't used in their jobs — for personal pleasure or with an eye to future career developments. ("Hidden talents" often come to the attention of potential employers or one's supervisors through one's volunteer activities.)

• Because they seek recognition not available from their jobs or families, no matter how well they are compensated or loved.

• Because they want to become more visible in the community, county, state or nation — depending upon the reach of the organization. (Some may lend their support *only* if they think it will help them to climb the social ladder.)

• Because a friend — someone they like, admire or owe a favor — asks them to take part.

The last is the most frequently cited and probably the most compelling reason why volunteers get involved in any given project. Most people won't take the initiative to join a benefit committee; they must be personally invited to do so. Even if they're aware of having any of the "wants" outlined above, they may be modest about their abilities or shy about thrusting themselves forward. Besides, most people think their lives are busy enough without taking on extra activities. When a volunteer recruits a friend for a benefit committee, her own commitment is reassurance that the recruit's time won't be wasted.

RECRUITING TACTICS

To illustrate how a skillful benefit chairperson might identify and recruit volunteers for her executive committee, we provide the following hypothetical dialogues.

Alice Willing, a longtime trustee of the Lakefront Beautification Committee (LBC), an organization that is responsible for creating an attractive beachfront park, marina and family recreation area in place of a deserted warehouse district in the city of Utopia, has just agreed to chair LBC's annual benefit. This summer marks the organization's 20th anniversary as well as the opening of a new attraction, a luxury cruise ship that will dock in Utopian Harbor and offer daily and evening excursions around the lake. LBC plans to join forces with the ship's owner, Portobello Cruise Lines, in turning its grand opening celebration into a benefit (see Chapter VI for an illuminating narrative on how LBC landed this once-in-a-lifetime opportunity).

A native of Utopia, Willing has been involved in community affairs since becoming a Candy Striper at the local hospital as a teenager. Whether hosting a coffee klatch to raise money for a mayoral candidate, organizing a school fair or mounting a black-tie benefit, Willing has earned a reputation as a gracious hostess, a capable leader and a persuasive advocate of worthy causes.

Willling's first choice for reservations/seating chairperson of the LBC benefit is Winnie Friend, a fellow volunteer who seems to know everybody in town and has in fact held this position on several other benefit committees. Upon accepting the LBC benefit chair, Friend is one of the first people Willing calls.

Willing:	Winnie, I'm chairing the Lakefront Beautification Committee's benefit on June 15th. We're going to unveil the new cruise ship that will be docked at the harbor, and it's going to be quite spectacular! We're expecting 900 people, so I need someone well organized and experienced to be reservations/seating chairperson, and naturally I thought of you. Can you do it?
Friend:	Oh, dear, that sounds like bad timing for me. My daughter's graduating from college on the West Coast in May, and my son's getting married two weeks later in Philadelphia, so I won't be around when you'll need me. I'll be back in time for the party, though, and I'd love to help. Is there anything else I can do?
Willing:	Well, I can see you're going to be busy this spring. Can I count on you to take a table, then? That would be a big help.
Friend:	Of course, Alice. Any benefit you're involved in is bound to be good; I won't have any trouble selling a table and I wouldn't miss it myself.

Willing hasn't solved her subcommittee problems, but she has just nailed down ten reservations. She has several people in mind for other positions on her executive committee and, in the course of her calls to these volunteers, she asks for suggestions about the reservations chair. One person gives her the name of a woman she has met recently on another committee, Edie Torr. Alice decides it's worth a try.

Willing:	Hello, Edie? My name is Alice Willing, and I'm chairperson for the Lakefront Beautification Committee's upcoming benefit on June 15th. Vera Handy is doing our decorations and she gave me your name; she thought you might be a good person to handle reservations and seating for the benefit because you're well organized and good with figures. Would you be interested?
Torr:	Did Vera say that about me? I don't know where she got the idea I'm good with figures; I can barely balance my own checkbook. I suppose it's because I work for a brokerage firm, but what I do is edit a newsletter. I guess you could say I'm well

organized, though. If Vera thinks I can do it, I'd give it a try.

Willing: (Backpedaling) Oh, I must have misunderstood what she told me. I'd hate to have you take on a job if you felt uncomfortable with it, especially with 900 reservations to keep track of.

Torr: Wow, that does sound like a lot. Would all those checks be coming to my house?

Willing: Yes, you'd be expected to keep accurate financial records and work closely with our treasurer. Since you're an editor, perhaps you'd rather work on our program book instead? Joe Pressman is chairing that committee, and he's looking for people who can write and do layouts.

Torr: Joe Pressman of Pressman Printers? Sure, I'd be glad to work with him. I'll bet I can get my firm to take an ad, too. Now that I think about it, maybe my boss, Jane Gaynor, would be a good person for your reservations committee. She's one of our vice presidents, and she really loves the lake — she sails in the summer — so she'd probably like to help.

Willing: Hmm, do you think she'd have the time? We need someone who'll be available from about April 15th on, and it requires a lot of telephone work in the last month.

Torr: That shouldn't be a problem. She doesn't make too many out-of-town trips and she's on the phone all the time, anyway. She's got a lot of clients who might want to buy tickets. Would you like me to ask her if she's interested and call you back?

Willing: By all means. I'd like to talk to her as soon as possible so I can firm up my executive committee by the end of next week. In the meantime, the printing committee is having its first meeting next Thursday at noon at the Downtowner Restaurant. Can I tell Joe you'll be there?

Torr: Sure thing. Give me your number, and either Jane or I will get back to you this afternoon. See you at the meeting.

In Gaynor, Willing has not only found a potential reservations chairperson with a whole list of new contacts, but she has also worked out a more appropriate assignment for Torr, who might have caused real problems in the reservations job.

But how would Willing deal with a recruit who's not so enthusiastic? Here's what she might say to overcome the objections of "Skeets" Howard, a nightclub owner whom she wants to be entertainment coordinator.

Willing: Hello, Skeets, this is Alice Willing. Joe Pressman told me that he asked you to help with the entertainment for the Lakefront Beautification Committee's benefit on June 15th. Let me fill you in on the details: I'm sure you've heard about the Portobello cruise ship that's docking here this summer. It's going to be very elegant and a good shot in the arm for all local business, don't you agree?

Howard: It sure will. The more places in town where people can go out and have a good time, the more they get in the habit of going. It's good for all of us.

Willing: You're so right, Skeets. Well, Lakefront has the privilege of putting on our benefit as the ship's grand opening and, to make it a memorable occasion, we'll need top-notch entertainment. Joe thought you'd be an ideal person to handle this, because you know so many show business people. Will you serve on our committee?

Howard: I don't know, Alice. What would I have to do?

Willing: Well, we need to hire a big-name band for dancing on the upper deck and something a bit different for our cabaret. We've had a few suggestions, which I'll give you, and we hope you'll come up with some others. We'd like you to follow up on them, find out who's available and what they charge and come to our executive committee meeting on the 20th with your recommendations.

Howard: That's all there is to it?

Willing: Of course, we'd like you to come to the benefit yourself and bring your friends.

Howard: Will I have to go to a lot of meetings? I haven't got much time for that sort of thing.

Willing: We'd only need you to come on the 20th. Then you won't have to come to any more meetings; just take care of the contracts and come on the day of the event to help the entertainers set up.

Howard: Let me check my calendar. Yes, I'm in town on June 15th.

Willing: Good. Do you think you can get us the information we need by the 20th?

Howard: I'll do my best.

Willing: Let me know immediately if you run into any snags.

Notice how Alice has given all recruits a specific assignment, meeting date and contact person so they're involved before they have a chance to change their minds. Subcommittee chairs can also use this technique to recruit their own volunteer forces.

Even at the subcommittee level, the benefit chairperson's reputation has clout. The first question a potential volunteer is likely to ask is, "Who's chairing the benefit?" If the would-be volunteer has had a bad experience with that chairperson or has heard that the chairperson is "difficult," she may suddenly find she's too busy to serve on the committee.

Never take a turndown from a potential volunteer (or donor) personally. First-time benefit chair R. Eric Kennedy's philosophical approach is worth emulating:

> While there will be people who are willing to lend their time, money and experience to your cause, there are others (some of whom you consider friends) who will have no interest. Don't get discouraged. Always remember that the fund-raiser's disappointment in the human spirit is soon overcome by the joy of meeting someone who is willing to dedicate himself to the success of your benefit.

Don't overlook the ready source of volunteer help that exists in your organization's established support groups. When dealing with such a group it is well to work through its president, who may appoint one of its members to serve as liaison or may assume this role herself. By observing this protocol you can take advantage of established communication channels to ensure the group's full cooperation. The liaison will help identify and recruit volunteers within the group for specific tasks. Sometimes a support group will assume responsibility for an entire subcommittee's work such as addressing invitations or collecting auction items.

ORDERLY PROCEEDINGS

When it comes to organizing the committee itself, the benefit chairperson may choose to have regularly scheduled meetings of the executive committee to hear reports on each subcommittee's progress or let subcommittee chairs handle most of their arrangements independently while maintaining frequent contact by phone with the chairperson.

Which procedure she follows may have as much to do with the set of circumstances surrounding a particular benefit as with the chairperson's personal style. Because The Ball at the Halle Building was a case of shared sponsorship, the executive committee consisted of several representatives of the corporate co-sponsor and all benefit subcommittee chairs. In addition, various consultants such as a lighting engineer and a theater production manager attended the biweekly executive committee meetings as needed. Both volunteers and co-sponsor felt it was desirable to bring everyone together so they could reach a consensus on important decisions, rather than risk having one group feel that the other was trying to run the benefit unilaterally.

The Fantasy committee, on the other hand, didn't have to share its decision making with a major underwriter. This committee prided itself on not requiring committee members to attend general meetings, instead allowing each subcommittee head to work independently and report back to the appropriate co-chair. When a committee is homogeneous, the plans straightforward or the volunteers simply too scattered for any meeting time and place to be convenient, this method may be more productive. However, lacking a regular forum, the chairperson should take care to communicate frequently with committee, board and affected staff members. Committee members especially need to be "hooked" on the benefit in order to keep up their own enthusiasm and sell tickets to their friends; so apprising them of plans as they unfold is a vital task. This can be done by sending out periodic progress reports or by distributing the minutes of executive committee meetings.

Minutes should be kept by the benefit executive committee and any other committee that has more than three members and meets regularly. Not only can minutes be sent out to inform absent committee members and other interested parties of what transpired at a meeting, but they also provide for future reference a chronology of decisions made and actions taken.

There may be chairpersons who prefer to assume all the planning responsibility rather than deal with the give-and-take of shared decision making. This may be the quickest way to get things done, but we question the efficacy of such a method. Nothing is more frustrating to committee and board members than to be kept in the dark about their own benefit. It's true that when you have open meetings you hear dissension; but usually it's better to let people have their say in committee than to reduce them to grumbling privately among their friends, which can be bad for ticket sales, to say nothing of morale.

MAKE EVERYBODY A WINNER

It's not necessary to have an entire 50- to 100-member benefit committee in place before you begin work on the event. In fact, it's easier to get new recruits started immediately and let their initial enthusiasm and ideas attract additional volunteers to the project. Usually the benefit executive committee is organized first; then each subcommittee meets separately, with the benefit chairperson in attendance, to establish procedures and designate responsibilities. From the beginning, advises Lynn Schmelzer, former president of the National Council of Jewish Women, Cleveland Section:

> Everyone needs to feel and be a part of the decision and planning process, no matter at what level they are in the organizational structure. Appropriate decision making at each level gives the person ownership of her own work. Everyone should participate in setting goals for her subcommittee. With clear, attainable goals, each volunteer knows how she "fits in." Knowing how her role influences the total picture gives the volunteer the inspiration to do her best...on time.
>
> Prompt, well-organized and FUN meetings make the volunteer feel her time is valuable. It's important to recognize publicly her time, talents and expertise. If the atmosphere is professional, the volunteer will come back for more.

Pride and belief in the sponsoring organization can also be a prime motivator. Any volunteers who are unfamiliar with the organization should receive informational brochures and perhaps a tour of the facilities so that they understand what purpose the benefit's proceeds will serve. The manager or artistic director should meet with the committee of the whole early on to thank volunteers for getting involved and explain why the organization needs their help. The development director should also attend to show how important benefit profits will be in meeting the organization's total operating expenses.

The benefit chairperson can use the benefit budget and reservation list as motivational tools, as well. By referring repeatedly to the goal and reporting the steady progress of ticket sales, she can promote a sense of achievement and mounting enthusiasm while helping members to focus on the main objective.

At the most basic level, though, words of encouragement and thanks have the greatest power to motivate volunteers — and everyone else, for that matter. Don't wait until the benefit is over to show appreciation. Be quick to praise interesting ideas, demonstrations of initiative and examples of good teamwork. Above all, show a sincere personal interest in each volunteer, letting her know how much you value her individual contribution.

DISCIPLINE WITH DISCRETION

Now that Alice Willing has her committee in place, how will she keep it moving toward the goal without losing momentum? One way is to give everyone a task that the chair believes the volunteer can complete successfully. Expect some, nonetheless, to have trouble getting their assignments done. Let's suppose Skeets Howard, the volunteer who reluctantly agreed to find and hire the LBC benefit entertainers, comes to the first meeting without the information about available groups that he was supposed to bring. He claims the agents he tried to reach didn't return his calls. The decision on what groups to book has to be made today; Willing doesn't want to lose momentum by waiting for another meeting. She excuses Howard to make his phone calls while the committee discusses another topic. (If Howard hadn't shown up at the meeting, she would have asked someone else to make the calls—without calling attention to Skeets' lapse.)

Some assignments are more formidable than others. Soliciting underwriting, for example, is a job few people undertake willingly. A volunteer may need help getting up the nerve to make the calls. In this case, the chairperson should offer to come along or send another experienced committee member. Volunteers rarely turn down such an offer. As Schmelzer notes:

> Working in pairs assures broader decision making and ideas. "Two heads are better than one" can have broad implications. Pair an experienced person with a newer volunteer and, most importantly, always have the chair give final approval. Then everyone feels that she is being supervised equally.

But what can you do if a committee member is downright disruptive? Firing a volunteer is a last resort to be taken only when the person's continued involvement could jeopardize the results of the entire benefit. Most offenses short of the criminal—persistently rude behavior, an unpleasant personal trait, incompetence—would be cause for dismissal of an executive committee member only; they would probably be tolerated in a person in a less critical position.

Disciplining a wayward volunteer is another matter. There are several steps that can be taken, depending on the severity of the problem. In the fairly common case of a committee member who simply doesn't get along well with others, the benefit chairperson or subcommittee chair should find some way to isolate her from the rest of the volunteers instead of trying to correct her. Give her a limited assignment that she can do by herself and have her report the results to you directly. If a volunteer behaves objectionably at a meeting or work session, draw her aside to ask her opinion on an important subject. If she is a constant complainer, set a time when you can talk with her privately and hear her grievances — that alone may resolve the problem.

When there is a problem with a volunteer's performance, simply make a telephone call to clarify the assignment or explain the reason why the job should be done in a specific way. This approach is less threatening than a face-to-face confrontation. Be sure to emphasize the importance of the volunteer's work as the reason for taking special care to do it well.

When a performance problem begins to affect the work of others, a face-to-face appointment is necessary. Lynn Schmelzer advises: "You should plan the meeting ahead of time in order to ensure that you cover the most important issues. It is always best to address the situation directly; this will clear up any mistaken impressions and set everyone in the right direction again, and I believe, in the long run, the volunteer will respect the chair's leadership."

When dealing with a serious offender, it's always best to have a third party involved for the purposes of listening to what is said on both sides, clarifying the issues and backing up the person whose unpleasant duty it is to be the disciplinarian. On those rare occasions when a subcommittee chair must be removed from her position, the decision should be made jointly with the president of the organization's board. The reason for backing up the chairperson's authority in this manner is that a disgruntled volunteer can lash back at the organization, harming its reputation in the community.

Schmelzer adds:

> Removing a volunteer from a position is the least favorite part of anyone's life. You will be unhappy and the volunteer will be mad, but the overall purpose and success of the project must be kept in mind at all times.
>
> This must be done with care, lots of thought and preplanning because it is important to be professional. Although it is extremely difficult, why you are asking the volunteer to step aside must be handled with honesty. If at all possible, suggest another area of responsibility where the volunteer's talents and skills can be better utilized. Many times a person has been misplaced (the chair must take full responsibility for this), her job description has been altered or the time commitment is not reasonable.

We repeat: The best way to keep committee members happy

is to give each a challenge she can manage successfully, keep each fully informed, let each have a say and assure all continually that their efforts are appreciated.

ROLE OF THE BOARD OF TRUSTEES

After the board members have appointed a benefit chairperson whom they trust to represent them, their job isn't over. As we mentioned earlier, the board's executive committee must also review the benefit budget to ensure that it is realistic and appropriate. Once the board is satisfied that the budget will achieve the desired goal, each and every board member is expected to support the benefit by buying tickets.

Often the majority of volunteers on a benefit committee are not trustees of the sponsoring organization, but they nonetheless lend their time, talent and money to help the board raise money for the organization. Board members can show their appreciation by assisting the committee in finding underwriters and by encouraging their friends to come to the benefit. Board members should not sit together at the benefit, but instead should use this opportunity to introduce the organization to outsiders by hosting tables.

Board members who are able should also "prime the pump" by buying the higher-priced tickets. (If some are too modest to call attention to this kind of contribution, the benefit chairperson can certainly make much of their praiseworthy example in her reports to the board and committee and in conversations with other prospective ticket purchasers.) The reasoning is, again: If volunteers who aren't members of the board are willing to buy the most expensive tickets, as well as giving of their time, trustees should do no less.

In addition, the board's financial officer might offer to work with the benefit committee treasurer to make certain that all income and expense records are in order. If necessary, he or she could help set up the benefit books in a way that conforms to the organization's bookkeeping system and would stand up to an outside audit.

The board also has an obligation to review the results of the benefit after it's over. The executive committee or standing benefit committee should take time to read the chairperson's final report, act on any recommendations and resolve any problems that come to light before placing the report in the organization's files.

Finally, the chairman or president of the board should send personal thank-you notes to the benefit chairperson, the co-sponsor and other major underwriters and anyone else who has played a principal role in the benefit's success. Gifts are not necessary, but words of appreciation are essential.

Department of Human Resources, Part II

The working relationship between volunteers and the sponsoring organization's management and staff can be a touchy one for those benefit committees that do not take the time to define its parameters beforehand. With forethought, a professional approach and a positive attitude, however, a successful and satisfying collaboration need not be difficult to achieve.

In the best of all possible worlds, volunteers and staff members would automatically have respect for and confidence in one another's abilities, because, in the best of all possible worlds, everyone would be hard working, well qualified, single-mindedly dedicated and conscientious. In such a world, of course, no one would ever get behind in her work, lose her temper, slight another's feelings, fail to communicate full and accurate information or forget to say thank you.

In the world we're familiar with, however, human beings are only too liable to lapse into behavior that falls short of the best possible, and it becomes necessary to remind ourselves that *both* volunteer and paid professional are motivated by a desire to serve the best interests of the organization.

Even though both sides won't always agree on what those best interests are, it's important to foster a spirit of cooperation. This means listening attentively to others' opinions and concerns, expressing one's own ideas and expectations clearly and treating everyone with courtesy and consideration. It is by far one of the benefit chairperson's most important responsibilities to establish lines of communication between volunteers and management and staff and to keep them free of static.

Among the sentiments to be communicated, none is more basic than appreciation. Volunteers thrive on it and so do paid professionals. Just as we can't afford to take for granted the contributions of unpaid workers who seek only intangible rewards, we mustn't assume that those who receive a salary don't also need verbal reinforcement.

KEEP IT PROFESSIONAL

Much of the misunderstanding that can arise between volunteers and staff is rooted in the very structure and dynamics of not-for-profit organizations. To begin with, the volunteer benefit committee, whatever else its members may do in their daily lives, is created for the express purpose of putting on the benefit, while the organization's full-time staff has many other ongoing projects and priorities that lay claim to their workdays. And, though both the benefit committee and the staff of an organization have established hierarchies, the two don't correspond exactly.

On the staff side, the hierarchy of authority is reasonably clear; employees presumably know who their supervisors are and to whom those individuals report in turn. Their duties are assigned to them by their supervisors and their continued employment depends on how well they perform.

Advising and guiding the executive director or general manager or similarly titled boss to whom all employees ultimately report is the board of trustees. Ideally, the board sets policy for the organization and sees that the executive director and staff have the wherewithal to carry out the organization's agenda, but trustees do not get involved in running the day-to-day activities.

When a benefit requires volunteers and management and staff to work together, the chain of command can get tied up in knots. Does the staff member answer to the volunteer chairperson (who may or may not be a trustee) or to her staff supervisor or both? What if there is a conflict? While staff members can, of course, think and act for themselves, they do expect direction from the top executive of the organization. It's unfair to ask employees to decide for themselves what the priorities are in the case of a conflict; while they probably have their own opinions on the subject, they are obliged to please their supervisors first. Therefore, it's up to the board to determine where the benefit stands on the organization's priority list, which is one of the reasons why we argue strongly for board evaluation and approval of the benefit plans and budget, as described in Chapter I. Then it's the director's job to allocate staff time accordingly and to make sure both staff and volunteers accept these terms.

SHARING THE WORKLOAD

We recommend that the benefit chairperson and the executive director meet as soon as possible after the event gets the go-ahead from the board, in order to discuss plans, anticipate needs and try to work out procedures in advance. (The board president or chairperson of the standing benefit committee may request this meeting, but doesn't have to be present.) The benefit chairperson needs to hear what other projects staffers are involved in during the benefit planning period, and the executive director needs to know how much staff assistance the committee will request and when.

At this point, the benefit chairperson should ask the director to appoint a staff member to serve as liaison with the benefit committee if one has not already been assigned. Some executive directors may want to handle this task themselves, but most more likely will delegate it to the director of development or public relations. As soon as the staff liaison is appointed, it's time for a three-way meeting of the benefit chairperson, director and liaison to work out the specifics of who will handle what.

Dean Gladden, managing director of the Cleveland Play House and former director of development of Great Lakes Theater Festival, notes:

> The way benefit duties are divided up will differ for every organization and volunteer committee. You have to find a balance that works in your situation. The key is for everyone to know what's expected and to agree on responsibilities. Staff and volunteers need to go in with the attitude that they're on the same team. You can help this along by meeting on a regular basis and sharing important information such as time lines and budgets.

In this chapter is a job checklist that you may use in this negotiating session. Rather than go 'round and 'round trying to decide whether volunteers or paid professionals are better qualified to do each of the tasks indicated, you will have to make compromises for the sake of getting things done. For each job, consider what volunteer or staff member could handle the work most effectively and then try to determine whether that person will be available to do it at the proper time. For example, will photocopying be done by a staff member or a volunteer? It really doesn't matter, so long as the staff member who usually operates the copier knows that he's responsible and when the work is likely to be needed or else has been informed that a volunteer has permission to use the machine and should be given directions on using it.

A more complex task such as coordinating the design and printing of all printed materials should be assigned on the basis of experience, interest, knowledge of the event, contacts, proximity to the print shop, etc. The assignment may also depend on who has the final authority to approve copy and design. The important thing is to agree on the procedures to be followed at the outset, so there is no confusion or misunderstanding later on.

These procedures should be discussed with the committee of the whole and all staff members who will be affected at the first opportunity for a general meeting. The completed checklist should be handed out for everyone to review at his or her leisure; it will provide a point of reference in case any questions come up later on.

ROLE OF PROFESSIONAL STAFF

The staff positions that are most frequently involved with benefit work are the following:

Executive director or general manager. In addition to the responsibilities discussed above, this individual, as the organization's chief spokesperson, must be a presence at the benefit. This means more than merely showing up. He or she should make an effort to greet and chat with as many of the organization's patrons as possible, especially those who are new to the fold.

Development director. This person most often serves as liaison between the committee and the organization's administration, since the benefit is primarily a fund-raising project. The amount of involvement by a development department depends to a great extent on how experienced and well staffed the committee is and the magnitude of the event. If the benefit is a first for the organization, the development director will probably want to exercise more control than over a repeat of a successful event. A take-charge staff member tends to stifle the initiative of the volunteer committee, however. Obviously, the more a benefit committee can do on its own, the more creative it will become, and the more it frees the development department for other activities.

Other considerations affecting the involvement of the development department include the percentage of the total fund-raising budget to be raised by the benefit, the time availability of the staff, the availability of computers or memory typewriters and the completeness of mailing lists and donor records.

Other than helping to set the benefit's financial goal, the development director's main concern is coordinating the event with the organization's other fund-raising activities to avoid hitting the same prospects with more than one appeal at the same time. He or she should help the underwriting committee identify potential donors and be able to provide up-to-date names, titles and phone numbers of contact persons at corporations. Likewise, he or she can advise the committee whether the organization has another request under consideration with a prospect the committee wants to approach. The development director should provide the underwriting committee with a written synopsis, to be used in donor solicitation, explaining how this event fits into the overall fund-raising effort, how the money will be used and how patrons will be recognized by the organization. If benefit proceeds are to be applied

CHECKLIST FOR VOLUNTEER/STAFF NEGOTIATION

TASK	PERSON(S) RESPONSIBLE	TASK	PERSON(S) RESPONSIBLE
COPYWRITING		WRITE CONTRACTS	_____
Save the date card	_____		
Kickoff party invite	_____	SECURE PERMITS	_____
Invitation	_____		
Press materials	_____	DEPOSIT CHECKS	_____
Solicitation letters	_____		
Other	_____	WRITE CHECKS	_____
COPY APPROVAL		PHONE INQUIRIES	_____
Save the date card	_____		
Kickoff party invite	_____	PUBLIC RELATIONS	
Invitation	_____	Compile press kits	_____
Press materials	_____	Make press contacts	_____
Solicitation letters	_____	Hire photographer	_____
Other	_____	File press clippings	_____
		Compile comp list	_____
PROOFING		Handle hospitality	_____
Save the date card	_____	Staff registration table	_____
Kickoff party invite	_____		
Invitation	_____	PHOTOCOPYING	_____
Press materials	_____		
Solicitation letters	_____	CLERICAL	
Other	_____	Take/distribute minutes	_____
		Meeting notification	_____
PRODUCTION		Typing	
Hire designer	_____	Correspondence	_____
Solicit type/key/print bids	_____	Committee list	_____
Coordinate production	_____	Written copy	_____
		Press materials	_____
MAILING LIST		Acknowledging reservations	_____
Compile list	_____	Guest list/seating chart	_____
Update list	_____	Final report	_____
Input corrections	_____		
Secure printouts/labels	_____		

toward a matching grant, such as a National Endowment for the Arts challenge grant, he or she must see that wording conforming to grant requirements is used on invitations, letters of solicitation and other written materials. He or she should certainly be present at the event to meet new patrons, so that these acquaintances can be cultivated in the future.

Other duties that may be assumed by the development department include helping draft solicitation letters, contacting underwriting prospects, providing mailing lists, typing and distributing minutes and announcements of meetings and helping with duplication of seating charts and reservation lists.

Dean Gladden feels the development department should take a leadership role in helping volunteers to organize their benefits: "If the professional staff doesn't challenge the volunteers' expectations, they may undershoot their goal. Benefit committees start from scratch every time; the staff can be the ongoing link with the organization." By contrast, Anthony J. Poderis, director of development of the Cleveland Orchestra, keeps a low profile in most of his organization's benefits:

> It's just not cost-effective for us to get involved in benefits. My job, and that of my staff, is to manage the annual corporate and individual sustaining fund campaigns, the endowment fund campaign and securing grants and underwriting for our concert series and various special projects. Our Women's Committee members are the real pros at benefits; their Scheherazade [see appendix] raises over $250,000 every other year without our help, and we couldn't do without them. In fact, we wish they would do it every year!

We hasten to add that it's a rare organization that boasts such a well-established team of volunteer fund-raisers. In most cases, the development director will want to provide support and direction.

Public relations director. Since an ancillary goal of a benefit is to create favorable publicity for the organization, the PR director should obviously be involved. To what extent depends on the personalities and qualifications of the participants. Some benefit committees prefer to take charge of their own publicity, making sure that the PR staff has up-to-date information on the benefit in case anyone calls the office with questions. If committee members write their own press releases and fact sheets, the PR director should edit them to make sure that information about the organization is accurate; but it's often more expedient for the PR department to write, produce and mail these materials, since staffers should already have a media mailing list and know the deadlines for various publications. Media contacts may be handled by the PR director or volunteers or both, depending on who has the best relationship with a particular reporter or editor.

The PR director should be present at the event to assist publicity committee volunteers in greeting media guests and helping them secure interviews and photographs.

Business manager or comptroller. The organization's top finance manager can, if it's deemed appropriate, assume the duties of benefit treasurer, receiving checks from the reservations chairperson and making disbursements from the benefit account. Otherwise, he or she should help the volunteer treasurer set up the books and review them afterwards, be available to answer questions and ready to assist the benefit chairperson with the final financial statement.

Artistic/performing staff. This group of employees appears to be a natural, creative resource just waiting to be tapped for a benefit. Do bear in mind, however, that artists and performers can be particularly sensitive to being asked to do their work for free. Many, of course, are quite willing to do so, but others will expect you to be aware of union rules and pay scales.

Clerical staff. Often these workers can be the biggest help to the benefit committee, though they may have the least authority to respond to volunteers' requests without approval from their supervisors. It's best to route clerical work through the staff liaison, who should take responsibility for seeing that the jobs get done properly and on time. Seasoned volunteer leader Lynn Schmelzer offers these tips for delegating clerical work:

> In order for the staff to type any information it must be in proper order, legible and come with clear instructions. The best method is to telephone in advance to the staff liaison and ask him or her to set an appointment for you with the typist to present the material and review the instructions. Setting an appointment when there is a great deal of material and information to review shows respect for both people involved. It is unfair for a volunteer to expect her material to be ready overnight. Allow enough time for the staff member to give it the attention and care that the volunteer put into it initially.

One person who should not be overlooked is the office receptionist or telephone operator, who needs to have regularly updated information about the benefit, as well as a list of names and numbers of people to whom calls can be referred.

Clearly, top-level managers of the organization, particularly those who have worked closely with the benefit committee, need to be present at the event itself not only to attend to specific details but also to "work the crowd." Usually the committee agrees to invite the executive or managing director, artistic director, development director and public relations director to attend gratis or for the cost of the meal alone, if it isn't underwritten. Whether this invitation should be extended to other members of the staff who have worked on the benefit is a matter of choice. Many committees like to give non-executive staff members an opportunity to take part in the event. If there is space available, they may offer a special ticket "at cost." As an alternative, they may ask them to perform light duties such as working at the registration table. Such assignments shouldn't be forced on staffers, but should be presented as an option for those who'd like to attend the party.

FINDING THE RIGHT SUPPLIERS

Here are the major suppliers most benefit committees will need to hire:

Caterer. After the committee itself, this individual or firm may have the biggest impact on the success or failure of a benefit. The reason is simple: Food is one amusement everybody notices. There may be those who don't drink, those who don't dance, those who ignore the entertainers or those who abstain from bidding on auction items, but almost everyone partakes of the meal. And everyone will have an opinion about it because, of all the intangibles that go into the price of a benefit ticket, the cost of the meal is the one figure that most people can estimate simply by comparing it to what they'd pay for something similar at a good restaurant. With so many differing opinions on how food should be cooked, seasoned and presented, the caterer who can serve the same meal to several hundred persons and satisfy most of them is a highly valuable associate.

Catering services have proliferated in recent years, thanks to the current interest in gourmet cooking coupled with more career-oriented life styles, so there should be several good caterers from which to choose in any city. The first question to ask those with whom you are considering working is whether they have done any parties of the size and type you are planning. A caterer who can execute a superb dinner for 200 may or may not be able to muster the equipment and trained personnel to serve a similar meal for 1,000. If the benefit location is outdoors or in a facility without a professional kitchen, find out how the caterer plans to function — again, by asking about the firm's previous experience.

Be sure to ask for and check out references. Also find out who if anyone on your benefit committee has attended one of the caterer's parties. Ask her about the quality of the food, the size of the portions, the presentation, the temperature (did the soup arrive hot and the baked Alaska frozen?). Were the waiters courteous, efficient and neat in appearance? Was the manager in evidence throughout the event to keep things running smoothly? Could he or she handle special requests with a minimum of fuss?

Be sure the caterer can follow your timetable — this means setting up well in advance of your guests' arrival and serving the meal on time so that it doesn't drag on and disrupt the entertainment. (You can help by calling guests to the table about 15 minutes before you want them to sit down, as it takes time for people to break up their cocktail-hour conversations.)

When discussing prices, find out what the per-plate charge covers in addition to food and beverages. Are tables and chairs, linens, service, tax and gratuity included? Can the caterer provide bar service and at what cost — per drink, per bottle or per hour? Are set-ups included or extra? Be sure that the contract notes all these details, as well as possible hidden charges such as labor, cleanup and overtime.

If you have any questions about quality control or are experimenting with new recipes, don't hesitate to ask the caterer for a tasting. Most caterers will be happy to offer samples. As Robert S. Pile, chairman of Hough Caterers of Cleveland, says:

> I like to do tastings because we all learn something. You have to keep in mind, though, that when you reproduce the same meal you did for eight for a benefit of 800, you may not get quite the same degree of perfection. But it should be pretty close.

If the meal is truly elaborate, you may want to have a complete dress rehearsal for a few select committee members. Have the caterer lay the table covers exactly as he or she plans to do the night of the benefit and serve the complete meal. Ask the florist to make a sample arrangement so that you can determine whether the colors and proportions are right: Can the guests see one another over or around the flowers? Is there room for all the china and glassware? Are the candles at the proper height to cast a flattering glow without setting anyone's sleeve on fire when the rolls are passed? If anything is out of place, adjustments can be made in time; if everything is great, the committee will surely convey its enthusiasm to prospective guests.

Facility manager. There are several advantages to working with a hotel ballroom, club, restaurant or hall with its own kitchen and staff rather than an independent caterer. In the first place, the tables and chairs are already there, and the staff is thoroughly familiar with the layout. Lobbies, dining rooms, cloakrooms and restrooms are designed for the comfort as well as the convenience of large numbers of people. The disadvantage of using such a facility is that you are usually obliged to buy its catering service rather than shopping around for the best quality and price. And you may not be allowed to bring in donated food or liquor, either, which limits your opportunity to reduce expenses.

So, in choosing a hall, you must take into consideration the capabilities of the chef and the manager. Benefits have to offer a more exciting menu than that served at the routine business luncheons and weddings that take place there every day. For this reason, don't select a menu from a standard list; discuss the theme of the party with the chef and ask him to suggest several special menus, always keeping in mind what the kitchen does best.

Be sure to go over your timetable with the manager, as you would with any caterer. Since these facilities book one event right after the other, they probably won't allow as much set-up time as the benefit committee would like. Remember to coordinate your florist's or other decorating professional's schedule with the manager's and insist on having enough lead time for the committee to add such finishing touches as table numbers, programs and favors before the guests begin to arrive.

Florist. If all you need are standard table centerpieces and a few ficus trees to fill in the corners of a fully decorated room, any florist can supply them. Shop around for a competitive price and make sure the quantity you need won't exceed the limits of the florist's resources. But if you have something more exotic in mind or especially if you are trying to dress up an unfinished space, you would be better off enlisting a creative floral designer—an artist who can create scenery and dramatic visual effects using plants, flowers and accessories. He or she should be brought in on the planning as early as possible, preferably as a volunteer member of the decorations committee. The decorations chairperson should discuss the theme and entertainment and the sort of atmosphere the committee wants to create; then she should walk through the facility with the floral designer, pointing out areas to be emphasized or screened from view. The designer can then work up sketches or sample displays to submit for the committee's approval. He or she should also see the graphics for the invitations and other printed materials and confer with any other designers working on the benefit, so a unified visual effect can be achieved.

Graphic designer. If you want to create a fresh image for your benefit's printed materials, you should probably start with a free-lance designer, graphic studio or an advertising agency. Interview several candidates and choose the one who seems to have established the best rapport, understands your concept and makes suggestions that appeal to you. You will, of course, try to persuade the designer to donate his or her services, but don't hesitate to pay a reasonable fee if that is the only way you can acquire this service.

For the sake of unity as well as convenience, have all the design work done by one person. Your designer may come up with a single graphic or logo that can be incorporated in every printed piece (even stationery and matchbooks), which could save money *and* make for a strong visual identity. This individual may also be willing to solicit competitive bids on the various phases of production and oversee the job from start to finish. Be sure the designer knows the limitations of your budget, so that he or she can plan for the most economical use of materials.

Printer. A full-service print shop also has typesetters and keyliners under one roof, so that you or your designer need only deal directly with one account executive to coordinate the production of your entire print job.

Before your first meeting with your designer, decide how many printed pieces you will need in what quantities and the purpose of each. A printer can help you establish a rough printing budget once you've established quantities for each piece and if you can show him or her samples that approximate what you want. Most will shy away from quoting any firm prices until all the specs have been determined by the designer, however.

If the printing of a piece is donated, don't forget to acknowledge the donor prominently on the piece itself and in your program book, unless anonymity is requested. Unfortunately, a generous offer of free printing from a third party—say, a company that's not in the printing business but happens to have a print shop—can sometimes complicate the picture. Naturally, you will want to accept the donation, but have your designer go over the specs with the printer to make sure the shop can handle the job. If the artist's design and the printer's capability aren't compatible, you'll have to give up one or the other. Find this out *before* the job is run, to avoid embarrassment, needless expense and loss of precious time.

Before the designer begins to work on each piece, write as much of the copy as you can. Type it neatly, double spaced, with headings and important phrases clearly indicated so that the designer will know what to emphasize visually. If you are missing some information, you can leave blanks, but indicate where that information will go and how many lines it will take (for example: "Committee list to come—approximately 120 names").

The designer or printer will help you work out a production schedule for each piece, working backward from the date you want it delivered. Be sure to build in time for copy approval and plan to be available for proofreading after type has been set and again after the piece has been keylined. Add three to four more days if you need to have several people sign off on the blueprint (the last chance you have to make corrections before the piece is printed). Remember, changes get more expensive the farther into production you go. Ask the printer to calculate how many days after he receives camera-ready artwork you can expect delivery of the finished piece; ten working days is standard as a minimum. Try to give the printer a few extra days' grace; if you give him a rush job and he has to rearrange his production schedule to fit it in, it will naturally cost more. And if the printer is doing your job as a donation, it's only reasonable to assume his paid work comes first.

SERVICE WITH A SMILE

When a benefit promises to be a prestigious affair that will bring favorable attention to any supplier who works on it, most will try hard to make a good impression. The attitude of Charles M. Phillips, floral designer for The Ball at the Halle Building, is typical: "When I know there's going to be a lot of publicity and that hundreds of people will see my work at a benefit, I'd be silly not to do it to the best of my ability." Adds caterer Robert Pile: "There is so much competition nowadays that I have to be willing to give more."

The important thing to remember in working with suppliers is that they expect a quid pro quo. Much as they may want to support good causes in the community, they are, after all, running businesses. The more generous and cooperative a supplier is known to be, the more requests for contributions of goods or services he or she will get. Unless he or she has a personal interest in the organization, a supplier has to weigh each request against two business considerations: Is the person doing the asking a good customer, one worth going out of my way to please? And am I likely to realize more business as a result of the visibility this benefit will give me in the community?

It's obvious, then, that benefit committees should be comprised of persons who frequently use caterers and florists for their personal and business entertaining. This enables the committee to pool knowledge of available resources and to approach suppliers through members who already have good working relationships with them. It's also fair to expect other members of the committee to patronize those businesses who contribute to the success of their benefit. Committee members can show their gratitude for a job well done by recommending the suppliers to potential customers whenever possible, and a benefit chairperson would not be amiss if she gently reminded her committee members to do so.

Just as there are volunteers who specialize in running benefits for various organizations, there are suppliers whose names come to be associated with the benefit circuit and, naturally enough, whose services are always in demand. Like the volunteers, these businesspeople enjoy the excitement, prestige and opportunity to contribute in a meaningful way to a successful community event. But their relationship with the benefit committee is still a professional one, and they do expect at least to cover their costs.

Charles Phillips puts it this way:

> I like to do benefits, especially when it's a good committee and an organization I support. The publicity is nice, but it only goes so far. I have to be responsible for my business; I have to have some return to show my accountant. Flowers are my main expense. I don't have an hourly rate for my own time, and I'm willing to absorb the cost of my employees' labor, so I never get back all the money I put into a benefit; in this sense, I think suppliers are also benefit patrons. So, each time I'm asked to do a benefit, I have to ask, "Can I afford to take a loss at this time of year?" I don't pad my retail costs to cover benefits, by the way, but I have to see if I'm likely to pick up enough other business in that particular month to balance my books.

In order to work effectively with suppliers, keep the following points in mind:

1) **Appoint one or two persons to deal with the supplier.** Many suppliers prefer to meet with two committee members, feeling that one person can be arbitrary, but they find it annoying to receive phone calls from three or four different people a day, all offering conflicting suggestions. Whether it's the benefit chairperson, subcommittee chairperson, co-sponsor or a staff member of the organization, make it clear to the designer from the outset who's responsible for making the decisions and paying the bills; that way there's no question whose orders take precedence.

2) **Be frank about your budgetary limitations.** It's better to tell a supplier up front how much you want to spend and find out what you can do with that amount, than to waste time talking about ideas you're ultimately going to reject because they're too expensive.

3) **Be prepared.** Richard W. Evans, president of Evans Printing

Company in Solon, Ohio, a supplier for many area benefits, suggests that you make an appointment with the supplier, telling him or her the name of your organization and what you want to talk about. Bring to the appointment examples of the type of materials you'll need printed, along with basic information such as date, size, location and theme of your event. Evans confides: "I hate it when I come out of the print shop up to my elbows in ink, and there's somebody waiting up front who wants to know if I've got a minute to talk. Of course I make the time, but I prefer to know she's coming, so I can try to look the part of the image I think that organization wants to convey."

4) **Be reasonable.** Don't ask for the moon if you expect the supplier to stay within your stated budget. Be willing to accept medium-grade supplies instead of demanding the most deluxe materials available.

5) **Be considerate.** Suppliers like to participate in the creative process but, generally speaking, they don't want to attend long meetings of the benefit committee. State what you want and don't equivocate if you're not happy with their first proposals. Once you decide on a plan, stick with it — minor adjustments are reasonable, but too many major revisions try a supplier's patience.

6) **Trust your supplier.** If you think enough of his professionalism to have hired a particular supplier, listen to his suggestions. Remember that his expertise is worth more than the cost of the supplies. It would be less than fair to ask for a lot of free advice, only to take the plans you have developed together and go shopping for a cheaper price from another supplier.

Maximizing Profits

With the cost of benefits escalating, securing underwriting is vital. If you have any doubt about this, your budget should convince you that it would be futile to proceed with your plans without having prospective underwriters firmly in mind. Setting a goal of 90 to 100 percent underwriting will assure underwriters, patrons, the benefit committee and the organization that the event will be "of benefit" to the cause. The best way to accomplish this is to find a co-sponsor *before* your plans are firm. An underwriter that takes on this role may offer its own facilities to the organization, as well as provide food and drink, entertainment and/or technical assistance.

We are primarily referring to corporations, because they seem to have the resources—manpower, materials and money. In many instances, they also have a reason to gain from the investment of those resources in a benefit. Corporations can be exposed to criticism from their communities if they spend too little on charitable or cultural institutions. Any such criticism can often be blunted if corporate promotional dollars are invested in deserving not-for-profit organizations.

This fact shouldn't deter committees from seeking individual contributions to help cover basic expenses or from using a supporter's personal resources to advantage. For example, a distinctive private home can be an ideal place to hold a benefit; an art object from a friend's personal collection can be a valuable addition to a benefit auction. But rarely, if ever, does an individual offer to foot the bill for a major benefit attended by 1,000 people. However, real estate developers and promoters of all kinds often do just that.

Mark Randol, president of Forest City Commercial Management (a division of Cleveland-based Forest City Enterprises, which co-sponsored The Ball at the Halle Building), has much hands-on experience with underwriting benefits, since his company regularly co-sponsors them in connection with the opening of office buildings and shopping malls around the country. He explains that co-sponsorship represents enlightened self-interest and the desire to be a good neighbor. Underwriting a benefit gives his company the opportunity to get to know influential members of the community and to defuse any opposition to its planned commercial development. Randol notes: "When we turn over a large amount of money to a community organization before we even open our doors to do

120

business, it creates good will you can't buy with advertising. Giving funds outright is one way to do this, but the only way to get the whole community involved is to have a benefit."

Co-sponsorship — that is, when a company pays most of a benefit's expenses in return for equal billing with the not-for-profit organization that will receive the proceeds — is clearly the most desirable form of underwriting. Not only does it work wonders for the profitability of the benefit, it can also increase the visibility and prestige of the event. Far from excluding other corporate support, such co-sponsorship can actually attract additional gifts, even from the company's competitors.

The offer of a co-sponsorship frequently arises when a company decides to become involved in one of three types of events:

Grand openings. Just about any kind of real estate or property development — condominiums, housing developments, apartment or office buildings, hotels, shopping malls, airports, even warehouses — seems to call for a public celebration that will attract attention to the new project and encourage the curious to come have a look at it. The company's objective is not necessarily direct sales, but rather to excite interest and to build a glamorous image for the development. Usually such promotion accompanies the completion of the project, though it's conceivable that a benefit could be held around a groundbreaking if the site were breathtaking enough.

As Randol observes:

> The owner of a new building feels like the father of a new baby — he's so proud of his offspring, he's giving away cigars. Many people want to be the first to see a project that they've watched under construction. They're more willing to pay the ticket price to see it when it's first opened than they will be when it's been around awhile.

Sporting events or shows. Some companies find that sponsoring highly visible special events such as auto races, golf tournaments or jazz festivals can have more impact than advertising when it comes to corporate image building. Rather than try to turn a profit on such an event, the firm can demonstrate its good citizenship by allowing a not-for-profit organization to reap the financial rewards. The company's chief aim is to link its own name with that of a popular event.

Fashion shows. Regardless of the type of merchandise shown, this is one business promotion that never seems to go out of style. A department store or specialty shop that wishes to promote its lines is a prime candidate for co-sponsorship. Usually the store has the contacts to bring in one or more well-known designers, hires the models, runs the show itself and may even underwrite the costs of the music, invitations and luncheon. Patrons may be given the opportunity to order garments on the spot, which is of obvious value to the co-sponsor, but if not, the publicity and the appeal of the featured designs should lure customers back to the store.

Sometimes a store will establish a long-term relationship with one organization and host a fashion show every year for that group; other times an organization will establish the fashion show as an annual event, but with a different store sponsoring it each year.

While these are the most common examples of co-sponsorship, benefit committees don't have to wait for one of these occasions to enlist corporate support. Sometimes a benefit has a theme that ties in with a particular type of business. For example, if the theme is "Arabian Nights," perhaps an airline, oil company or foreign trade mission would agree to become a co-sponsor. Other related businesses that might also be approached for donations include travel agencies, Oriental rug dealers and importers, to name but a few.

The important thing to remember about underwriters is that their largess is intended to advance their own ends as much as yours. If community good will is the intangible result they're after, public acknowledgment, in the form of publicity and printed credits, is the tangible means to that end. In order to gain maximum exposure, major underwriters usually want their names included on the invitation and mentioned in all press releases. (A few companies prefer to remain anonymous, fearing that they'll be inundated with requests from other organizations, but such donors are rare.) Co-sponsors want their names in the benefit's title or listed alongside that of the not-for-profit organization, and if you're fortunate enough to find such support, you should be only too happy to agree. Your chances of getting large corporate donations diminish once the invitations are printed and mailed.

FINDING A CORPORATE ANGEL

Whether you are going after a single co-sponsor or a number of smaller underwriters, the process of securing underwriting is similar. That's why it makes the most sense to put your effort into finding and working with a big one. If successful, you'll not only be relieved of responsibility for the major expenses, but you'll find it's easier to attract additional support for the remaining items. Committee members will also be more confident when talking with other prospects when they can mention that you have a serious backer.

As with all forms of solicitation, you need to do your homework *before* approaching prospective underwriters. Finding a corporate angel can be a matter of luck, but more often it is the result of advance planning, creative use of contacts and persuasive ability. That is one reason why an organization should establish a standing committee on benefits consisting of several committed volunteers who keep in touch with the business community and on the lookout for opportunities. However, that committee is only the starting point for soliciting ideas about prospects. Consult the other members of your board and your benefit committee: What contacts and resources can they bring to the quest for a co-sponsor and additional underwriters?

The organization's development department should be involved in the search, as well. The development director should have an up-to-date list of the names of business contacts and an overview of which companies are currently being solicited for special gifts, the organization's annual fund drive, etc. It is vital to check with the development office before approaching any company or individual, even for small donations. Not only can these staffers help you avoid overlapping solicitations, they can tell you if any recent request was turned down with reassurances that the company would love to help in some other way. They may know that company A has already allocated its annual contributions budget, but has money available in its promotions or advertising budget that could be applied to a special event. Or they may be aware that company B is looking for an opportunity to gain some favorable publicity.

When is the best time to approach a potential underwriter? As soon as you hear about a new building project or as soon as you have developed a benefit concept for which you want to propose a co-sponsorship. Count yourself fortunate if your prospect says yes immediately to your request. The proposal process usually takes time—figure at least three weeks from the day you first spoke or met with company officials until you hear their decision, more if you're asked to submit a written proposal for a formal review. Be sure to ask when the decision will be made; the company may be operating on a different timetable from yours. If so, politely let them know your time requirements for doing a top-notch job.

Face-to-face contact is always best for initiating a big request. Go straight to the top executive or owner, unless you know that another executive has decision-making authority in these matters. Let the person who knows the prospect best call or write for an appointment. If no one in your organization has a personal relationship with the prospect, have the highest-ranking board member or the chairperson of the standing committee on benefits make the approach. If it seems appropriate, send a delegation consisting of the board president or standing benefit committee chairperson, benefit chairperson and executive or artistic director.

If your prospect requests a written proposal, it should be prepared by the development director and the benefit chairperson. The proposal itself should consist of a one- to two-page letter on the organization's letterhead (if you're still in the process of finding a co-sponsor it's too early to have printed benefit stationery) describing the type of event you wish to mount and explaining why you believe the company will benefit from co-sponsoring the project.

Enclose supporting materials that will convince the corporation that your organization is deserving: a descriptive brochure or annual report that details the organization's mission and activities, a roster of trustees, a budget for the current fiscal year showing how crucial benefit proceeds are and any particularly favorable press clippings. Don't forget to include any stories on previous successful benefits your organization has held on a scale similar to that being proposed. Note that the emphasis should be on what your benefit can do for the corporation. You want to impress the company with your organization's ability to create an event that the company will be proud to co-sponsor.

Let's trace how our fictional Lakefront Beautification Committee might approach a prospect for major underwriting:

In September LBC learns that an Italian cruise line, Portobello Internazionale, plans the following summer to initiate a new lake route with Utopian Harbor as one of its ports of call. LBC board member Alice Willing is waiting for this news; Portobello president Alessandro Soave has been in negotiations for some weeks with city officials and businesspeople including LBC president Solomon "Old Salt" Boatman to bring the ship to their port. Willing has already discussed with Boatman and several other trustees her idea for having the organization's next benefit on board this ship, and all agree it is a splendid idea. Boatman informs the board of Portobello's plans at a regular meeting about a week before the official announcement is to be released to the media. The next morning, Willing is on the phone with Soave's secretary, Ms. Largo, at the cruise line's temporary headquarters in the Harborside Hotel.

Willing: Good morning, Ms. Largo. My name is Alice Willing and I'm a member of the Lakefront Beautification Committee's board of trustees. I'd like to make an appointment to meet with Mr. Soave to discuss the possibility of a joint venture—a benefit to launch your new cruise ship and help improve the lakefront at the same time.

Largo: How did you find out about that? We haven't announced anything yet.

Willing: (Realizing she has spoken out of turn) Of course, we're aware that your company has been exploring the possibility, and I recall reading that you were expected to announce your decision soon. Naturally, all of us at LBC are optimistic you'll decide in favor of coming here. I wanted to make our proposal as early as possible so that there would be plenty of time to plan the event. Would you tell Mr. Soave I called and ask him for an appointment at his convenience?

Largo: Well, Mr. Soave is very busy right now, and he leaves for Italy in a week. We're setting up a press conference with the mayor on Friday to announce our decision. I'm sure he couldn't speak with you before then.

Willing: I see. Well, here is my number, in case something opens up in his schedule. Thank you for the information.

Willing realizes she's not going to get anywhere with this approach. The secretary is obviously trying to run interference for Soave; probably she won't even give him the message. Still, from what Boatman has indicated, Soave sounds like an agreeable fellow. Maybe there's another way to get through to him. Willing calls Boatman for help and he agrees to make the contact.

Boatman: (Whose call is put through immediately) I can't tell you how pleased we are at the lakefront that you've made the decision to dock the ship here, Sandro. Of course, I'm planning to attend the press conference. Let me assure you again that our group will do everything we can to promote your efforts. I imagine your next step is going to be to plan a big opening, and this is one area where we'd like to help. I want to introduce you to a member of our board, Alice Willing, who's one of the best benefit planners in town. You know, it's customary in this country to have a benefit in connection with an event like this. It'll be very good for business.

Soave: Yes, I suppose that would be a good idea. But I must fly back to Italy and I won't return for several months. This can wait until spring, no?

Boatman: Actually, our committees have found it takes the better part of a year to get the wheels in motion and sell the tickets. That's why I think you should talk to Alice before you leave. If you like her ideas, she can take it from there. Can you meet us for lunch any day this week?

Soave: Really, I'm afraid I have no time. But if you like, you can talk to my chief of North American operations, Fred Pesca, who will be coming from New York in a few weeks to take over for me. I'll tell my secretary to set up the appointment for you.

Boatman: That will be fine, thank you. We'll look forward to meeting him.

The meeting takes place three weeks later in Fred Pesca's Utopia office. Accompanying Boatman and Willing is LBC executive director Art Fine; Portobello's regional marketing director, Erica Sharp, is also in attendance.

Willing: As Sol explained when he set up this meeting, we would like to discuss the possibility of a joint venture — a benefit to launch your new cruise ship that would raise money to help improve the lakefront at the same time.

Pesca: So would about 15 other organizations that have called us in the last three weeks. Really, I had no idea there were so many not-for-profit groups interested in our ship — if we get such a response from the paying customers, we'll be in business. This puts us in a rather awkward position. Why should we choose your organization out of all those that expressed interest?

Willing: I can sympathize with your position. Obviously, you want a group that can show off your new ship to its best advantage. We know you're supportive of all the worthy causes in our community, just as we have supported your efforts and other business developments along the lakefront. After all, it was the Lakefront Beautification Committee that cleaned up the harbor in the first place and turned a dingy warehouse district into a beautiful, clean park for family recreation.

We have a good track record in this community. Our benefits usually attract between 800 and 1,000 patrons, and there are a lot of people in town who think of our annual event as the official beginning of summer. Here are some clippings from our last benefit on the stage of the new amphitheater we built with the proceeds from the previous year's benefit. You see, we turn all our profits directly back into improvements to the lakefront, which ultimately makes the area more attractive to your passengers.

Pesca: Very impressive. But we really hadn't planned to make a decision this soon. We have a great deal to do between now and next summer.

Willing: In my experience, now isn't too soon to begin planning, if you want to have a really spectacular event, as I'm sure you do. We'd be happy to work with your team to come up with a suitable concept. Suppose I come back to you in two weeks with a more detailed proposal. Would that make your decision easier?

Pesca: Why, yes, it would give us something to go on. But I can't make you any promises; the final decision would be up to Mr.

	Soave and his partners. I'll tell you what: I'll be out of town for a few weeks. Why don't you confer with Erica and the next time I'm back, let me see what you've got.
Sharp:	(Studying the clippings) This looks as if it was a great party. We'd want to do something like this, but with a more romantic feel, to launch our Moonlight Magic cruises — like something out of a Grace Kelly movie.
Willing:	I think I know what you mean — with lots of flickering lanterns and the band playing tangos and the smell of gardenias in the air.... I'll need some information as to the capacity of the ship and the layout of the various decks. Can you get that for me this week?
Sharp:	Yes, in fact if you can stay for a few minutes after we finish here I'll go over the deck plans with you.
Pesca:	All right then, let's meet again as soon as I return and see where we are.
Willing:	Very good. Let me just leave you this board list and annual report to look over in the meantime. We certainly appreciate your time and interest.

In the case of a more routine solicitation, say, a pitch for corporate tables, it's acceptable to make the request by letter instead of meeting with the executive in person. The letter, however, usually has to be followed up by phone calls; otherwise such requests are easily ignored.

When going after additional underwriting once your benefit plans are underway, you will need to be prepared with several alternatives in case a prospect turns down your first suggestion. If your presentation is carefully organized, the contact may agree to one of the following contributions, listed in order of priority:

Straight donation. Always ask for a specific amount, and be sure that amount is greater than your top ticket price. If the highest patron ticket is $1,000 and corporate tables are $2,000, ask for $5,000.

In-kind donation. If a company or professional can donate any of the goods or services that you need, everyone comes out ahead, as their cost is less than what you'd pay at retail. Just be sure what the donor offers to provide really meets your specifications. He or she may come up with a good idea you hadn't thought about, but on the other hand, he or she may try to press something on you that just doesn't fit into your plans. You will have to weigh the value of the offer and decide whether it's worth altering your plans to accept it.

Printing is one of the easiest donations to secure, as many corporations have in-house print shops. A commercial printer can sometimes be persuaded to donate benefit invitations or programs, particularly if he has an existing business relationship with the organization — he then has a stake in its continuing existence. In the case of invitations, be sure to note that they will be seen by many more people than will actually attend the benefit.

Other possible in-kind donations include decorating or design services and materials, costumes, entertainment, food or beverages (from restaurants, delicatessens or wine shops), auction items or prizes. Advertising and public relations firms will sometimes donate their time for a benefit as a public service. And don't forget that any supplier who provides his or her goods for the cost of materials alone is also making an in-kind contribution of labor and professional consultation.

Though we are not aware of any previous instances of this, we would like to suggest that corporations might make in-kind donations of a secretary's time, in much the same way that they "loan" executives to not-for-profit organizations to provide accounting, managerial or other expertise on a temporary basis. A good case could be made that an executive secretary needs to be as involved in community projects as his or her boss and could make useful contacts for the company through a benefit committee assignment. Such service would likewise make a challenging internship for a secretarial or business administration student.

Corporate table. This doesn't qualify as direct underwriting support, but it does give you a fallback position in case the prospect rejects your first or second requests. After someone has turned you down twice, how can that person then refuse to buy a few tickets? While this kind of support won't directly help to reduce your expenses, it does count towards realizing your income projections.

Naturally, you hope that corporate underwriters will also buy a table. They may, however, expect free tickets; then you'll have to decide whether their donations warrant such a gift. If an underwriter provides all the food and beverages, as well as the space, it certainly deserves some consideration. If a company's contribution is less than you'd expected, you may honor its request in the hopes of developing a long-term relationship. In any event, don't let your ticket sales committee approach any prospective underwriter until you have first made your pitch for special support. Given the alternative, most prospects will choose the less expensive option.

CORPORATE CONCERNS

Great as has been the generosity of corporations across the country in supporting the activities of not-for-profit organizations, business leaders are beginning to express alarm that they cannot keep up with the demands being made on them to attend fund-raising dinners. The following quote from a report titled "Philanthropy for Dessert: The Corporate Fund-Raising Dinner," which appeared in Issue 4, 1985, of the Better Business Bureau publication *Insight*, makes plain the dimensions of the problem:

> First Interstate Bank of California was represented at 96 such events last year. Ruth Jones-Saxey, vice president, manager of charitable contributions for the bank, [said], "$1,500 per table was the norm just two to three years ago [in California]; it is now $2,500 to $3,000 for a table of ten. There are even ones that start at $25,000!
>
> A New Jersey-based food manufacturing firm reported...that it received more than 240 invitations to special events last year. In an effort to "determine what the potential impact would be if we had the resources and the stamina to attend each event," the firm kept track of the invitations and the lowest cost table for each event. The total hypothetical cost came to $520,000.

In response to the proliferation of fund-raising dinners, corporations are beginning to scrutinize more closely their involvement in these events. The Greater Newark (New Jersey) Chamber of Commerce is one group that has squarely addressed the issue. In April 1985 a task force consisting of representatives of five major Newark-based firms and the chamber enlisted the cooperation of the Center for Non-Profit Corporations, Inc., in order to study the problem and try to arrive at a mutually agreeable solution.

Their concern, to quote the task force's resulting report, was not only with the "inordinately heavy strain on both the human and financial resources of the business community," but also that "the running of these events may well be siphoning off the energies and resources of the sponsoring organizations, thereby cutting back on their ability to be as effective as they wish to be." The task force developed guidelines for both business and not-for-profit organizations to follow in order to "bring about an immediate, continuing and orderly control of fund-raising events."

Task force chairperson Frederick G. Meissner, Jr., assistant vice president of external affairs of New Jersey Bell, assesses what the impact of the guidelines have been:

CORPORATE SOLICITATION LETTER — THE BALL

Standard business letter

Dear Mr. Jones:

The Ball at the Halle Building, a benefit for the Great Lakes Theater Festival, will take place on Saturday, November 2nd. I am inviting you to be a part of this event by sponsoring a corporate table.

As the developer and major underwriter of the benefit, Forest City Enterprises is ensuring that every aspect of the evening is as elegant as one would expect of the grand opening of a building that has been known as "Cleveland's most fashionable address."

As a $4,000 corporate sponsor, you can choose to receive complimentary limousine service in grand style to and from The Ball. Or, you may choose a complimentary check-in on Saturday afternoon at Stouffer's Inn on the Square, limousine service both to and from the party, plus your wakeup call, coffee and morning paper and Stouffer's famous Sunday brunch.

Or, as a $2,000 corporate sponsor, your corporation will be listed in the program, and all your guests will receive valet parking as well as cocktails, dinner and dancing.

Please fill out the enclosed form and join us at The Ball.

P.S. Make reservations early — we have only 120 tables available and 90 have already been reserved.

CORPORATE RESERVATION FORM

Yes! I will support The Ball at the Halle Building for the Great Lakes Theater Festival by (check where appropriate):

_____ Hosting a table of eight
_____ Having my company host a table
_____ Asking my company to be a corporate underwriter of items such as the orchestra, decorations, cocktail-hour entertainment, special guests, sound, lighting, etc.
_____ Other (please specify) _____

Name _____
Company _____
Address _____
Phone _____

PATRON SOLICITATION LETTERS — A STERLING SPECTACULAR

Handwritten personal notes

Dear Irene,

The Women's Committee of the Great Lakes Theater Festival invites you to be a patron of A Sterling Spectacular, our fashion show honoring the 25th year of GLTF, to be held on February 26, 1986 at the Ohio Theatre. Your purchase of a $100 Sterling Patron ticket will entitle you to a program listing. You will also receive a complimentary invitation to our patron luncheon in October.

We further invite you to join our patron committee which entails selling one or more Sterling Patron tickets, or Special Friends tickets at $55 each or general tickets at $35.

In order to list you as a committee member on our invitation, we need your commitment before November 10th. Please write or telephone me soon.

Your support is greatly appreciated.

Dear Irene,

Thank you for attending our patron luncheon and generously supporting Great Lakes Theater Festival by becoming a patron of our Sterling Spectacular fashion show.

(Repeats last three paragraphs above.)

Dear Mary Lou,

We missed you at our patron luncheon, but thank you for generously supporting the Great Lakes Theater Festival by becoming a patron of our Sterling Spectacular fashion show.

(Repeats last three paragraphs of first letter.)

Dear Irene,

It was great seeing you at the kickoff party. We certainly were all very excited when it was revealed that our designer will be Mary McFadden.

As you are a staunch supporter of our event, we want to remind you that the checks of all other Sterling Patrons and Special Friends must be in by February 12th in order for the names to be printed in our program.

We look forward to seeing you and your friends at the Ohio Theatre.

Since our guidelines came out we've had requests for them from 30 to 35 chambers of commerce, and several are considering adopting them. We've had excellent response from not-for-profit organizations, too: As long as the corporations will hold up their end of the deal, giving straight contributions in lieu of attending dinners, the organizations will come out ahead. I can think of several dinners in Newark that were cancelled as a result of the guidelines, and the organizations netted more from straight contributions than they would have from the dinners.

From my point of view, the results have not been as dramatic as I would like, but greater attention is being paid to the issues we've raised. It's only fair to the organizations to phase out gradually: We're telling people that this is our last year to buy a full table, that we'll cut back on the number of tickets next year. There are some events that you can't abandon, though. Mostly they're the ones that attract individuals as well as corporate ticket buyers, that have a wide community involvement. The ones we're trying to discourage are the "first and second annual" events.

I honestly believe that if organizations, particularly young ones, show more dedication to standard fund-raising procedures, they'll do better in the long run. Of course, we have to do some indoctrinating of the corporate community, as well: If we want the organizations to give up the dinners, the corporations have to give up something ourselves in the way of increased contributions.

It is worth writing to the chamber for a copy of of the New Jersey guidelines not because they offer an ideal solution, but because they represent the kind of intense corporate scrutiny that requests for benefit underwriting may increasingly undergo. Though at first blush it may appear that the guidelines are in direct contradiction with the purpose of this book, we feel that their underlying message supports our own: In order to attract continued support from the corporate community, benefits must be well run, highly profitable and purposefully integrated into comprehensive fund-raising programs for the organizations that sponsor them.

ETIQUETTE FOR CO-SPONSORS

The co-sponsor/volunteer committee relationship is, at heart, a business relationship. Though the emphasis may be on building good will between the company and the organization, the reason you have come together is because each side has something to offer the other. The company has money and resources, while the organization's volunteers have influential friends and a sterling reputation in the community. Rarely in diplomatic relations is power precisely balanced; in this case everyone is aware that the side with the money has the edge. A tactful benefit chairperson will allow the co-sponsor to show leadership without ceding control of her committee and its plans. A reasonable co-sponsor will take a low-key approach to working with the volunteer committee, deferring to its judgement on matters of style, taste and community interest.

The big question on everyone's mind will be: Who is paying how much for what? Sometimes a co-sponsor will offer a lump sum to be spent as the benefit committee sees fit. More often the company will provide certain goods and services for which it pays the bills. This gives the co-sponsor more control over the actual arrangements, but it can also mean a bigger financial contribution in the end, since the company may be able to donate some items at cost for which the committee might otherwise have to pay full price. The problem is that while you can safely assume that the company has its own budget for this event, you can also be fairly sure company representatives won't disclose it.

When the co-sponsor has experience with benefits and knows what it wants to accomplish, it should tell the volunteer organization up front what expenses it plans to assume. Forest City Enterprises, for example, usually draws up a list of responsibilities, financial and otherwise, that recognizes and takes advantage of the different resources each side has to contribute. Mark Randol always suggests that the volunteer organization pay for all mailings because its not-for-profit status qualifies it for a lower postal rate. The organization is also in a better position to compile the mailing list and sell tickets. For its part, the Cleveland-based developer prefers to oversee the design and printing of invitations and other promotional materials, subject to approval by the volunteer committee, since these affect the company's image as well as the organization's. The particulars will vary with each benefit, of course.

If the co-sponsor doesn't speak up first, however, the benefit chairperson should take the initiative in negotiating finances at the earliest possible moment and put the agreement in writing. As a starting point for the discussion, use the checklist in this chapter, which has been adapted from Forest City's model.

Try not to leave out any details, or there may be confusion and possible conflict later. Does the co-sponsor need tickets — if so, how many and at what patron level? Be explicit about what is included in each expense category. If the co-sponsor is paying for food and beverages, does that mean a sit-down dinner or a cocktail buffet? Do beverages comprise just coffee and tea or table wine, liquor, set-ups and bartending service? As you discuss your ideas and divide up the responsibility for various line items, you'll quickly discover whether or not you and your co-sponsor agree on the benefit's basic style, tone and degree of opulence. If there are disagreements, it's easier to make compromises before either side has gone too far with its plans. The benefit committee is free to seek underwriting from other sources for any item not covered by the co-sponsor, of course.

To what degree co-sponsors will get involved in the actual party planning depends on the company representatives' interest, experience and enthusiasm. Many corporations are fairly new to the benefit scene and look to the volunteer committee to set the tone. They may be unfamiliar and impatient with the committee process and may, for that reason, seem peremptory to volunteers. The benefit committee must be extremely tactful but assertive about its own needs and concerns so as to give the co-sponsor confidence that the volunteers know what they're doing.

According to Randol, working effectively with a volunteer committee demands a different management style than that with which corporate executives are familiar. Executives don't personally supervise their trained employees, as a rule, but in the case of a benefit, volunteers often are doing jobs for the first time. A co-sponsor, he feels, has to be willing to spend time and commit experienced staff to working with the committee, making sure that the details are done right. After all, the corporate image is very much at stake.

If the relationship between co-sponsor and volunteer committee is to be satisfying and productive, each side must find a way to exchange information, make decisions and express opinions freely. Formal communications channels must be established through regular meetings and periodic updates or memos, and all participants should agree on how information will be acted on and how decisions will be reached. As long as everyone maintains a professional attitude and acts courteously, the collaboration should be harmonious and satisfying.

But sometimes misunderstandings and even hostility can arise. When this happens, benefit and corporate leadership must try to bring the issue out in the open so that a compromise can be reached. In most cases, the side holding the purse strings has the final say—this is a fact of life. But since the responsibilities are divided, there is room for give and take. When there is a difference of opinion, a well-researched, calmly stated position can often be persuasive.

In planning The Ball at the Halle Building, there was much discussion about the question of commemorative gifts for $500 patrons. Forest City's Randol argued that patrons who give at that price level deserve a nice present, and the Great Lakes Theater Festival committee countered that the cost of a gift would eat up

CHECKLIST OF CO-SPONSOR'S RESPONSIBILITIES

EXPENSE	PERSON(S) RESPONSIBLE	EXPENSE	PERSON(S) RESPONSIBLE
DESIGN, COPYWRITING, PRODUCTION		Valet parking	_____
		Tent (if required)	_____
Save the date card	_____	Equipment (PA system, coat racks, etc.)	_____
Kickoff party invite	_____		
Invitation	_____	Attendants	_____
Program	_____	Insurance/permits	_____
Signs	_____		
Other	_____	FOOD/BEVERAGE	
		Caterer	_____
POSTAGE	_____	Liquor/wine	_____
		Equipment	_____
PUBLICITY			
Kickoff party	_____	ENTERTAINMENT	
Press kits	_____	Performers	_____
Other	_____	Stage	_____
		Sound/lighting system	_____
COMP TICKETS		Stagehands	_____
Co-sponsor's list	_____	Piano	_____
Media	_____		
VIPs	_____	DECOR (list items)	_____
FACILITY RENTAL		RAFFLE/AUCTION ITEMS	_____
Fee	_____		
Security/maintenance	_____	FAVORS/GIFTS	_____

the extra contribution that donors intend to support the organization. The committee felt this was a financial issue, not a matter of taste, and therefore wasn't willing to defer; eventually it prevailed.

There is no room, however, for pettiness or internal squabbles. Meetings should be well organized, with both sides prepared to contribute to an agenda established in advance. The benefit chairperson should get a feel for committee members' opinions before the meetings, so that time isn't wasted in dealing with irrelevant objections. When a sticky issue does arise, try to table discussion until it can be researched carefully and you can be sure of committee support. The co-sponsor, for its part, should remember that its goal is to engender good will. As Randol puts it: "It behooves us to see that we don't get so emotionally involved that we upset the volunteers. The only way they'll enjoy the event is if they've had a wonderful time putting it together." We might add that the only way the underwriter will want to co-sponsor another benefit is if the committee demonstrates its ability to accomplish the task at hand in a thoroughly professional way.

SELLING OUT THE HOUSE

From the moment you begin planning your benefit, ticket sales should be uppermost in your mind. Every activity you undertake, from securing board approval and drawing up your budget through recruiting your committee to executing the minutest details, must lead ultimately to the realization of your income projections. The only way to make your underwriters', volunteers' and organization's investment of time and money pay off is to sell every available ticket at the highest possible price level.

Your ticket sales strategy starts with the members of your benefit committee; each is both a potential ticket buyer and seller. One of the reasons why you recruited as large a committee as you could, representing every geographical corner of your region and every possible social, professional and civic group in your community, was to build a solid core of ticket buyers and to assure entree to their constituents. This has long been one of the unwritten rules of benefit committee work, but volunteers new to the benefit scene may need to be apprised of the ticket-buying protocol at the time of recruitment. Those who have been previously involved in benefits have less of an excuse for shirking their obligations.

The benefit chairperson should encourage participation by talking up ticket sales at every meeting, reporting the number of tables and/or individual places sold to date and urging committee members to make their own reservations early, "to avoid disappointment." She should also be prepared to follow up, politely but persistently, in private conversations with committee members who are slow to respond. Some volunteers will work on the committee but will be out of town the night of the event. They should be encouraged to buy tickets, anyway, and give them away to friends or to make a straight donation. There isn't much you can do about those few committee members who will resist appeals to their sense of duty, except to avoid them in the future. One rule that absolutely must be enforced is that committee members who want to attend the benefit must pay their own way.

From buying their own tickets and encouraging their friends

to attend, it's a short step for committee members to make the more serious commitment of becoming a table host or hostess.

TABLE HOSTS AND HOSTESSES

Let's say you have to sell 800 tickets to realize your income goal. How can you begin to find that many takers, much less keep track of their reservations and make sure they send their checks in on time? The answer is to reduce the job to a manageable size: Instead of looking for 800 ticket buyers, you find 80 table hosts or hostesses, each of whom promises to round up a table of ten. If the hosts or hostesses each come with a spouse or date, they are responsible for lining up only four other couples. It's as simple as hosting a dinner party in their own homes, but without having to cook. The trick is to persuade their friends to buy tickets.

In the "good old days" it may have been common to treat one's friends to a benefit evening, but it's not as easy with the high cost of benefits today. Actually, it's better if each couple pays its own way. That way the organization acquires more individual donors and, if some patrons wish to donate at a higher level than their companions, those tables become more profitable.

The heart of your benefit sales force, then, consists of the hosts and hostesses who are responsible for filling the tables. It is the benefit chairperson's responsibility to see that an adequate number of table hostesses have been recruited, although she will need to enlist several influential members of her executive committee to help with this important and time-consuming task. There is no substitute for a personal appeal to each benefit committee member, trustee and support group member. You should also approach other friends of the organization and people who are known to support benefits in your community.

If prospective hosts or hostesses are concerned about rounding up an entire table, encourage two friends to go in together — then they only have to find three more couples. Since you're asking for a definite commitment, you may have to give the prospect a couple of days to think about it, but don't leave your request open-ended. Arrange to call back within a week.

The list of table host/hostess reservations is the simplest and most important marketing tool you have. The benefit chairperson should make a point of taking the list with her wherever she goes, to show prospective hostesses and corporate table buyers who is coming. It's easy to monitor progress from day to day as you add names to the list: If sales are going well you can report it with satisfaction to the committee and prospective underwriters, urging them to act quickly before the party is sold out. If sales are slow, the list will serve as a constant reminder to keep working until all tables are filled.

Be aware that you must overbook table assignments, just as the airlines do with seats. Figure that at least 15 to 20 percent of your table hosts and hostesses may not attend. They may have to go out of town on business or to attend a wedding, or they simply may not get around to selling the required number of tickets. Also expect that some may need help at the last minute in filling out their tables. Fortunately, there are always a few guests who will attend without being part of a preset table group.

By all means, list the names of committed table hosts and hostesses on your invitations as a demonstration of support for the benefit. This is another incentive to have a large number signed up by the time your invitations must go to press. Sometimes table hosts and hostesses are listed with the regular committee members, but if you have a great many who aren't working committee members, you may want to list them separately.

KICKOFF PARTIES

Is it really necessary to have a party to announce an upcoming benefit? While it's possible to do without one, if properly handled, a kickoff party is a valuable marketing and promotional tool. In fact, think of it as such; you will be more inclined to focus on the business at hand and downplay the refreshments and entertainment.

The purpose of a kickoff party is to give advance details and create enthusiasm for the upcoming benefit and to recruit new committee workers and table hosts and hostesses, which generates ticket sales. The theory is to show how much support the benefit has already garnered so that others will jump on the bandwagon. Sometimes a kickoff party will consist of a luncheon or tea in the benefit chairperson's home, at which she recruits more volunteers to work on her committee and/or to reserve tables. We recommend gearing the kickoff party to a wider audience — including board members, committee members' spouses, business representatives and the media — and staging it in a convenient facility such as a downtown club.

A kickoff party should be held a minimum of eight to 12 weeks before the invitations are mailed so that table hosts and committee members who sign up at that time (and as a result of your immediate follow-up) can be added to the official list before it goes to the printer. If invitations go out eight weeks before the benefit, that means the kickoff party should precede the benefit itself by at least four months. You need to start working about six to eight weeks before that in order to muster an impressive committee and a substantial number of table hosts/hostesses by the time of the kickoff party.

The invitations to the kickoff should alert guests to the fact that they're being let in on the ground floor of an exciting project. While you may send out press releases and several hundred invitations, you need to speak personally to everyone whose commitment to attend you really want. Not everyone will be able to, of course, but those who do should be primed to spread enthusiasm about your plans. Reporters in particular will be quick to pick up on the excitement of the crowd and pass the word to their audiences.

Kickoff parties should be informal, convivial and to the point. You need provide only light refreshment and perhaps some quiet but upbeat music. A few short speeches by benefit principals (chairperson, board president or executive director and co-sponsor) should suffice to announce details of the forthcoming event. Have a registration table at the door supplied with an alphabetical guest list and ask anyone else who shows up to sign in. Prominently display the list of committed table hosts and hostesses (the benefit chairperson and board president head the list) so that other guests can add their names on the spot. Provide mail-in forms for corporate tables so that the executives in attendance have a written document to take back to the office for consideration.

The kickoff party for The Ball at the Halle Building was a cocktail party held on a weeknight almost six months before the benefit at Cleveland's Union Club, across the street from the Halle Building itself. The location and the hour (5 to 7 p.m.) made it possible for downtown workers to attend on the way home from work. Drinks were essential, but food was limited to nuts and chips to hold down expenses and to discourage lingering. A trio provided background music. The atmosphere was not unlike that of a vendor-sponsored reception at a convention, where guests are aware that their hosts have invited them for the purpose of soft-selling their product. Marilyn prepared a long scroll that she asked guests to sign. Already inscribed with the names of 15 table hosts or hostesses, the scroll picked up more at the kickoff party. More importantly, Marilyn and her executive committee later called everyone who had attended and as a result brought the number to 35 out of a possible 100 tables.

The highlight of the Fantasy kickoff party was a four-minute videotape (produced for only $25) of Le Masquerade in performance. The tape proved more effective than words in selling the novel entertainment planned for this benefit. It succeeded in capturing the imagination of the guests, especially several society writers, whose eyewitness accounts published later in the newspapers served as an endorsement to those readers who couldn't be there in person. This kickoff was held at the Play House Club, a facility owned and operated by the Cleveland Play House, which on this occasion allowed benefit committee volunteers to bring in their own hors d'oeuvres. The procedure for signing up was essentially the same as that for The Ball.

ADVERTISING AND PUBLICITY

This brings us to the marketing role played by advertising and publicity, an issue that is not clearly understood because their impact is hard to assess. Whether or not publicity sells tickets is debatable. Nonetheless, committee members and media watchers tend to believe that a powerful society columnist can make or break a benefit. Frequent or favorable mention of your benefit in the press helps to convey the impression that everyone is looking forward to this event, but without an active sales force to follow up, good publicity alone does not produce ticket sales. Should you rate coverage in a national publication (except for listings in the "Chronicle" section of *Town & Country* magazine, this is a rare occurrence), it may make people sit up and take notice. But don't expect ticket buyers to flood the phones.

Lack of publicity, on the other hand, should never be totally blamed for a poor turnout. If you can't interest your friends in this event, who can? They're the people who'll be buying the tickets, usually not strangers who read a favorable mention in the paper. But if, on the other hand, you manage to stir up enough grass-roots excitement, perhaps even the media will jump aboard.

For similar reasons, paid advertising plays even less of a role in benefit sales. Generally speaking, we believe it doesn't generate sufficient ticket sales to pay for itself. The exception is when you're trying to sell thousands of tickets to a popularly priced concert or sporting event. Opportunities for *free* advertising should not be overlooked, however. If your organization has a newsletter or program book that reaches your target market, ask to have a free ad run as a reinforcement of your marketing efforts. Public service announcements, or PSAs (in the form of copy that is read or simple video- and audio tapes, all of which you must provide), are the equivalent of free advertising. Unlike newspaper stories, which appear only once, PSAs run numerous times over a period of weeks.

You have no control over when or how often your message will run, however—on TV, especially, PSAs are used to fill in those spots, usually at odd hours, that haven't been sold to advertisers.

Another source of free radio and TV publicity are community affairs calendars, which can be asked to mention your upcoming event, and public affairs programs, which may want to interview your benefit chairperson. If your benefit features an interesting speaker or performer, try to book him or her on local radio or TV talk shows. (Be aware that stations are highly competitive and may request an exclusive appearance.) In the case of an important speaker, you may even be able to arrange for a live broadcast of the address. If your celebrity will not be available until the day of the event, a talk-show appearance won't do much for ticket sales. In fact, your organization may only be mentioned in passing. But even a nod will please patrons and committee members and will contribute to raising community awareness of your cause.

Publicity after the fact—the photo spreads of radiant party-goers in newspapers and magazines—can add to the euphoria of a successful benefit, but it does nothing for your net profit. It may help to sell your *next* benefit, though, by letting those who weren't there know that they missed a great time. For an organization struggling to establish its image in the community, a good review of a benefit can indicate that the group has "arrived" as a force on the social and cultural scene. That image, however, will persist only if your next events succeed.

Possibly the most beneficial thing publicity does is boost the morale of the benefit committee. For this reason alone, you should go about publicizing the event with the same professionalism you apply to the rest of your efforts. This doesn't mean you have to hire a PR firm; many volunteers have some experience in this area, and it's easy to learn. Your organization's PR department should be able to provide information and assistance. Talk to the department head early on about proper procedures and appropriate media contacts. Be sure everyone agrees on the PR timetable and who's supposed to call on whom.

Karen Strang, publicity co-chairperson for both Fantasy and Scheherazade, has this advice to offer benefit committee publicists:

Knowing reporters personally is not necessary, but I must say it makes the job much easier. Example: A telephone call placed to a member of the media will be returned more quickly if the person is familiar with and has respect for the caller. If you are new to publicity, you may want to send a letter a few days before you make your initial call. Include information about who you are, why you are calling and when you will call.

The best way to cultivate a media person is always to be totally honest and do your homework. Providing enough information in many different areas is important. Some of those areas are fashion, "funsy" news, gossip, photo opportunities — the more time and study of your event you do, the better you'll be able to present it. Give them only information they can use, not reams and reams of unimportant detail.

Remember that reporters are busy information handlers who like to have data presented in concise, logical form. They are accustomed to receiving press releases, fact sheets and, where appropriate, glossy black-and-white photos clearly captioned on the back. Like anyone else, writers like to be taken out to lunch, but no amount of socializing will change the fact that they will reserve the right to judge for themselves how newsworthy your event is. If possible, point out an angle that ties your benefit in with a current news story.

TOOLS OF THE PR TRADE

A professional publicity campaign makes use of all of the following elements:

Press release. This is the basic tool for conveying information to all print media. Sometimes a newspaper or magazine will print the release verbatim; other times it will edit the release for a listing section or have a reporter call for an interview. A press release should be no more than two pages long, typed double-spaced on organization or benefit letterhead, and should answer the standard news questions: who, what, when, where and why. All of these answers should appear in the first paragraph, if possible, and can be elaborated upon in succeeding paragraphs. The name of the (co-)sponsoring organization(s) should appear in the introductory paragraph, and the chairperson(s) should be identified toward the release's end. Try to create an interesting lead sentence (e.g., "Ten thousand silver balloons launched by Mayor James Winner will mark the long-awaited opening of the Futuristic Building....") rather than a straight recitation of the facts ("The Community Cultural Association will sponsor a benefit....").

Date the release and give it a headline. Always type the name and phone number of at least one contact person at the top of the first page, for the editor's use. The last paragraph of the release should also contain a number to call for more information, which may be the same as your contact number, but doesn't have to be. For example, the contact may be the committee's public relations chairperson or organization's PR director, while the number you want potential ticket buyers to call may be the reservations chairperson. The number given in the body copy is the one that will be published. Type "more" at the bottom of the first page and "-30-" at the end of the release.

Fact sheet. This contains the same information as a press release but in outline form, usually on one page with headings in upper-case letters and the information opposite for easy reading. Benefit fact sheets should list the names and phone numbers of the chairperson(s) and key executive committee members. Often a press release and fact sheet are presented together, at the kickoff party, for example. Fact sheets are also useful when talking to reporters in person and in recruiting committee members and table hosts and hostesses. Anyone who answers telephone inquiries concerning the benefit should have a copy of the most recent fact sheet for ready reference. Like press releases, fact sheets should be dated and have a contact name and number at the top.

Public service announcement. This is a spot radio or TV announcement that not-for-profit organizations don't have to pay for; you will have to write and sometimes produce it. (The Federal Communications Commission requires radio and TV stations to air such spots gratis in the public interest.) As radio stations have differing length requirements, the safest bet is to write two or three separate announcements of ten, 20 and 30 seconds' duration. Type each one on a separate page (double-spaced and all upper case) and enclose all of them in the same envelope. After you have composed the spots, read them aloud several times to make sure they flow smoothly and include all the necessary information in the allotted time. Put phonetic spellings in parentheses after any difficult words or names so that the announcer can pronounce them properly. At the top of each page type the name and number of the contact person, the length of the announcement (e.g., "30-second PSA"), the kill date (the last day you want the announcement to be read) and a headline. Most radio stations will read your item verbatim, but some may ask to have a representative of your organization record the message over the phone or in the station.

To make a simple PSA for television, have a photographic slide made of the benefit logo superimposed on an appropriate picture and write a ten-, 20-, or 30-second message as above. If you want to produce a more elaborate videotape, consult your local stations' public affairs departments about what formats they accept. The station may offer to help you produce the spot; if not, perhaps an advertising agency or video production house can be approached to donate its services.

Photographs. You may want to hand out good-quality, black-and-white glossy photos of your benefit entertainers to newspapers and magazines, along with your press release. The identities of the subjects in the photos should be typed on a strip of paper taped to the back. Include your address if you want the photos returned. Suburban newspapers are more likely to use photos of benefit committee members who live in their circulation areas than are big-city dailies. Any journals that cover the event itself will send their own photographers, if visuals are deemed necessary.

Press kit. This is simply a folder containing a copy of all press releases, a fact sheet, photos and any other pertinent information such as committee lists, seating charts and brochures about the organization. Press kits look more impressive than a straight press release, but they are also more expensive. Your organization's PR department may have printed folders suitable for this purpose; if not, use plain-colored folders from any office supply store or have some printed with your benefit logo or, as a less-expensive expedient, print stick-on labels to adorn plain folders.

Press kits may be handed to media representatives at the kickoff party or press luncheon and updated versions mailed just prior to the event to those who will be covering it. You can also mail press kits to reporters who don't attend the kickoff to try to interest them in the story. Have extra copies of the materials on hand so that when you follow up by phone a couple of days after the kit should have arrived only to learn that it has been misplaced, you can send the reporter another.

TIMED-RELEASE ACTION

You should pace your PR campaign so that new information is released throughout the benefit's entire planning period. Let's say your organization lands the opening of an important new office building. This rates an immediate call to the writer you think will be most interested in the scoop, even if the benefit isn't going to occur for a year or more. (Be sure you have the co-sponsor's approval before releasing the information.) When plans are ready to be announced officially, invite all appropriate society and feature writers to a kickoff party or press luncheon. Call the various newspaper and magazine writers who cover benefits, identify yourself and briefly explain that you're going to send them an invitation so that they'll be expecting it (reporters receive dozens of communications every day; advance notice will help to make yours stand out from the rest).

Once the formal announcement of the benefit has appeared,

SAMPLE FACT SHEET — FANTASY

BENEFIT NAME:	Fantasy
CELEBRATING:	The 70th anniversary of the Cleveland Play House
DATE:	Saturday, June 14, 1986
TIME:	6:30 Cocktails and entertainment, 8:00 Dinner and entertainment, 9:30 Dancing and entertainment Open bar
PLACE:	The Cleveland Play House, 8500 Euclid Avenue, Cleveland, Ohio
PRICE PER PERSON:	The Phenomenals — at $1,000 per person ($950 tax deductible) Includes cocktails, hors d'oeuvres, dinner, dancing, program listing for underwriting one performer with special attention by same and a chance to win a Fantasy weekend for two in New York.
	The Spectaculars — at $500 per person ($450 tax deductible) Includes cocktails and hors d'oeuvres, dinner, dancing, program listing, a special surprise and a chance to win a Fantasy weekend for two in New York City.
	The Fantastics — at $250 per person ($200 tax deductible) Includes cocktails and hors d'oeuvres, dinner, dancing, program listing and a chance to win a Fantasy weekend for two in New York.
	The Fabulous — at $150 per person ($100 tax deductible) Reservations limited. Includes cocktails and hors d'oeuvres, dinner and dancing.
CORPORATE TABLES:	$4,000 — Spectacular Corporate Patrons ($3,600 tax deductible) A table of eight ($500 per person). Includes cocktails, hors d'oeuvres, dinner, dancing, program listing, a special surprise and a chance to win a Fantasy weekend for two in New York City.
	$2,000 — Fantastic Corporate Patrons ($1,600 tax deductible) A table of eight ($250 per person). Includes cocktails and hors d'oeuvres, dinner, dancing, program listing and a chance to win a Fantasy weekend for two in New York City.
ENTERTAINMENT:	The World Fantasy Performers of New York City, "Le Masquerade"
CATERER:	Simply Elegant, Elaine and William German
DRESS:	Elegant-fantastic apparel
SEATING:	Eight to ten patrons per table
FOR MORE INFORMATION CALL:	The Cleveland Play House Development Department 000-0000 ext. 00

CHAIRPERSONS:

Mrs. Paul Brentlinger, Shaker Heights
000-0000

Mrs. Joseph T. Meals, Hunting Valley
000-0000

Mrs. Douglas Richardson, Chagrin Falls
000-0000

FOR RESERVATIONS CONTACT:

Mrs. David A. Cowan, Cleveland
000-0000

Mrs. William J. Pappas, Shaker Heights
000-0000

Please make checks payable to:
The Cleveland Play House Fantasy

you can continue to feed tidbits to the press via phone calls or in writing. The strategy here is to keep the event in the public eye in order to build a sense of anticipation. Don't badger reporters by repeating information you've already sent, but a friendly call to bring them up to date is usually acceptable. Say one of your committee members is going on vacation in Thailand, where she will buy silk and statuary for decorations, or a celebrity has agreed to put in an appearance, or a well-known artist has donated a painting to be used on the invitation and auctioned off at the benefit—if you follow the society or gossip columns in your local papers, you'll see that these are the kinds of follow-up news items they are happy to print. Be selective in your calling, however; most reporters want exclusive information, and if one is scooped by a rival at another publication, to whom you've given the same story, he or she will never trust you again. Try to time the release of the most important new developments to coincide with the mailing of invitations.

If your event is especially significant or offbeat, it may rate a spot on that evening's TV news. Though weekends tend to be slow news times, TV news directors will rarely make a firm commitment to cover a benefit—fires and other unplanned disasters take precedence. If a crew is sent, its arrival may be timed more for its convenience than to jibe with your schedule. The PR chairperson should know the whereabouts of important guests at all times, so that she can lead the cameras to them or vice versa. TV crews tend to breeze in and out, sometimes without warning, and they usually don't expect to stay for the meal.

Any reporter who has written an advance story or is likely to cover the event itself should receive complimentary tickets. Some newspapers will pay for tickets, but unless you know this to be true of a particular paper, expect to assume this expense. In some cases, the writer and photographer will come together, but sometimes one or both will expect to bring a date. They'll let you know. A benefit committee would be within its rights to deny such comps on the grounds that space is limited and it can't afford to give away places that could be sold. But when you consider that raising community awareness and generating good will is an ancillary goal, it makes sense to comply with all such ticket requests.

Station PR committee members near the door to greet media guests. You may want to assign one PR committee member to each media person—to make introductions, set up photos and provide information as needed. Don't seat reporters together unless they request it. As volunteer PR pro Karen Strang points out: "Society writers want to be treated as guests and sit with interesting and fun people. Each writer wants a unique angle — one only she may have heard or seen because she happens to be sitting in a particularly good spot. If the writers have a good time at your benefit, they will express just that in their columns."

INVITATIONS AND OTHER MAILINGS

The more the competition from other events around town, the more you have to remind people about the importance of attending yours. That's why benefit committees are putting increasing effort into mailings: invitations to kickoff parties, save the date cards, personalized sponsor solicitation letters and preview copies of auction catalogues — all in addition to the actual invitation.

Save the date cards — a notice mailed as much as six months in advance to prospective patrons — are a recent invention arising out of stepped-up competition. Their purpose is as much to stake a claim to the community's attention as it is to reserve a spot on the calendar. They can be as simple as a well-designed postcard or as elaborate as enclosing tiny favors. (A few years ago, a benefit for the Akron [Ohio] Symphony Orchestra called Topaz mailed ersatz yellow gems to be glued to the appropriate day on the recipient's calendar.) The copy on a save the date card should be carefully worded so as to be provocative without giving away all details about the benefit itself.

Personal notes are an important way of reaching potential ticket buyers, especially those upper-level patrons whose support should never be taken for granted. The patron committee usually undertakes the job of selecting prospects for the higher-priced tickets from the general benefit mailing list. Some committees jot notes on the invitation itself (first-class postage is required for those pieces that have handwritten addenda), while others prepare separate letters on benefit letterhead, to which they add a few lines in their own handwriting. These letters are mailed out before the invitations to avoid the risk of their arriving after the recipients have already sent in their reservations. This personal touch is important. Clevelander Lindsay Morgenthaler, indefatigable benefit chairperson and trustee of many Cleveland and national organizations, including the Kennedy Center in Washington, D.C., points out: "If an invitation or letter appears to be untouched by human hands, it's easy to ignore. People won't respond if they think nobody will know the difference."

The printed invitation. Though very large, public and geared in part toward developing new supporters, the most successful benefits convey a feeling that most of the guests are one another's friends. Attending a benefit is not the same thing as attending a concert; there the performance is the main event and chitchat is confined to a brief intermission. It's fair to say that socializing *is* the main event at a benefit, and usually it's more fun attending accompanied by friends. The high ticket price alone makes most invitees think twice about accepting, unless a friend urges them to.

For these reasons, the printed invitation should be considered as merely an announcement, not a personal solicitation. As such, it serves several important functions: First, the committee and table host/hostess listings tell the recipient who's going to be there. It also gives the table hostess an icebreaker ("Did you get your invitation?") when asking friends later whether they plan to attend. It can be kept as a reminder of the particulars of time, place and price, which are easily forgotten. Because it may provide the first visual cue as to what the party will be like, an attractive piece can engender excitement. Last but not least, it includes the all-important reply card and return envelope, which allow checks and reservation information to reach their proper destination.

Take great care in composing the copy for your invitations. You need to include *all* the pertinent information here: once they're printed, there's no opportunity for correcting mistakes or changing your mind. The main body of the invitation contains the who (name of the sponsoring organization and corporate co-sponsor, if any), what (title and brief description of the benefit), when (date and time), where (location) and why (for the benefit of...), along with a cordial request to join in. Sometimes the agenda for the event is included, complete with the names of the entertainers and, if noteworthy, the caterer. A listing of committee members and table hosts and hostesses is usually placed on the back or inside flap. The "how much" is revealed on an enclosed reply card, which may also detail the special perks awarded the purchaser at each ticket price level. The reply card should have space for filling in the ticket purchaser's name, address, phone and the names of the other patrons with whom he or she would like to be seated. It should also provide the option of making a straight donation in case the recipient can't attend the benefit. Finally, an unstamped return envelope addressed to the reservations/seating chairperson is enclosed.

Even with those who don't buy tickets, the invitation has the potential to make a good impression — assuming it's read. Which brings us to the reason why we insist that benefit invitations be hand-addressed: Most people receive several computer-labeled communications every day, most of which they automatically toss away unopened. A handwritten address on the envelope conveys the impression that there's a living, breathing human being behind this message, making it more likely that the addressee will be curious enough to open it and find out who it is. (The committee list on the invitation should provide the answer.)

Strange as it seems, those very people who complain about getting too many solicitations are the first to be offended if they don't receive an invitation to a benefit about which their friends are talking. Such lapses are, of course, unintentional; what not-for-profit organization can afford to exclude any potential supporters? Even more likely to take offense are those who receive incorrectly addressed invitations—to "Mr. and Mrs.," for example, when the couple has recently divorced. That's why committees need to take the care and feeding of their mailing lists seriously.

COMPILING AND MAINTAINING A MAILING LIST

There is no guaranteed percentage of return from a direct-mail campaign, so we can't tell you how many invitations you'll need to send in order to sell a specific number of tickets. Lacking a more precise system, most major Cleveland organizations rely on a mailing of 6,000 to 8,000 pieces for benefits of up to 1,000 guests. The size of the mailing will also be determined by the number of volunteers who can be mustered to prepare it—remember that all those invitations have to be hand-addressed, stuffed, sorted and hauled to the post office. Some benefit planners maintain that the quality of the list—how up-to-date and accurate it is and how familiar the benefit planners are with the names on it—has more to do with success than quantity. At any rate, it stands to reason that the more you work with your list, the more closely you can follow up on your invitations.

If you have access to a good mailing list, preferably one that's been used for your organization's previous benefits, take some time to update it before you prepare your first mailing. (If you skip this step, you'll waste postage and miss potential patrons by sending pieces to the wrong addresses.) Recruit six to eight regular benefit-goers and, at a joint meeting, have each go over one section of the list, looking for persons who've recently moved or changed their marital status. Questions and information should flow freely around the table, and no doubt everyone will think of names to add to the list. Have telephone books and current club directories handy for reference.

If you have to create a benefit mailing list from scratch, allow a good two to three months for this project. Most organizations have some sort of mailing list, but it's not likely to be usable as is for the purposes of a first-time benefit. If the organization has identified different categories of donors and subscribers by computer code, you're in luck. Begin with a printout of the most likely prospect categories, including board members, volunteer support group members, season subscribers and donors of $100 or more. Ask your co-sponsor and underwriters if they wish to contribute names and try to obtain lists from special-interest groups that would have an interest in your event (say, the Print Collectors' Society, if you're having an art auction). Then have committee members bring in membership directories of any clubs, professional organizations or neighborhood associations to which they belong and cull them thoroughly for the names of individuals known to attend benefits. You can also glean names from published donor lists of other organizations. And don't forget the backs of other benefit invitations!

And as long as you're going to all this trouble, input the mailing list on computer disk (use a volunteer's home computer equipped with mail-merge software if the organization doesn't have one). Because 8,000 names constitutes a lot of data entry, it would be worthwhile to hire a temporary secretary to handle this chore. It will save time in the long run by allowing you to print out labels (acceptable for save the date cards, auction catalogues, etc.) and cull, update and cross-reference the list more easily than you could if the list were in a card file. Proof the list carefully to make sure there are no duplications — a computer will read two variants of the same name ("Mrs. J. Smith" and "Mrs. James Smith") as two different individuals; ditto variants of the same address. If you have both the home and business address for the same person, the home address should be used.

ORGANIZING BULK MAILINGS

For the same reason that invitations should be hand-addressed, it would be nice to send them first class — but postage rates make that prohibitive for large mailings. There's no question that bulk mailings are cumbersome to prepare and slow to arrive at their destinations, but the savings are usually worth the inconvenience.

To qualify for bulk rate, a mailing must consist of at least 200 identical printed pieces — any pieces containing extra enclosures or handwritten notes are ineligible. Bulk-mailing sessions can be reasonably pleasant and relaxed, if you are well prepared. Mailing requirements clerks in the main post offices of most cities can explain bulk mailing procedures and supply you with the approved forms, bags, rubber bands and stickers. Not every post office substation accepts bulk mailings — find out which ones in your area do, how many bags they will handle at one time and what hours their bulk mail departments are open. The addressing/mailing chairperson should stop in for supplies and information well in advance of addressing and sorting sessions so that she won't get flustered trying to interpret complex instructions under pressure of time. Check in with the post office every time you prepare a mailing, as the regulations seem to change frequently.

Your not-for-profit organization should already have a bulk-rate permit number that must be printed on the mailing envelope (the printer or designer can help you with the proper placement of this indicia). Ascertain that the permit is current; it must be renewed every year. Be sure you know the procedure for payment; you may have to deposit a check in the organization's account before the bulk mailing section will accept your bags. It's a good idea to print "address correction requested" on the envelope, too; you will be charged first-class postage for every piece returned, but it's essential for keeping your list up-to-date.

Mary Abbott, chairperson of the Western Reserve Antique Show featured in the appendix, offers these additional tips for expediting bulk mailings:

> Allow two to two-and-a-half weeks ahead of the date when you want the mailing to reach individuals, for your mailing to be complete and at the main post office. Bulk mailings can be held at substations for several days before the local carrier will deliver them [because first and second class mailings take priority]. Plan to do a mailing during the middle dates of the month as the first and last three to four days are heavy with Social Security checks and bills.

Invitations should go out eight weeks before the date of the benefit — no less! Most people won't make up their minds until they've found a quiet moment to study all the particulars, and time is needed for table hosts and hostesses to follow up by phone. Kickoff party invitations can go out two to three weeks before that event; again try to follow up so that you'll know how many guests to expect. Acknowledgements and tickets, if mailed, should be sent out as soon as reservations come in; these require first-class postage. If the patron committee does a separate mailing to upper-level ticket prospects, it should also go first-class.

Production snags are usually the major obstacle to getting your mailings out on time. It's extremely frustrating, if not disastrous, to have to reschedule mailing sessions involving 20 or so volunteers because the printed materials aren't ready. You must be scrupulous about keeping your own deadlines and impress upon the printer the necessity of delivering the finished job on time. Then allow several extra days' grace.

Mailings that involve stick-on computer labels can be done in a day if the labels are delivered in zip code order, but hand-addressing sessions require a place where materials can be left out undisturbed overnight. A volunteer's home is usually the most convenient place, as long as the rooms used are out of the way of family traffic. You'll need plenty of space, light and work tables; one printout of the mailing list (in zip code order); all the pieces to be stuffed; boxes for sorting; post office supplies; coffee and non-sticky snacks for volunteers. You'll also want to line up someone with a station wagon or van and perhaps a couple of strong teenagers to hoist the mailbags when it's time to deliver them to the post office. Assign volunteers to specific shifts; if they're told to come "any time this week," some will never get there. Have one person, preferably the same one at all times, available to assign pages of the printout to each volunteer and to make sure everyone understands the procedures and follows them precisely. The post office will reject any mailing that doesn't conform strictly to its rules, which will cause delays or higher rates being charged.

THE PERSONAL TOUCH

Telephone follow-up should begin one to two weeks after invitations are dropped in the mail. If you sent them eight weeks before the benefit, you have six weeks to track down all those friends and acquaintances who, you are certain, wouldn't want to miss this event. The obvious place to begin your follow-up is with the table hosts and hostesses. Rather than try to reach each one of them herself, the chairperson should divide up the list among members of her executive committee. Then call members of the committee, board or support groups who haven't yet responded. A board member should call fellow trustees, the president of a support group should call members of that group and so on. The chairperson herself might want to talk to committee members. The underwriting committee is responsible for following up on corporate table solicitations; the patron committee calls individuals who have not yet responded to a written appeal to purchase upper-level tickets.

The purpose of the follow-up call is to give and get information, as well as to spur on the organization's most loyal supporters to come and bring their friends. You need to know how quickly the guest list is coming together, whose table is accounted for and who's likely to need help. Here's how our fictional chairperson Alice Willing would elicit that information from table hostess Dolly Madison:

Willing: Hello, Dolly. This is Alice Willing. I'm calling to see whether you received your invitation to Cruisin' in the Moonlight.

Madison: Oh, yes, I got it, it's right here on my desk somewhere. Well, I know I put it in this pile, I'm sure I'll find it again. I've just been so busy lately I haven't had a chance to send in my reservation.

Willing: That's good. I'm so pleased that you're coming. I just like to be reassured that the invitations are reaching everyone. Do you know who's sitting at your table?

Madison: I asked the Andersons, but they haven't called me back, and I was going to ask the Bakers, but I think they'll be out of town that week, and I was planning to call the Clarks....

Willing: Well, the benefit is only three weeks off, and the reservation list is filling up fast. I wouldn't want you to be disappointed. Would you like me to help you fill out your table? I know of several couples who are coming but don't have table assignments yet.

Madison: What a nice idea. Yes, I'd love to meet some new people. But I do still mean to ask the Douglases and the Edisons; I'm sure they'll come.

Willing: Will you call me back as soon as you know for sure? Then I'll know if you need any additional people to sit at your table.

Occasionally you'll learn that a table host or hostess has completely forgotten about his or her commitment or has simply made other plans. If your call comes early enough, he or she may still have time to complete a table — or, perhaps, to send a contribution. If not, you won't be unpleasantly surprised.

Table hosts and hostesses are supposed to remind their friends to send in their reservations, but there are always some guests who will wait until the last minute to write their checks. It's not a good policy to hope those individuals will pay at the door. Some may arrive in full regalia but without their checkbooks, making for an awkward situation. Others may fail to show up, resulting in your having to pay the caterer for uneaten meals. It's the reservations/

seating chairperson's responsibility to make sure that *all* guests have paid in advance for their reservations. Here's how Willing's subcommittee chairperson Jane Gaynor handles the task:

Gaynor: (Calling table host Arthur Round one week before the benefit) Arthur, Alice tells me that Sally and Bill Fuller are sitting at your table on the 15th, but I still haven't received their reservations. Could you jog their memories, please? We need to have all checks in by the tenth.

Round: I'd be happy to, Jane, but I'm leaving this afternoon on a business trip. I'll be out of town the rest of this week.

Gaynor: I see. Well, if you don't mind, I'll give Sally a call myself.

Gaynor: (Calling the Fullers immediately) Sally, I have you and Bill listed as guests at Arthur Round's table, but I haven't received your check yet. Are you still planning to come? I'm afraid I can't hold your place much longer.

Fuller: Don't worry, I put the check in the mail yesterday.

Gaynor: (Three days later, when the check still hasn't arrived) I'm afraid we still haven't received your check. Could you look again to be sure you mailed it?

Fuller: Oh, I'm so sorry. I gave it to Bill to mail on his way to work, but I guess he forgot.

Gaynor: Well, it's getting so close to the date, do you think you could drop it off at my house?

Fuller: I'd like to, but my car is in the shop.

Gaynor: Well, I'll tell you what. I have to run an errand in your neighborhood this afternoon on my way home from work. Why don't I just swing by around 5:30 and pick it up?

Fuller: Well, it's awfully nice of you to go out of your way. Now, remind me, to whom do I make the check payable?

There may even be occasions when you sell out early and have to turn people away. In this case, the chairperson can delegate to the benefit secretary or the reservations chairperson the responsibility of calling those who are supposed to come but still haven't sent in their payments to inquire whether they wish to be placed on a waiting list.

SAMPLE RECEIPT FORM

Name of event: _____

Date: _____

DATE REC'D	NAME	TICKET PRICE			DONA-TION	TOTAL
		$	$	$		

TOTAL this page
TOTAL previous page
TOTAL to date

Page no. _____

Date prepared _____

By whom _____

Directions: Reservations/seating chairperson should compile list of receipts at least once a week, making copies to give to benefit treasurer (along with checks to be deposited) and chairperson. Enter names of individuals and corporations in alphabetical order for ready reference. Enter number of tickets purchased in each price category and total dollar amount in last column. Be sure to note any straight contributions and carry over previous weeks' totals to determine new counts. Example below:

DATE REC'D	NAME	TICKET PRICE			DONA-TION	TOTAL
		$500	$250	$125		
10/3	M/M John Q. Adams			2		$ 250
10/1	Bountiful Foundation				$100	100
10/4	Cosmic Corporation		8			2,000
9/30	Ms. Gloria Day	1				500
10/2	M/M Westin East			2		250
	TOTAL this page	1	8	4	$100	$3,100
	TOTAL previous page	3	24	5	$700	$14,700
	TOTAL to date	4	32	9	$800	$17,800

A Sense of Occasion

Now comes the fun part—mixing concept, budget and talent together to create the party of your dreams, the event of the season, the "ultimate benefit!" We hope we've shown by now that it takes as much creative talent and energy to come up with a knowledge-able, dedicated committee, a sound budget and underwriting and marketing plans as it does to choose a theme and conceive the decorations. That doesn't mean, however, that the latter assign-ments are unimportant. Herewith we offer a few pointers to consider when fleshing out the benefit concept. For further inspiration, turn to the capsule descriptions of 20 successful Cleveland-area benefits in the appendix.

CHOOSING A THEME

The bare outlines of your benefit concept don't tell much about what the party's going to be like. The committee needs to invent a theme that will convey a sense of the occasion—whether it will be colorful, exciting, glamorous, informal, elegant, dignified or humor-ous. The difference between producing a routine event and a memorable one is in carrying out a well-defined, appropriate, unifying theme in every detail from start to finish.

Often the occasion itself or the location of the benefit in-fluences the choice of a theme. It makes sense for a theater or ballet company's opening-night benefit to spin off the theme of the performance, perhaps even borrowing its color scheme, decorations and props. For several years Cleveland Opera held benefits on its home stage at Cleveland's State Theatre between performances of such colorful productions as *The Mikado*, *Die Fledermaus* and *The Merry Widow*. The stage provided a built-in dramatic backdrop, and patrons enjoyed mingling with some of the soloists and feeling as if they were part of the production.

Anniversary benefits are even more common; you can either use the traditional silver, gold and diamond themes or ignore them in favor of something more imaginative. The Great Lakes Theater Festival celebrated its 25th anniversary with a simple Silver Ball theme that worked, in part, because it played off the more elaborate Ball at the Halle Building, held the previous year.

In that case, location alone determined the benefit theme. The former Halle Bros. department store, then newly renovated and reopening as a luxury office building, had developed such a strong carriage-trade identity during its 90-plus years in business that a theme of "elegance from a bygone era" seemed to emerge naturally.

Choosing a name is your first elaboration on the theme. It should be a simple title, easy to remember and pronounce, and one that instantly calls to mind a host of images. The right name will galvanize the committee and its supporters around a single idea and make it easy for committee members to talk about the event to their friends, while a party with no name or one that is not particularly evocative has to be described in a roundabout way. Some of the best names consist of a single word (the Cleveland Orchestra's biennial auction night, Scheherazade, is a good example, even though hardly anybody can spell this word; the title of the popular Rimsky-Korsakov symphonic suite, it evokes images of a night of a thousand fantasies). Other good titles can be taken from books, shows, songs, places or phrases. Just be careful the title you choose isn't copyrighted or a registered trademark.

BRAINSTORMING

Before you settle on a theme or title, do some brainstorming with a few of the best creative minds in your organization. Participants in the first couple of brainstorming sessions don't have to constitute a formal executive committee, nor are they obliged to serve on the benefit committee later. You may get some excellent ideas from people who aren't able to commit themselves to a year's worth of planning; others with more time may be able to act on their inspirations.

Good candidates for a brainstorming session are people who love to travel or seek out offbeat experiences; who read widely and take in every play, movie, concert and exhibition they can; who are always turning up interesting artifacts and have a sense of daring and adventure. It helps if they are visually oriented, too, for what you need to do at this point is dress the stage for the entire event.

If possible, walk your brainstorming group through the benefit site, taking note of architectural features, focal points, traffic patterns, sight lines and the location of electric outlets, restrooms, kitchen facilities, parking lots, entrances, ramps, elevators and so on. What kinds of images and activities seem to fit the place? Think about what your organization has done with past benefits—then try to come up with something that's different but still in line with supporters' interests.

The rule in brainstorming is that anybody can throw out any idea, no matter how farfetched. No criticism that could stifle creativity is allowed at this stage. The best ideas will automatically generate the most enthusiasm and elaboration. It helps to bring in pictures, reference books, found objects, swatches of cloth, taped music—anything that will help participants visualize the finished product. Encourage the brainstorming team to think big, to dare to suggest the impossible. (Later, when each subcommittee works out the details, you will have to confront the limitations of your facility and especially your budget.) You'll discard plenty of ideas as you go along, but in the meantime you'll have more to bounce around. And sometimes the most outrageous-sounding notions can turn into the unexpected flourishes that lift a benefit out of the ordinary into the spectacular.

To illustrate how a theme develops in the hands of a skilled committee, we'll briefly describe the creative process that produced, in more than a year of planning, The Ball at the Halle Building.

The Ball's underwriters, Forest City Enterprises, owners and developers of the Halle Building, wanted to revive the elegant image of the family-owned department store that once catered to fashion-conscious Clevelanders. This seemed to dictate a strictly formal affair, with guests in white tie and tails, white-gloved waiters, white table linens, gleaming crystal and silver. The benefit committee, likewise nostalgic for the gracious personal service that went hand-in-hand with high fashion at Halle's, agreed that only the most sophisticated production values were appropriate.

Because the grand reopening of this historic building was an event in itself, the committee and underwriters agreed that a ball was the ideal entertainment. A fine dinner and a lively dance orchestra would enhance patrons' enjoyment of the setting. Committee members originally wanted to call the event the Geranium Ball, after the well-known Halle Bros. Company emblem; when they learned that members of the Halle family were already planning a Geranium Ball to benefit another not-for-profit institution in Cleveland, they dropped the geranium motif and decided to call their benefit, simply and definitively, The Ball.

Early on, Forest City executives, the executive committee and caterer Robert S. Pile had worked out a floor plan that provided for a bandstand and dance floor visible from all 125 tables, plus space for two temporary kitchens, waiters' stations and bars. Then it was the benefit committee's responsibility to turn a two-dimensional sketch into a three-dimensional environment, full of music, color and life. An historical treatment focusing on Halle's famed personal service and high-fashion image gradually evolved.

The task of translating Halle's past elegance—now only a memory—into a coherent interior design fell mainly to the decor subcommittee chaired by Audrey S. Watts, a past president of the Great Lakes Theater Festival board of trustees. A former Halle's fashion buyer, Watts was intimately familiar with both the store's tradition and the building itself. She also had experience working with unfinished spaces, which proved to be a boon when the committee learned that the entire second floor, to be used as the benefit "ballroom," would boast no more than a coat of paint and a few lights—no carpeting, no finished ceilings, no dividers. Watts met with her large subcommittee every two weeks for eight months. At every meeting, she reiterated the committee's goal: to create an "ambience that is formal, elegant and gracious with a simple, unique and dramatic impact."

Marilyn recalls the experience as:

> ...not unlike trying to decorate the shifting sands of the Sahara. Even though we were given floor plans to scale, they were in a constant state of flux. Walls moved or were never built, exits and entrances changed, power sources appeared and disappeared. One wall went up and was painted (with custom paints we had specially prepared, by the way) as we were installing decorations at the last minute. Message: Expect the unexpected, especially when you're opening a new building.

For expert assistance in conveying Halle's fashion image, Watts called on Barry Bradley, curator of costume and textiles at Cleveland's Western Reserve Historical Society, which has an excellent couture collection. Bradley offered to create eight "vignettes" consisting of mannequins dressed in gowns, furs and accessories— some with the Halle label—from each decade of the store's existence. Professional interior designers Mary Wasmer and Jean Vosmik assisted in locating period furnishings, while amateur horticulturist Jeanette Evans designed flower arrangements to complete the displays, which were installed on custom-designed, carpeted platforms underwritten by The May Company, a local department store.

To recapture the distinctive atmosphere of the Halle Bros. Company, Audrey Watts sought out its former fashion director, Dixie Lee Davis, who, in turn, sent out a call to other former Halle's employees, who had held annual reunions ever since the downtown store closed in 1982. They responded with an outpouring of memorabilia—everything from old shopping bags to Christmas catalogues to employee training manuals—from which Davis assembled displays on the main floor to be viewed during the cocktail hour. The committee invited several Halle "alumnae" to recreate their former roles as elevator operators on the night of the benefit. Davis found old photographs of the elevator girls' uniforms, which were reproduced by students at Cleveland's Virginia Marti Fashion Institute and the Krause Costume Company. Davis, who was now working for the May Company, enlisted its Glemby salons to do the elevator girls' hair and makeup in an authentic Thirties style.

Various other experts contributed to the overall effect. General Electric Company senior lighting engineer John Kennedy, who had designed new exterior lighting for the renovated Halle Building, helped the decor committee solve problems of insufficient interior lighting on the "ballroom" floor and harsh exterior lighting coming through the windows from the street. Great Lakes Theater Festival production designer John Ezell and production manager Greg Tune helped install scenery from two of the season's productions. Several scrims from the set of *Twelfth Night*, reproductions of 18th-century pastoral paintings, were recycled into panels that would add visual interest to the bare walls. And the set from the last act of *The Game of Love*, outlining a trellised courtyard in turn-of-the-century Vienna, became a backdrop for the bandstand.

Interior designer Chaille Tullis concentrated on the table settings, which she had realized would become a major design element when repeated 125 times throughout the room. It was Tullis who recommended using pale pink tablecloths and pink flowers, instead of stark white, to create impact in the cavernous unfinished space. Tullis, Watts and benefit chairperson Brentlinger worked with florist Charles M. Phillips to come up with dramatic centerpieces consisting of tall wooden platforms from which pink anthuriums and white alba lilies cascaded, crowned by 30-inch white candles.

No opportunity to create a dramatic impression was overlooked. Forest City not only refinished and installed two of the store's original mahogany display cases, but also cleaned, reassembled and hung three of Halle's enormous crystal chandeliers to greet guests as they emerged from the elevators on the second floor. GLTF Women's Committee member Helen Lybarger wrote a short history of the Halle Bros. Company for the benefit program and retired advertising executive Clay Herrick dug up old photographs and documents to illustrate it. Another GLTF trustee, Robin Gunning, helped arrange memorabilia in the display cases and outfitted the restrooms with guest soaps, towels, hand lotion and other amenities. GLTF Women's Committee volunteers stuffed souvenir packages of perfume donated by the May Company into white bags decorated with The Ball's logo.

The result of all these labors was a consistent and thoroughly enjoyable experience for benefit patrons. From the moment they were ushered into the brightly lit, polished marble lobby by doormen wearing Halle Bros. uniforms, they entered a bygone era that conveyed both a wonderful feeling of nostalgia and an exciting sense of optimism about the future of a beloved landmark and its neighboring theater district.

COMPENSATING FOR DEFICIENCIES

As the story of The Ball indicates, there are many problems to be solved in the process of translating a theme to three-dimensional reality. Some of the thorniest are caused by deficiencies in the benefit site. Since no building or outdoor location is perfect, you'll have to size up the problems that "go with the territory" and find a way around them before proceeding to decorate — just as you'd have to repair cracks in the walls of a house before repainting and papering. Here are some suggestions for dealing with specific problems without or putting too great a strain on the benefit budget:

Hard to find location	Include a map in the invitation or mail later (be sure it's up-to-date and accurate).
Insufficient parking	Use shuttle bus, trolley, limos or antique car parade to transport guests between lot and building. Multiply time of round trip by number of guests per trip to determine how many vehicles or valet parkers you need.
No porte-cochere	Rent an awning or station doormen with golf umbrellas to escort guests from car to door.
Too large a room	Create false wall across one end with drapery, folding screens, flats, scrims or tall potted plants.
Interior looks dingy	Hire a cleaning service to spruce up before event; use lighting to emphasize tables and decorations while de-emphasizing ceiling, walls and floor.
Poor lighting	Install extra fixtures or theatrical lighting; use mirrors to reflect light. Use candles with caution due to fire hazard.

Not enough electric plugs	Use heavy-duty extension cords, taped down to prevent tripping. If necessary, install 220-volt line.
Poor acoustics	Don't have a program that requires speaking. Consult acoustician for proper placement, sound levels of band.
No locked storage area	Store items in nearby secure facility; deliver day before event. Hire round-the-clock security on site.
Dangerous steps, holes	Rope off or shine lighting in front to create visual "curtain." If steps must be used, light adequately and mark with reflective tape.
Not enough elevators	Provide something to do near elevators on all floors, so guests don't feel they're waiting. Hire operator to move people along.
No cloakroom	Rent racks, hangers and numbers; convert a small room or closet near entrance; lock all but one door of room; provide enough checkers to keep lines moving quickly and avoid mix-ups.
No kitchen	Hire caterer with portable kitchen equipment and proven experience dealing with this situation. Determine in advance where you will get fresh water for coffee, plug in equipment. Have fire extinguishers handy.
Not enough restrooms	If outdoors, rent portable facilities; indoors, rent a trailer outfitted for this purpose and install near building.

PEOPLE MOVING

Unfortunately, benefit patrons are more likely to be annoyed by delays and omissions than charmed by all the little extras you provide. The truly well-planned benefit is one in which all the logistical details have been taken care of, so that everything works smoothly and moves at the proper pace.

Of all the areas in which planning ahead counts, people moving is the most crucial. The more times and the greater the distance you must relocate patrons for different activities, the greater the potential for getting behind schedule and losing guests' interest. If dinner is just a bit late and everyone goes for another cocktail instead, the festive mood will change imperceptibly; once the momentum is lost, it may not be regained. It's the benefit chairperson's responsibility, with the help of the entertainment and food and beverage chairs, to make sure all programmed activities begin on time. The hospitality committee's main function—to be executed with the lightest possible hand—is crowd control.

To work out traffic patterns and table arrangements, you'll first need an accurate floor plan. As soon as you've chosen the location for the benefit, ask the building manager to provide one; it should be drawn to scale with all doors, windows, supporting columns, elevators, telephone booths and restrooms indicated. With the aid of your caterer, equipment rental agent or an interior designer, pencil in the exact location of every table, the stage, bandstand, bar and so on, so that you can see exactly how these facilities will fit. (This exercise will also help you determine the maximum number of tickets you can sell.) Avoid bottlenecks by placing serving tables, bars and activities away from narrow passageways. Set buffet tables so that lines can form on both sides at once.

There are four things for which benefit patrons hate to wait around. They are: liquor, food, the coat check and their cars. Begin rounding up patrons for dinner early, so that their food will be just arriving by the time they sit down. Calculate exactly how long it takes for a valet parker to drive a car to the garage, park it and return for the next one; then provide enough attendants so that there's always someone waiting for the patron who's pulling up to the curb. Getting rid of all the potential snafus will leave your guests no choice but to be relaxed and happy so that they can enjoy all the beauty and entertainment you have provided.

Finally, be sure your floor plan and electrical installations are approved by the city fire marshal and your traffic routing and parking arrangements by the police department. Those officials may seem to impose unnecessary constraints, but it's better to have enlisted their cooperation in case you need them.

DRESSING THE STAGE

Once you've worked out the logistics, you can concentrate on creating an atmosphere that will draw people into the party mood. Chet Edwards, owner of Chet Edwards General Home Furnishings in Aurora, Ohio, who has worked on the decor of many Cleveland-area benefits, says:

Ambience is one of the most important ingredients of a benefit. Most committees tend to underscale their design or think only of the table settings. Whether it's a formal affair or not, static decorations are old hat. People go to a party to be taken away from today. You need to create a mood with lights, sound, movement and color.

According to Wally Gbur, former display artist for the Higbee Company department store and longtime designer of the Pavilion, a temporary dining room created in Cleveland's Public Auditorium for patrons of Northern Ohio Opera Association's annual Metropolitan Opera Week:

> You have to fantasize and dream — don't think of the budget when you start out. When I do a benefit, I take the theme and a color scheme (benefit committees always have certain colors in mind) and then look at books and souvenirs from the places suggested by the theme. I used to travel on my vacations to get ideas. I'd bring back typical items from the countries I visited — not expensive things, but a tile with an interesting design, a piece of fabric or a foreign-language book, if it had good illustrations. Sooner or later, an occasion would come up to use them.
>
> I recommend that a committee consult a design professional. He or she can do a lot for you to create an illusion with light and color.

When it comes to specifics, floral designer Charles M. Phillips, who created the dramatic centerpieces for The Ball, offers the following tips for decorating on a budget:

> The first thing you have to look at is the room itself — what is there to begin with? In a way it's easier to work in a naked room — because you can do anything you like with it — than to work in a heavily decorated room. If that's what you're dealing with, it would be best to stick with good linen and traditional centerpieces. Some themes just wouldn't work in a place like that; to try to make it look Oriental, for example, would wind up looking gimmicky.
>
> If you have only $1,000 to spend, don't spread it too thin. Go for the big impact. Use either one zillion balloons or a single, very large shape — like a sculpture or an imitation Calder mobile — with a spotlight on it so it dominates the room. Rather than spend just ten dollars per table on fresh floral centerpieces, put the money into one fabulous arrangement on the buffet.
>
> Simple things done in quantity, and done well, make an impact. Commercial flowers are expensive, but anyone can cut Queen Anne's lace by the side of the road — just be sure you take the whole committee out and cut buckets and buckets of it. A big basket of apples can make a gorgeous centerpiece if you get the prettiest basket and the shiniest, most perfect apples you can find.
>
> When deciding where to put decorations, look at traffic patterns and concentrate on focal points people will see when they're eating,

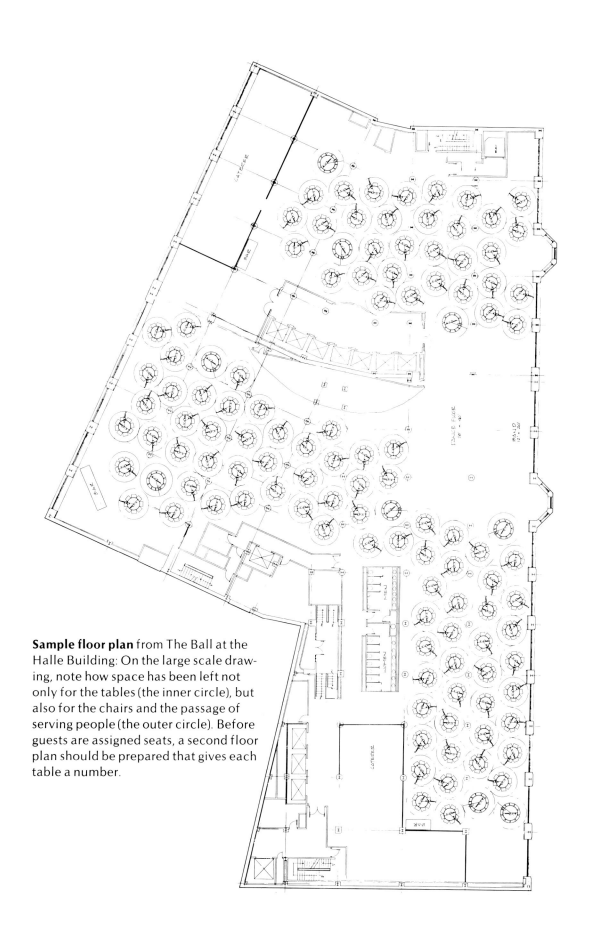

Sample floor plan from The Ball at the Halle Building: On the large scale drawing, note how space has been left not only for the tables (the inner circle), but also for the chairs and the passage of serving people (the outer circle). Before guests are assigned seats, a second floor plan should be prepared that gives each table a number.

dancing or walking by certain areas. Don't put things in corners where they won't be noticed.

Keep in mind that you can achieve wonderful effects with lighting. If the room has bright lights and no rheostat, it would be better to keep them off. Candlelight on the tables and soft lights in the corners will make the room seem more intimate. Some other treatments you could use: If the building has pillars, you could make fantasy capitals out of foamcore [a lightweight, easy-to-cut material similar to styrofoam, available in art supply stores] and bathe them in lights. You can hang colored cellophane or fabric frames over the dance floor and shoot lights onto them for a flattering effect. You can create shadows on the ceiling by lighting big pots of bare branches or palms from underneath. You can simulate moonlight with blue lights or starlight by shooting spotlights through cutout gels.

If your benefit is outdoors, let the setting "do" itself. Keep it informal, with baskets of flowers and candelarias — lots of them. Again, the point is to take advantage of what you have, rather than trying to transform it.

In Le Papillon, a benefit for the Shaker Lakes Regional Nature Center, we have another good illustration of how a benefit committee can pool its resources and make judicious use of professional consultants to create an appropriate outdoor setting based on a simple, unifying theme. The following narrative of the benefit's evolution is adapted from the final report of the decorations subcommittee submitted by its chairperson, Bobby Griesinger.

To mark the occasion of its 20th anniversary, the Shaker Lakes Regional Nature Center, an environmental education facility in one of Cleveland's eastern suburbs, wanted to bring back its popular "Party in the Park" benefit. Abandoned several years previously after having grown unwieldy, the Party in the Park had in the past featured a wide array of delicacies prepared by as many as 100 professional and amateur gourmet chefs.

As in previous versions of this event, the benefit committee wanted to showcase the center itself. Marilyn, who served as publicity chairperson for this benefit, suggested the butterfly as a happy symbol of nature's beauty. She brought to a brainstorming session several examples of butterfly art on napkins and kites to illustrate its visual potential. When benefit chairperson Phyllis Baker happened to hear *Papillons,* a piano piece by Robert Schumann, a few days later, she remembered Marilyn's suggestion and the French title clicked as the name for the event.

The decorations subcommittee began with the idea of adorning the tent in which dinner would be served with large butterflies. Volunteer Patty Chapman designed a pattern that could be used to mass produce the butterflies, but the committee eventually decided that it would be easier to purchase them after Marge Drollinger steered them to the butterfly kites featured in a catalogue of the Go Fly a Kite Company in East Hadden, Connecticut. The committee ordered 24 kites, some silk (preferable but more expensive), some paper. All had to be ironed and assembled before the party.

Because of the vastness of the benefit's outdoor setting —cocktails were to be enjoyed on the winding All People's Nature Trail—the committee felt the need to consult a professional florist. Rocco Gioia of La Fontana Florist met with committee members at the center and advised them to use wildflowers (including asclepias, commonly known as butterfly weed) in fall colors of orange, yellow, gold, red and crimson to convey the desired feeling of natural beauty and color. He showed them where to place arrangements around the tent and on the trail and helped them choose coordinating tablecloth and napkin colors.

Green benches and wicker plant holders were rented from Mutual Display Manufacturing Company of Cleveland to create a park outside the tent. For the birthday-cake centerpieces on each table, Lucy Meacham found just the right accent: small feather butterflies that fluttered on long stems. Graphic artist David Rankin offered to make a large version of his butterfly logo design (used on the invitation and program book) to put at the entrance to the center's driveway. Volunteer Linda Johnson cut out butterfly shapes on innumerable paper-bag candelarias, which were used to line the drive. With lighted candles inside, they produced a fairyland effect after dark. The gourmet tables, set up along the nature trail during the cocktail hour and spread with appetizers contributed by 25 volunteer chefs, needed a spot of color. (Recipes for the items served—such gourmet delicacies as galantine of duck, maki sushi and miniature vegetables with herb filling—were printed in the benefit's souvenir program book.) Sunnybrook Farms Nursery of Chesterland, Ohio, was asked to make up four-inch pots of herbs, which later served as the chefs' take-home gifts.

The total cost of decorations came to roughly $1,200, which was donated by an individual patron. In her final report, Griesinger noted only one oversight: Some decorations that had been left unattended after the party disappeared overnight. The committee recommended that a cleanup crew be appointed for future events. "I can't close," Griesinger concluded, "without thanking the moon for showing up—so visible through the see-through tent!"

TYPECASTING

Remember that the visual theme of a benefit should be expressed in the design of its printed materials as well as in its decor. In fact, the printed pieces establish the benefit's image long before the big day arrives. Invitations go out to thousands of people, and souvenir programs provide a permanent record of the occasion. Auction and show catalogues will be shown in the future to prospective donors and advertisers. So the benefit's graphics are perhaps as important as its decor.

All of your printed pieces should be coordinated visually. A good way to accomplish this is with a logo — either a simple, stylized drawing, or the name of your benefit spelled out in a distinctive typeface or some combination of the two. A strong logo not only helps promote name recognition, but can give the decorations committee something concrete on which to elaborate.

Once you have a logo, it's a good idea to print benefit stationery for use in solicitations, acknowledgements, press releases, meeting announcements and other correspondence. Custom stationery conveys the subtle message that yours is a well-planned and substantial event.

Good graphic design is seldom inexpensive, but it's worth paying for professional work. Amateurish-looking materials would hardly convince potential patrons that the benefit's high ticket price is justified. Perhaps you can economize in other areas, such as using a lesser grade of paper, fewer ink colors or a standard size and shape for your invitation, instead of one that requires extra cuts and folds. Allow some flexibility in the design specifications to take advantage of materials the printer may have on hand, if you can do so without sacrificing quality. For example, ask if the printer has a suitable paper in stock — that is, left over from another job; it will be much cheaper than placing a special order. The understated look in printed materials impresses potential underwriters and patrons with the idea that the benefit committee is being frugal and therefore has its priorities in order.

Whatever your printed materials, take great pains to ensure that their carefully executed graphic design isn't spoiled by copy or proofreading errors. Those misspelled words and names will come back to haunt you.

STRIKE UP THE BAND

Music, the quintessential mood enhancer, should be a part of every benefit. Just as decorating sets the visual scene for a benefit, music provides an aural backdrop, like the sound track to a movie. No single element contributes more to a sense of occasion than the presence of live musicians appropriate to the style of the party.

The Great Lakes Theater Festival
and
The Developers of The Halle Building
request the pleasure of your company
for dinner and dancing at

The Ball

at

The Halle Building
for the benefit of the
Great Lakes Theater Festival
on Saturday, the second of November
at half past six o'clock
Twelve Twenty-eight Euclid Avenue
Cleveland, Ohio

R.s.v.p.   *White or Black Tie*

PLEASE
COME TO THIS
WHITE TIE
GATHERING.

BUT
DON'T WEAR
ONE.

Just join us to talk about white ties and black; and a fine formal affair we are planning, to benefit the Great Lakes Theater Festival.

That will be November 2, 1985, at The Halle Building — once again Cleveland's most fashionable downtown address.

But we'll be gathering to talk things over, over cocktails and such, from 5 P.M. until 7 P.M. on Thursday, June 6, 1985 at The Union Club.

We need you to help us do things right.

Please say you'll be there, with a phone call to the Great Lakes Theater Festival at 241-5490.

Sample invitations: (Top left) Formal invitation from The Ball at the Halle Building; (top right) invitation to the kickoff party for The Ball; (bottom left) save the date card for the 11th Annual Western Reserve Antiques Show; (bottom center and right) informal invitation to the Third Annual Cleveland Wine Auction and its accompanying response card.

Reserve the Date

Thursday,

October 23, 1986...

Third Annual Cleveland Wine Auction
for the benefit of the
Cleveland Center for Economic Education

WHERE:	The University Club 3813 Euclid Avenue Cleveland, Ohio
WHEN:	Saturday, September 19, 1987
6:30 p.m.	Wine tasting and open bar. Silent Auction begins.
8:00 p.m.	Dinner with fine wine, of course.
9:00 p.m.	Live Auction with Auctioneer Patrick C. O'Brien. (Silent Auction will close 15 minutes after Live Auction concludes.)
DRESS:	Black Tie (optional)
RESERVATIONS:	$125 per person ($75 tax-deductible)
	Each guest will receive $25 scrip for use in either the Live or Silent Auction.
	Auction catalogue will be mailed prior to the Auction.

**Third Annual
Cleveland Wine Auction***
Benefiting the Cleveland Center for
Economic Education
September 19, 1987

Name _____

Address _____

_____

Phone _____

Please make checks payable to CCEE-Wine Auction.
Tables of eight/ten.

☐ We are planning to sit with:

_____
_____
_____

☐ Please arrange seating for us (me).

Number of tickets		**Amount**
	$125.00 per person ($75.00 tax-deductible). Free parking, wine tasting, cocktails, dinner, and auctions.	
	Sorry I can't join you — but wish to toast you with a contribution to the CCEE.	

*Reservations will be held at the door.

There are three different ways to make use of them: for dancing, in concert and as background. Some benefits may incorporate all three.

When creating a concept, one of the basic questions that must be resolved is whether or not there will be dancing. If the answer is yes, it's essential to hire the best band you can afford. Music is going to be the force that carries the evening; it must be lively enough to draw people out of their chairs and onto the floor. If, on the other hand, you're offering other entertainment as well, you can hire a smaller or less well-known ensemble than you would if dancing is to be the main event.

The best way to judge a band is to catch it in performance at a party or club—that way you can see what kind of stage presence the players have as well as hear their sound. If you can't see the band live, request an audition tape. If your toes don't start tapping immediately, keep looking. Bear in mind the ages and tastes of your potential patrons and by all means tell the bandleader your preferences.

If you're planning a concert performance, choose a musician or group whose name and repertoire are well known to your patrons. Explain to the artists (or their agents) the nature of your event so that they can suggest an appropriate program; you should usually steer away from anything too heavy. Consider hiring a small combo for dancing at the post-concert reception; it will help to keep the afterglow alive following a great performance.

No matter what your main entertainment, you will still need background music during periods of socializing. We don't mean the kind that massages our ears all day long in elevators, offices and supermarkets, but something with presence that will enhance, not overwhelm, conversation. Strolling musicians—madrigal singers, gypsy violinists, a flute and guitar duo, whatever is appropriate to the style and tone of the party—may be the answer when you have a large space to cover. An alternative is to set up a cocktail pianist, harpist, woodwind quintet or jazz combo in a prominent spot so the performers can be seen as well as heard by all.

Be sure to require that the musicians dress in the same manner as your guests unless they have truly stylish costumes. This goes for a big band as well. If the guests are in black tie, the band members will look tacky in brightly colored blazers.

Dramatic moments call for fanfares or drum rolls. Do plan to use them to call attention to important activities such as a raffle or to announce dinner.

The only benefit with which we are acquainted that used taped music to advantage was Fantasy, at which live dancers performed elaborately costumed and choreographed routines to popular songs. If you must use taped music, be sure you have an excellent sound system and an experienced engineer or disc jockey to operate it.

WHAT'S FOR DINNER?

Menu planning is one area in which it doesn't pay to be too original. Here, carrying out the benefit theme is more a question of matching the style and service to the tone of the affair, rather than offering exotic or gimmicky food. When serving a large crowd, you need to keep these principles firmly in mind: quality, consistency, presentation and conservative tastes. Though restaurant patrons and gourmet chefs may be experimenting with foreign cuisines as never before, benefit patrons still seem to prefer simple, recognizable dishes. They appreciate food that's cooked to the proper degree and served at the proper temperature. Portions shouldn't appear skimpy, but you don't want patrons to eat so much that they fall asleep during the ensuing entertainment. If the meal is being served buffet-style, be sure there are servers to fill patrons' plates; otherwise you may run out of food before everyone gets through the line.

Robert S. Pile offers the following menu-planning advice based on his nearly 60 years' experience in serving Cleveland benefits:

> Innovation is all very well; I like to provide it in an interesting soup or salad, but not the entree. People are going to more benefits these days, so you need variety, but you still have to please the majority of patrons. As I always tell my committees: "Think of the people who are paying the tab! They're furious if they get a cold dinner." I never serve a cold meal at a benefit, even in the summer.
>
> Most of the major benefits in town still serve beef tenderloin. In spite of the trend away from red meat, everybody raves about a perfectly cooked filet. You can get around those who won't eat red meat with a simply prepared fish such as sole, red snapper or swordfish (I always anticipate that some will request fish and I have it on hand). For vegetarians or those who keep kosher, I offer a plate of four or five different vegetables or fresh fruit—these patrons usually make their needs known in advance.
>
> Before I begin working on a benefit menu, I need to know the time of year and the theme or color scheme, because I do plan the food for eye appeal and color. The season of year obviously affects the availability of certain foods. And if I'm doing two big benefits in a row I'll steer clear of the same menu. I need a realistic estimate of the size of the party, too—it's not a nice surprise when the committee tells me there will be 500 patrons and we end up with 250. It's not as much of a problem for a big catering firm if you have *more* people than you anticipated.
>
> I love it when committees make suggestions, but one thing I

don't like is when they try to outdo everybody else and get too exotic. Of course, everyone wants to have some twist that no one else has, but you have to be a little bit practical when you're serving large quantities. The little frills, like vegetables cut in the shape of flowers, that are exquisite at a small party, simply can't be done for 800 and still keep the price down to what the committees are willing to pay. Most people couldn't care less about eating something exotic. If the food is good and hot, you're in business.

That sentiment was echoed in a newspaper item that appeared as part of the publicity for Xanadu, a benefit for Cleveland's Golden Age Center. Clearly the benefit committee wanted to try something more adventurous than standard benefit fare, but felt the need to reassure the gastronomically timid:

> We knew that the food for Xanadu, like the poem, should be mysterious, elusive, memorable, primitive, sensuous, slightly Oriental, exotic, adventurous *but also unintimidating,* said committee member Jane Herget [italics ours].

So what did Xanadu's caterer, Jerry Wilke of Bradley Catering, suggest? Georgian grilled lamb kabobs in pita pockets, grilled sliced Carpathian chicken, Middle Eastern spinach pies and roast suckling pig surrounded by sliced pork cooked in coconut milk; with accompaniments of Moroccan eggplant salad, Indian potato fritters and cold rice pilaf with dried fruits and nuts. A far cry from steak and potatoes, but still recognizable dishes.

Though space forbids our offering menu suggestions for every occasion, here are three enticing examples—a luncheon, a cocktail buffet and a formal dinner—culled from the benefits featured in the appendix:

LUNCHEON MENU: A Sterling Spectacular

Hors d'oeuvres
Choice of two hot soups: cream of broccoli or tomato bisque
Cheeses and crackers

Luncheon
Tortilla basket salad
Filled with julienne of chicken, baby shrimp,
lettuce, tomatoes, shredded cheese,
garbanzo beans, artichokes, black olives
Choice of dressing
Assorted rolls and butter

Dessert
Chocolate top hat with sauce anglaise

COCKTAIL BUFFET: Una Notte Sensazionale

Mussels provencal
Calamari with yogurt and green onion sauce or horseradish sauce
Huitres a l'americaine
Swordfish grilled with roasted red pepper sauce
Cracked crab claws
Cajun shrimp
Smoked salmon with lemon and capers
Carpaccio
Canard grille on radicchio with warm balsamic vinaigrette
Capellini with sauce poireaux (cream, leeks, purple onion,
peas and parmesan cheese)
Tortellini with tomato-basil sauce
Fresh mozzarella with sun-dried tomatoes and herbs
Assorted cheeses
Fresh fruit
Melon with prosciutto
Old World breads

DINNER: Light of Day

First course
Fresh asparagus and tomatoes on bibb lettuce with basil vinaigrette
Warm Stilton-leek sauce, passed

Main course
Grilled veal chop with sauteed wild mushrooms
Green bean timbale with pecans
French-fried pita wedges with parmesan cheese
Small pumpernickel rolls
Butter

Dessert
Boule de chocolat with tangerine sauce
Assorted cookies
Coffee, tea, decaf

STAR GAZING

Celebrities always seem to add an aura of glamour to a special
event. One of the lures of a benefit is the possibility of rubbing
elbows with someone you've read about or seen on TV or in the
movies. That's one of the reasons why benefit committees sometimes go to great lengths to have a few on hand. The other is their

publicity value. As Lindsay Morgenthaler, chairperson of DAZZLE, a benefit for the Kent State University Museum, succinctly puts it: "You can't beat titles and tiaras for attracting attention."

In rare instances, celebrity appearances can truly make a benefit. When the movie *Light of Day* was on location in Cleveland, fans trying to catch a glimpse of star Michael J. Fox created traffic jams. Later it was announced that Fox, a regular on TV's *Family Ties*, and rock star Joan Jett would return for a true Hollywood-style world premiere of the film to benefit Cleveland's Playhouse Square and the Spina Bifida Foundation. The tickets sold out within the week—without a single invitation having been mailed.

Sometimes important alliances are forged with celebrity guests. When Great Lakes Theater Festival's artistic director Gerald Freedman invited his longtime friend, Jean Stapleton (the actress best known for her role as Edith in the television series *All in the Family*), to be his guest at The Ball at the Halle Building, she was a great hit .Later she agreed to star in a festival play produced by Freedman the following spring. The resulting revival of *Arsenic and Old Lace* played to full houses in Cleveland and Houston before opening for a lengthy run on Broadway and a national tour.

Don't feel you have to be on first-name terms with a celebrity to invite him or her to your benefit. Many well-known personalities are delighted to accept such invitations for publicity reasons. If you can "borrow" a celebrity who happens to be in your vicinity for some other reason at the time of your event, you may be able to save on transportation costs and take advantage of publicity about his or her other activities. Marilyn recalls one felicitous occasion when the Brevard Symphony Orchestra of Florida invited renowned violinist Isaac Stern to attend a thank-you party planned for the organization's Gold Key membership (donors of $500 or more). Stern, who had a few hours free from an engagement in West Palm Beach, 150 miles away, agreed to come if his transportation would be provided; one of the symphony's supporters made a company plane available. The famous guest didn't arrive empty-handed, either—he brought a print of the film, *From Mao to Mozart*, about his historic tour of China, which was just being released around the country. As it turned out, the showing was an area premiere and Stern himself was extremely ingratiating. The planners' only regret was that they didn't find out about the film in time to capitalize on this exceptional opportunity for a major benefit.

Light of Day chairperson Diann Scaravilli suggests approaching celebrities through their agents; involve an acquaintance of the VIP, if possible. (Perhaps the manager of a local theater or concert promoter in your area, who has had occasion to work with the celebrity, would be willing to act as go-between.) "If the cause is appealing and a personal contact is used, no fee is usually necessary," Scaravilli adds. She also notes that you may be able to avoid running up large hotel and restaurant bills by asking a major local hotel to play host in exchange for program credit.

The chance one takes with celebrities guests is that they may not show up. Check whether they have a good or bad track record. Another downside to celebrity participation is the extra energy that must be devoted to "pleasing" them. Some are accustomed to receiving star treatment. This can include a desire for constant entertainment, special provisions such as their favorite brand of champagne or services such as babysitting their children and pets. It is important to be gracious about fulfilling requests, for, as Fantasy co-chair barb Richardson points out:

> Remember they will take with them an impression of your city, your organization, your committee and your guests. Celebrities travel nationally and internationally and meet thousands of people. It would be nice if their memories of your city, organization and event were positive.
>
> Also, keep them posted of your advance press coverage—make them eager to live up to the city's expectations!

DRESSING THE PART

Dress codes are a bit hard to enforce, but many committees like to suggest them, anyway, as encouraging guests to dress up is an important way to foster a sense of occasion. Forest City's Mark Randol says he always insists on black tie for his company's grand openings: "How often do most people get a chance to wear formal clothes? It makes for a more memorable occasion."

Some benefit committees find clever ways around the confusion about what constitutes a man's formal attire and a woman's "ball gown" by suggesting guests wear a particular color. Cleveland Ballet's Puttin' on the Ritz benefit, held in honor of the opening of a new penguin exhibit at a nearby Sea World theme park, boasted the most original dress code we've seen. The invitation said simply: "Feathers optional."

One dress request that doesn't seem to go over well is the costume party. Many people feel too embarrassed or uncomfortable in costume to have a good time. Those who are daring enough to buy exotic costumes on their travels will find excuses to wear them, anyway, and this, too, adds interest to a benefit.

PERKS THAT WORK

Inventive names for different patron categories are another way to express the benefit theme. Le Papillon, for example, used "Admirals," "Viceroys" and "Monarchs"—all names of butterflies—to indicate its three ticket price levels. These appellations are mainly used on the invitations to identify the perks that go with each ticket level. And perks are offered as inducements to buy the higher-priced tickets, though their value should never approach the amount of the corresponding contributions.

The most important perk is one that costs the committee next to nothing, and that is recognition in the benefit program. All corporate and individual ticket buyers above the base level should be listed as special patrons. If a few sizable contributions come in early enough, those donors can even be listed on the invitation. Listings are gratifying both to the donor, whose generosity is thus publicly acknowledged, and to the organization, as a demonstration that it has broad-based community support.

Personal attention is the key to creating other low-cost, attractive perks that will make your upper-level patrons feel appreciated. A private cocktail reception with the celebrity guests is always an enticing offer. Preferred seating at dinner and/or during the entertainment is also desirable. You might promise invitations to a future event, such as a dress rehearsal-preview of your performing arts organization's next major production. If your benefit entertainment permits it, offer patrons the opportunity to be in the spotlight. At Fantasy, the costumed dancers paid special visits to upper-level contributors during the dinner hour. At a mystery-weekend benefit, special patrons might be given secret identities or important clues.

Valet parking makes an excellent perk if it isn't necessary to make it available to everyone attending the benefit. If it is, how about offering upper-level patrons limousine service to and from the event? You may be able to get the perk donated by an auto leasing agency or limo service or perhaps by an individual who collects fancy cars. The Ball at the Halle Building committee persuaded Stouffer's Tower City Plaza Hotel to provide reduced rates for overnight accommodations for patrons at the highest ticket level; in the end, only two couples took advantage of this perk, but it gave the benefit committee something of real value to offer.

Commemorative gifts are fine if they can be supplied at minimal cost to the committee. If the benefit entertainers have a book or recording, perhaps they would sell autographed copies to the committee at cost.

LITTLE TOUCHES MEAN A LOT

In the theater, every gesture reveals a great deal about a character; small details of scenery and costume can transport the audience into a different time and place. If you think of a benefit as a theatrical production, then you won't neglect the little touches that create a truly memorable event.

Lindsay Morgenthaler believes that the benefit stage extends to the street outside the building in which the main event takes place. For This is Opening Night, a benefit marking the official opening of the restored Playhouse Square theater complex in downtown Cleveland, Morgenthaler (who served as vice-chairperson) literally rolled out a red carpet on the sidewalk. There she and benefit chairperson K.K. Sullivan created excitement with musicians and jugglers, floodlights and even a giant TV screen that allowed patrons to watch themselves arriving. A crowd of onlookers and photographers heightened the sense of anticipation.

For DAZZLE, Morgenthaler arranged a different kind of welcoming committee:

> We had 40 Kent State University students in formal dress with pink ties and cummerbunds lined up about four feet apart, from the parking lot to the front door, to meet and greet guests. We had chosen the students well and trained them in hair and makeup and manners; we told them it was their school, their museum and they were the hosts and hostesses. They turned out to be what most people talked about afterward and seemed the hit of the evening. Each one spoke and smiled to each guest.

Patrons themselves will want to make a grand entrance. Having to trudge through rain or mud in long gowns and evening sandals would ruin the effect. Have doormen (with golf umbrellas ready, in case of rain) at the entrance to assist the ladies as their escorts pull up to the curb. Provide valet service for everyone if parking is inconvenient. Have cloakrooms and umbrella stands near the door so that patrons can shed their outerwear quickly and move right into the crowd.

The registration table, where patrons pick up their table assignment cards, is the next stop; it should be clearly visible and attractively arrayed with a tablecloth and simple decoration. Provide registration workers, hospitality committee members and other benefit "officials" with identifying hats, boutonnieres or badges in keeping with the spirit of your theme.

Directional signs are very important in a large, crowded space. Clearly identify entrances and exits, restrooms, telephones, cloakrooms, first aid stations and any other unmarked areas in which important activities will take place. It may be a good idea to mount poster-sized floor plans near entrances, stairways or elevators and just inside the dining room to help guests find their tables (or, if there is room, reproduce the floor plan in the program). Have signs printed or lettered by a professional in a style that coordinates with your other printed materials. Don't neglect to install signs explaining any special displays; these should acknowledge donations wherever appropriate.

Keeping the restrooms spotless is an important consideration; patrons will appreciate seeing an attendant on duty. Providing pretty guest soaps, hand lotion and linen towels in place of institutional liquids and paper is a gracious gesture. Add a small basket of sewing supplies, pins, combs, emery boards and hairspray for emergency repairs, and your guests will be impressed that you've thought of everything for their comfort.

THOUGHTS OF AN INVETERATE BENEFIT-GOER

Anyone who attends benefits regularly is bound to have formed strong opinions as to what makes a benefit work. Ben Shouse, community representative of Cleveland's United Labor Agency, is such an individual; he has attended 17 of the 20 benefits featured in the back of this book, in addition to many others. Here are a few of his comments on how to keep patrons happy:

> I would stress the importance of being made welcome at the entrance. This is not only in terms of greeting the individual, but in terms of the ambience, the atmosphere of the affair. Patrons should be given a truly warm welcome, so develop a plan whereby practically each new arrival immediately sees familiar faces. You'd be surprised how reassuring this is to quite a few people.
>
> I believe valet parking is helpful, especially in areas where parking is relatively difficult or scarce. Personally I like it very much, not for status but for *comfort* and *convenience.* Seating is also a consideration — I am not talking so much about locations as the seats themselves. I find that quite often the seats are not very comfortable and therefore detract from maximum enjoyment.
>
> If there are speeches, they must be controlled. Do *not* invite speakers who are not amenable to suggestions about subject and length.

In short: Provide for the needs of patrons as if they were guests in your own home.

The Final Countdown

At last the event you've been planning for months is only a week away. If you've followed the guidelines in this book and kept up with the responsibilities enumerated in the time line, you'll arrive at this point in good shape. From here on in, you'll need to coordinate activities on almost an hourly basis to make sure everything gets done on time and in the proper sequence. To assist you, we have outlined the executive committee's last major tasks in a second sample time line to which you can add your particular schedule for deliveries, decorating and equipment set-up.

The subcommittees that will be the most active during the last week are reservations/seating, decorating, hospitality, PR, food and beverage, auction (if any) and entertainment. The chairpersons of these subcommittees should review their individual time lines with the benefit chairperson before the beginning of the final week. They should also talk with the benefit chairperson at least once a day during this week, keeping her informed of their progress and problems and giving her a number where they can be reached. Naturally, the chairperson herself must be available at all times to answer any questions.

The appropriate executive committee members should find out when the caterer, sound and light technicians, florist and entertainers are planning to arrive and make sure they have access to the loading dock and freight elevator. The decorating chairperson should make a list of supplies and equipment his or her committee workers will need — ladders, tools, tape and extension cords — and be sure those items are either available on the site or make arrangements to bring them. Security guards may go on duty at this point; they should have a copy of the schedule and the names of all volunteers and paid workers who are authorized to enter the site. If necessary, arrange for parking passes for these workers.

The hospitality committee should meet on site a couple of days before the benefit, to review the floor plan and agenda. These volunteers must be familiar enough with the facility to help guests find their way around; they should know the location of the first aid station and every entrance, elevator, restroom, cloakroom and telephone, in addition to the areas in which the main activities will take place. If the floor plan is complicated or guests will be moving through several areas during the event, it may be a good idea to prepare information packets for the hospitality committee members' reference. These kits should include the evening's agenda, a map of the area (if the site is hard to find), a floor plan, notices of where and when to check in and where to pick up messages, as well as any special instructions concerning the evening's activities or patrons' comfort. This material will be especially helpful to those who can't make it to the meeting—but don't let the written summary substitute for an in-person session with as many hospitality committee members as possible, so that they can ask questions, clear up any confusion and pass information along to absent volunteers the day of the benefit.

The reservations/seating committee will stay close to the telephone this week, tracking down stray checks and piecing together table groupings from the sometimes sketchy information provided on the reservation forms. Count on a few hosts and hostesses not making up their minds about who's sitting at their tables until the day itself and be prepared to make some last-minute substitutions. Remember to tell the caterer not only the total number of people to expect, but the exact number seated at each table. If tables of ten are the norm, there will inevitably be odd groups of seven to 12 that will have to be accommodated. Note that groups of eight to ten can be seated at a 60-inch round table, but groups of 12 need a 72-inch table. Be sure your caterer or rental company can provide the number you need in each size.

Corporate tables are often the hardest to pin down. Many times a corporation will take a table and then neglect to invite enough guests to fill it. Occasionally no one will show up, which can be embarrassing to both the benefit committee and the corporation, particularly when the empty table is prominently placed and bears the corporation's name. To avoid this contretemps, either the reservations/seating committee or the underwriting committee should call the contact person at each corporation that has reserved a table and request the names of its guests. Usually you will talk to the contact's secretary, who will have to confer with his or her superior and call back. If even four guests are ultimately identified, it's safe to assume the company intends to fill the table. If no one knows who's planning to come, you may ask: "Am I to understand this is a contribution to the organization and that I may fill this table with complimentary ticket holders such as reporters and foundation representatives?" The corporation will usually be pleased to have this opportunity to help the cause.

In the meantime, the PR committee should contact those on its invitation list who have not yet responded to find out which writers

TABLE ASSIGNMENT FORM

TABLE NUMBER _____	TABLE NUMBER _____
TABLE HOST _____	TABLE HOST _____
CONTACT PERSON _____	CONTACT PERSON _____
Phone _____ No. at table _____	Phone _____ No. at table _____
1. _____	1. _____
2. _____	2. _____
3. _____	3. _____
4. _____	4. _____
5. _____	5. _____
6. _____	6. _____

Directions: To prepare a seating chart, first assign numbers to tables drawn on the floor plan. Then fill in guests' names in table groupings (according to hosts' requests) on this table assignment form. Then assign groupings to numbered tables, taking into account special needs insofar as possible (e.g., placing two tables hosted by same person together, giving upper-level patrons most desirable locations, seating handicapped patrons in easily accessible areas).

are bringing photographers and how many are bringing escorts. The committee chair should confer with the reservations/seating committee to ensure the appropriate placement of these guests. By a day or two before the benefit, the guest list and table assignments should be sufficiently completed to have them typed. The reservations/seating chairperson should allow enough time for the typist to produce two accurate reservation lists. One, in alphabetical order, will be used at the registration table to identify paid guests as they arrive; the other, in numerical order by tables, will help committee members and reporters locate patrons once they've been seated. Proof the typed lists carefully to be sure no one has been left out or seated in two places and that all names are spelled correctly. Here's another instance in which a word processor would come in handy to correct the minor changes that will invariably come up overnight.

No matter how carefully you've anticipated every contingency, expect the unexpected. Good advance planning should allow you to be flexible and respond quickly to problems, especially if you've built in time to make the last-minute changes in seating, decorating or programming that will inevitably occur.

Once the benefit begins, executive committee members will

want to mingle with the patrons, but resist the temptation to get lost in the crowd. Designate a message center, preferably located near one of the security posts, where subcommittee chairs can check in frequently during the cocktail hour and any other time when guests are away from their tables. The benefit chairperson and key members of the executive committee should also keep the numerical seating chart handy so that they can find one another during dinner, if necessary. Most of the problems you'll have to deal with involve dissatisfaction with the service or seating arrangements, but be prepared for medical emergencies by arranging in advance for a doctor to be on call.

Finally, don't depart without securing the site for the night. Several members of the executive committee should plan on staying until the very end, and a representative of the co-sponsor will probably want to stay as well, especially if the benefit has been held in its building. The benefit treasurer will remain long enough to distribute checks to those executive committee members responsible for paying the entertainers and hourly workers such as security guards, maintenance, etc. The food and beverage chairperson should count and secure any leftover liquor bottles that have been paid for by the committee, as these have a tendency to disappear overnight. The decorations chairperson may have to put away valuables, and the auction committee, if there is one, will have to gather up bidding records and store and secure unclaimed items. The benefit chairperson or someone appointed in advance should make a final round of the facility, including restrooms and cloakrooms, looking for personal belongings that may have been left behind after the last guest has said good night. The benefit chairperson should watch the security guard lock up and only then go home for a well-deserved rest.

FINAL TIME LINE

Name of event: _____

Date: _____

DATE/ TIME	TASK	PERSON(S) RESPONSIBLE

One week before

_____ Benefit executive committee meets to review schedule and procedures. Orient everyone to floor plan, by walking through site if possible. _____

_____ Executive committee assigns members to troubleshoot in key areas during event. Designate message center/ emergency meeting place. _____

_____ Hospitality committee has orientation meeting on site, reviews event schedule and traffic flow strategies. _____

_____ Reservations/seating committee continues phoning expected guests whose checks haven't come in; completes table groupings; prepares alphabetized guest list and numerical seating chart. _____

_____ Reservations/seating chairperson gives approximate head count to caterer with number seated at each table. _____

_____ Decorations committee reviews plans and installation schedule; assembles materials. _____

_____ Technicians install special lighting and sound systems, if necessary. _____

_____ Personnel manager reconfirms arrangements with all paid and volunteer workers, e.g., maintenance, security, parking lot operators, bartenders, coat checkers, etc. _____

_____ Designated committee members arrange local transportation for out-of-town VIPs, entertainers, etc. _____

Two days before

_____ Reservations/seating chairperson gives final head count to caterer. _____

_____ Facility cleaned and ready for decorations committee to begin delivery and installation of scenery, props. Locked storage room available or security guards on duty. _____

_____ Rental equipment agency installs dance floor, stage or platforms, coat racks, etc.; curtains off non-public

_____ areas; pitches tent, if required.

_____ Caterer or rental company delivers and sets up tables and chairs; installs temporary kitchen, if necessary. _____

_____ Designated committee members wrap and store favors or commemorative gifts in secure spot. _____

The day before

_____ Staff liaison has liquor license, permits, etc. ready in case of questions. _____

_____ Decorations committee installs decorations. _____

_____ Liquor and wine delivered, counted and locked in storage area. _____

_____ Piano delivered or moved, then tuned. _____

_____ Technicians check sound and lighting. _____

_____ Entertainment coordinator meets performers and brings them to site for orientation and rehearsal. _____

_____ Auctioneer checks sight lines, microphone; confirms placement of spotters. _____

Day of benefit

_____ Building supervisor adjusts heating/cooling system to proper temperature in a.m. _____

_____ Caterer sets and numbers tables, dusts chairs (volunteers may help with this). _____

_____ Reservations/seating chairperson makes last-minute adjustments in guest list and seating chart (cancellations, extra guests). _____

_____ Florist delivers centerpieces and other floral displays; committee puts finishing touches on tables and other decorations. _____

_____ Decorations committee installs directional signs for restrooms, telephone, other important facilities. _____

_____ Designated committee member checks that restrooms have been adequately cleaned; lays out guest soaps, towels, etc. _____

_____ Caterer sets up bars. _____

_____ Reservations/seating chairperson reconfirms head count with caterer in a.m.; sets up registration table near entrance; keeps track of actual number served vs. reservations. _____

Two hours before benefit

_____ Reservations/seating committee distributes typed guest lists and seating charts to registration table, PR committee and benefit chairperson; arranges table assignment cards at registration desk. _____

_____ Personnel manager arrives early to supervise details of final setup such as lighting. Final restroom check; have attendant on duty to keep clean throughout event. _____

_____ Hospitality committee members arrive at least half-hour before doors open; review any last-minute changes in schedule or floor plan; light candles; go to assigned areas to greet guests. _____

Zero hour to party's end

_____ Doors open; hospitality committee sees to guests' enjoyment while moving crowd along on schedule. _____

_____ PR committee members greet media guests, make introductions, help to set up photos, answer questions, as needed. _____

_____ Chairperson and designated troubleshooters circulate and bring problems, complaints (e.g., sound system too loud, car blocking entrance, etc.) to attention of appropriate workers. _____

_____ Chairperson resists guests' pleas to let the band play on past closing time (remember the budget!). _____

_____ Benefit treasurer distributes checks for workers whose contracts specify payment that night. _____

_____ Designated committee members secure or remove decorations, equipment, lost and found items; have security guards lock up. _____

It's a Wrap

You did it! The months of planning paid off, the benefit went off without a hitch and everyone—patrons, press and committee members alike—is raving about what a great success it was. The executive committee members are thrilled, of course, and also exhausted. It takes a day or two for your adrenalin level to return to normal; you don't sleep nearly as well as you expected you would, even though for the last three weeks you've longed for nothing more than to fall into bed. Whether you've entertained notions of moving on to new projects or escaping to some remote tropical island as soon as the benefit was over, you suddenly find yourself without the energy to do anything but vegetate.

This emotional and physical letdown is completely normal and you need to give in to it. But don't let it be an excuse to avoid the responsibility of tying up loose ends, thanking your committee members and underwriters and evaluating your results. It's important to do this while the details of the event are still fresh in everyone's minds, before the glow fades and the benefit records are relegated to the back files. You should plan ahead for the wrap-up of your benefit just as you have for the event itself; that way, it won't seem like too much effort.

CLEANING UP

The morning after the event you'll probably have decorations to take down, borrowed or lost items to return and still-attractive flower arrangements to give away to nursing homes or hospitals. The catering staff should be responsible for cleaning up all food, dishes and barware; the rental company will pick up its equipment. You should have arranged for the building maintenance crew to do a thorough cleanup; meanwhile, you'll at least want to leave things in reasonable order out of courtesy to your building hosts and to be sure you haven't left anything behind. Why not arrange a morning-after brunch as a reward for those committee members, staff and paid workers who have to return to do these chores?

If an auction was part of your benefit, there will still be many details to which you must attend, including determining the winning bidder for each item, informing him or her of the winning bid (going on to the next highest bidder if the winner changes his or her mind), arranging to collect for any unpaid items and delivering the items.

The treasurer's job will be to record any receipts earned at the event itself, pay outstanding bills and draw up a final income statement and balance sheet as soon as possible (this shouldn't take more than two weeks). The development director should enter the amounts of all patrons' and underwriters' donations in the organization's donor records and add new names and addresses to the general mailing list.

Besides reminding her executive committee members to take care of these tasks, the benefit chairperson has the duty of smoothing any feathers that became ruffled during the course of the event. No matter how close to perfection the benefit came, some patrons will have been unhappy about something—the location of their table, the food service or loss or damage to their personal effects. The chairperson can ameliorate bad feelings by offering to resolve the situation personally, although sometimes just listening to the complaint and apologizing is enough. In the case of personal injury or damage, facilitating a claim on the benefit's or facility's insurance policy and solicitous attention to the injured party may head off a lawsuit, though you can never rule out that possibility.

Some disgruntled committee members may wait until after the benefit is over to sound off; again the benefit chairperson must listen sympathetically and, if the problems aired are serious enough, address them openly in her final report and recommendations. If the chairperson attended to problems as they came up during the planning period, however, there shouldn't be too many complaints afterward. Instead, the benefit chairperson should be hearing compliments that will make her happy to turn her attention to the next important obligation, that of thanking everyone who helped.

THANK YOU, THANK YOU, THANK YOU

Now that it's all over, how can you possibly show your appreciation to the many generous volunteers, underwriters and patrons who made the benefit a success? It would be lovely to send each flowers or a commemorative gift, but that would either break the benefit chairperson personally or wipe out the benefit's net profit. An expensive gift may be justifiable in the case of a co-sponsor, but a modest souvenir for each of the co-sponsor's representatives would be equally appreciated: say, a laminated or framed copy of the benefit invitation or a glowing press clipping. A scrapbook compiled by the benefit executive committee might also be appropriate; it could be sent to the corporate co-sponsor to circulate to the various employees who were involved in planning the benefit before going on display as testimony to the company's generosity.

The simplest, least expensive and most satisfying thank you is still a handwritten note on personal or benefit committee stationery. No gift, no matter how lavish, can substitute for this important gesture. You can never go wrong in thanking too many people nor in seeing that an important volunteer or donor receives more than one note from different members of the organization.

It's unrealistic to expect that the benefit chairperson will write to every single member of the benefit committee, in addition to the co-sponsor, every underwriter, supplier, reporter and staff member who contributed to the benefit's success. The benefit chairperson should certainly write to the co-sponsor and every member of her executive committee, asking them to convey her thanks to the individuals who worked on their subcommittees. The subcommittee chairpersons, in turn, should individually thank their own helpers, as well as any underwriters who assisted in their particular areas. The rest of the list can be divided up among the chairperson and subcommittee chairs. Major underwriters deserve a note from the benefit chairperson, as well as from executive committee members who worked with them. Don't leave out the organization's staff members who worked on the event or suppliers who provided their services at cost. It's the benefit chairperson's responsibility to go down the list and make sure that *someone* has written to everybody who needs to be thanked.

The organization owes the volunteer committee thanks for its work. Letters from the executive director, development and public relations officers can appropriately be written on the organization's letterhead. The executive director can thank the entire committee through the benefit chairperson and should write separately to every major underwriter. The development director should acknowledge all in-kind and cash donations other than ticket sales. Both development and PR officers, who have presumably worked more closely with the committee, should thank the subcommittee heads, as well as the benefit chairperson.

The chairman or president of the board, as chief volunteer officer of the organization, is especially obligated to express appreciation to the benefit chairperson and major underwriters. Co-sponsors, volunteer committee members, paid consultants and patrons aren't expected to thank the benefit chairperson in writing, but letters of congratulations are certainly appreciated.

You don't have to wait until the benefit is over to begin thanking individuals and corporations that have donated money or in-kind services; this includes table hosts and hostesses and those who buy upper-level tickets. They should receive acknowledgements as soon as you accept their contributions. A brief, typed form letter reproduced on benefit stationery is minimally acceptable, but it would be far better to use a word processor in order to individualize the salutation and contents. Whether a form letter or not, this acknowledgement should be personally signed by the benefit chairperson, patron chairperson or the underwriting committee member who solicited the contribution or, better yet, by two of these three.

The day after the benefit is a good time to tackle the remaining names on your list; your outpouring of appreciation will never be more spontaneous and sincere. Don't take any chances of leaving anybody out. Begin addressing envelopes for thank-you notes (referring to your notebook for lists of donors, committee members, etc.) during spare moments before the benefit takes place. Then you'll have only half as much work — and by far the pleasanter part of the job — to do on the day exhaustion sets in.

SUMMING UP

Before the sharp edges of memory have dulled, it's time to summarize and evaluate the results of your benefit. Between two and three weeks after the benefit, hold your executive committee wrap-up meeting. This final meeting can be combined with a thank-you luncheon or tea hosted by the benefit chairperson, providing an informal, relaxed atmosphere for discussion as well as encouragement for everyone to come and take part in the evaluation.

Each executive committee member should submit a final report in writing at this time. It's a good idea to pass out evaluation forms a week or two before the benefit, so that all committee members can begin to think about their responses in advance and so that you get back the essential information in reasonably consistent form.

The evaluation questionnaire that we've included in this chapter, a tool prepared for Red, White and Bravo!, a benefit for the Akron-based Ohio Ballet, is a good model. In addition to soliciting a general description of the work done and time commitment required by each subcommittee, it asks for listings of community contacts made, in-kind contributions, special equipment that was needed and itemized expenses. It also asks for specific recommendations for improving the committee process as well as the event itself. The evaluation form reflects a particular interest in the role of publicity and the community's perception of the benefit. Finally, it asks flatly whether or not the event should be repeated the next year and, if the answer is yes, what form it should take.

Note that the question is immediately followed by a test of depth of interest: a question asking the respondent whether he or she would commit to working on the benefit again.

At the evaluation meeting, you may wish to dispense with oral reports except for the treasurer's ("How much did we spend and how much did we make?"), reservations committee's ("How many patrons came at each ticket price?") and the reading of correspondence. Instead, give participants a chance to make any comments they like about any aspect of the benefit and wait to see what issues come to the surface. The benefit chairperson should listen carefully for the general mood that emerges from these comments and take notes that can be used in future planning. Were committee members generally satisfied with their experience? Do they feel triumphant, frustrated, angry or vaguely unfulfilled? What areas seemed the most troublesome?

If they feel frustrated, find out exactly why and correct the situation if possible before repeating the event. If the concept was new, volunteers may feel that, even though they didn't have enough time or information to develop it properly, they have learned from their mistakes. If the benefit was a repeat of a previous success, a sense of malaise may be an indication that support for the entire benefit is waning. Though it's difficult to face this possibility, an event that has been run by the same organization in the same way for years may have reached a point of diminishing returns. Interests change and you must be sensitive to the signs that your benefit's appeal is wearing thin. You may have to perform radical surgery on your benefit concept, removing parts that are no longer functioning well and infusing it with fresh blood and vital ideas. Or you may simply need to retire the old concept and try something entirely new.

Sometimes problems can be dealt with more effectively once the pressure is off. The benefit chairperson should show committee members how complaints and dissatisfactions can be couched in terms of positive changes that should be implemented next time. Instead of noting that a committee member insisted on getting her way, "even though I told her it wouldn't work," the benefit chairperson should say: "Perhaps we should consider doing it this way next time." Others can support her recommendation without appearing to oppose the person who had previously prevailed.

Occasionally there are problems that participants are reluctant to discuss openly because they involve personal criticism. Once the benefit chairperson becomes aware of these problems, she should be willing to address them confidentially, perhaps recommending that better controls be built into the planning process or considering

SAMPLE EVALUATION FORM
— RED, WHITE AND BRAVO!

Name: _____

Committee area: _____

1. Describe (in grueling detail, please!) duties you performed in your job area.

2. List all business and community contacts (including phone numbers) you used in the completion of your job. _____

3. Itemize expenses incurred in your area. _____

4. List in-kind contributions of goods and/or services used in your area. _____

5. What special equipment was necessary for your area? _____

6. Approximately how many hours (*excluding* regularly scheduled committee meetings) did you spend on Bravo!? _____

7. Was publicity and promotion essential to the success of your endeavors?

8. If so, please describe the methods used (radio, TV, placemat, *Beacon Journal* insert, etc.) _____

9. Suggest additional or increased publicity plans which would be beneficial in your area. _____

10. Describe alternate ways you would structure your job. _____

11. How might committee meetings better serve chairpersons? _____

12. Suggest improvements in execution, management and planning of your area *and* entire Bravo! project. _____

13. Do you feel the community people you worked with have a positive feeling about their participation in Bravo!? _____

How about the recognition they received? _____

How about volunteers, staff or other committee members they worked with?

14. Should Ohio Ballet consider a Red, White and Bravo! for next year? _____

15. If so, would you suggest the same format? (black-tie dinner, performances, Grand Finale event) _____

16. Please describe an alternate format, if you would like. _____

17. If Ohio Ballet would do Red, White and Bravo! next year, would you be part of the steering committee? _____

In what area? _____

18. General comments: _____

Thank you — your comments and follow-up are invaluable! Please complete and return to Ohio Ballet by May 16th.

whether a carefully worded job description (e.g., "Must be even tempered, good humored and able to work under pressure") would rectify the situation in the future. Perhaps certain individuals will be duly noted as troublemakers and the information quietly passed on to the next chairperson so that she can simply avoid them.

The benefit chairperson must discuss any problem that can't be resolved at the benefit committee level with the appropriate authority — the executive director (if it's a management issue), the chairperson of the standing committee on benefits or the president of the board. If the problem is — dare we say it? — with the benefit chairperson herself, one or two committee representatives, preferably board members, should go directly to the board representative. It's tempting to wash one's hands of a bad situation once the benefit is over, but the problem won't go away unless someone brings it to the attention of a person who can do something about it.

No evaluation is worth the trouble unless it includes a hard, honest look at the final income statement. This is very important, because the development goals that go on the organization's books for the following year are based on this year's results. Even if the benefit achieved its goal, the organization shouldn't assume that it can automatically increase next year's goal. It will need to go once again through the process outlined in Chapter I in order to evaluate the potential of its next benefit. The evaluation you're preparing is designed to aid that deliberation.

The treasurer and benefit chairperson are jointly responsible for preparing this document comparing projected income and expenses with the actual results. If the two don't jibe, they need to determine what went wrong and discuss what can be done about it next time.

Never falsify your financial records or report one figure internally and a different one publicly. It shouldn't be necessary to say this, but some organizations may slip into this trap in an effort to save face or ensure a co-sponsor's continuing support. Though its intent may be harmless, such deception seriously damages the credibility of the organization when it's exposed, as it inevitably will be.

When the benefit chairperson has collated all the executive committee reports and written her own summary, she should request a meeting with the appropriate board committee (fund-raising, standing committee on benefits or executive) to present the evaluation, along with a check for the sum of the net profit. The benefit process isn't over until she has discussed her recommendations frankly with the appropriate trustees and urged them to take

SAMPLE FINAL INCOME STATEMENT — LE PAPILLON

RECEIPTS

Tickets (251)

80 Monarchs $125		$10,000
45 Viceroys $100		4,500
126 Admirals $75		9,450
		$23,950

Contributions (44 gifts under $500)	5,088
Underwriting (14 gifts over $500)	21,972
Cash bar	106
Gifts in-kind	3,724
TOTAL	$54,840

DISBURSEMENTS

	Actual cost	Underwriting	SLRNC cost
Invitation (5,500)			
Design/keylining	$ 970	$ 970	$
Typesetting	132		132
Paper/printing	2,344	2,344	
Tickets (300)	95	95	
Computer lists	400		400
Bulk mail postage	355		355
First-class postage	61		61
Address corrections	61		61
	4,418	3,409	1,009
Program (400)	929	929	-0-
Music	1,270	1,270	-0-
Lolly the Trolley	410	110	300
Bar			
Liquor/wine	787		787
License	63		63
	800	-0-	800
Hough Caterers			
269 dinners	7,397	7,397	
Tables & chairs	518	518	
Fogging	75	75	
	7,990	7,990	-0-
Decorations	1,274	1,274	-0-
Shaffer Tent Co.	2,550	2,550	-0-
Acme Rents			
Band platform	108	108	
Dance floor	294	294	
Astroturf	1,000	1,000	
Electrical outlets	320	320	
	1,722	1,722	-0-
Insurance ($500 rider)	150	-0-	150
Publicity (postage)	4		4
Security	783	150	633
TOTAL	$22,300	$19,404	$2,896

EXCESS OF RECEIPTS
OVER DISBURSEMENTS $32,540

whatever actions are necessary to carry them out. After filing a copy of her benefit notebook and final report in the development office, she can toss the chairperson's hat back to the organization, confident that she has not only discharged her duty to everyone's satisfaction, but that she has provided valuable information and new ideas as a starting point for the next benefit committee.

Since a benefit is an important component of the organization's fund-raising program, as well as a major event in its calendar, it deserves acknowledgement in the organization's annual report. Not only should the benefit's net profit be broken out under "contributed income," but all patrons should be recognized in the listings of donors. (The way to figure the total donation is to add the tax-deductible amount of a patron's benefit ticket to the amount given in other campaigns.) Alternatively, the annual report could include separate benefit-patron listings. In any case, a discussion of the event, accompanied by photos, belongs in the narrative of the organization's activities during that year.

BENEFITS OF THE FUTURE

Whenever people who plan and patronize benefits get together, sooner or later questions are posed about the future of benefit fund raising. Are there too many benefits for our community to support? Are there too few volunteers and too few patrons to go around? Are people getting tired of these events? Are they too expensive, too elitist and not productive enough for the organizations that sponsor them?

While we believe that this method of fund raising will endure, only the best-run benefits will survive in the long run. These will be the benefits mounted by volunteers with management expertise and the commitment to accomplish clearly articulated financial goals for genuinely deserving causes. They'll demonstrate fiscal responsibility by developing sound budgets, attracting underwriting support for up to 90 percent of expenses, selling the maximum number of tickets at the highest possible price and showing a healthy profit of at least 65 to 70 percent of gross income. They'll also be sensitive to human needs, taking pains to keep volunteers, underwriters, trustees, staff members and the community informed and above all enthusiastic about the cause behind the benefit. The events themselves will be dramatic, informative and fun — truly "special occasions" that build lasting friendships and achieve lasting respect for the creativity, resourcefulness and professionalism of the organizations they sustain.

Appendix

TWENTY TERRIFIC BENEFITS

APRIL IN PARIS   For the benefit of Cleveland Opera, founded in 1976 to present an international repertoire of operas performed in English or with English supertitles. Held in April 1987.

ATTENDANCE   455 at $150 each

NET PROFIT $60,000

CHAIRPERSONS   Sue Peay and Elaine Gilbert

Carrying on the tradition of its predecessors, Cleveland Opera's annual black-tie benefit was inspired by one of the 1987 season's productions, *The Merry Widow*, which is set in Paris. Held in a local bank's new 300,000-square-foot operations warehouse, the party required the services of a professional display company and a theatrical stage manager to pull off the elaborate illusion of spending an evening on the town in the romantic capital of France.

Guests first entered "the Left Bank," where they found market stalls filled with sausages, fresh breads and cheeses, a fishing boat from the Seine full of smoked fish and a table of crudites, filled croissants and pates topped with an ice sculpture of the Eiffel Tower. During cocktails, five street mimes entertained while artists drew portraits of the guests and a trio provided le jazz hot. Dinner was served in the "Moulin Rouge" to the accompaniment of nonstop music from a seven-piece orchestra and the ten-member Amazement Park Review. A professional trapeze artist from Ringling Bros. circus launched the evening's high-flying entertainment; she was followed by the Moulin Rouge Revue, complete with show girls and boy, the cancan girls from the company's *Merry Widow* production and the singers, dancers and band of the Amazement Park Review. A limited raffle with a top prize of a trip to Paris was held at midnight; 100 of the 200 tickets sold (at $100 apiece) were bought that evening. When the party ended at 1 a.m., 400 guests still lingered.

MOST VALUABLE LESSON LEARNED   "Soliciting underwriting is the job most people 'hate,' yet it is crucial to financial success," says Elaine Gilbert. "This year we tried a new idea that made approaching prospective donors easier. We gave them a list of specific items to underwrite, complete with prices. People loved the idea of underwriting the cognac or the valet parking, the wine or the cancan girls — right on down the list of all the expenses which are incurred to present the kind of magnificent party our supporters have grown to expect."

"*APRIL IN PARIS*"

THE BALL AT THE HALLE BUILDING

For the benefit of Great Lakes Theater Festival, a 26-year-old not-for-profit professional company presenting an international repertory of dramatic and musical-theater classics, in residence in Playhouse Square Center, a renovated vaudeville and movie theater complex in downtown Cleveland. Held in November 1985.

ATTENDANCE

39 Carriage Trade patrons at $500 each
233 1228 Club patrons at $250 each
510 Friends at $125 each

NET PROFIT $151,000

CHAIRPERSON   Marilyn Brentlinger

The grand reopening of the Halle Building, a magnificent marble and brass-lined edifice that once housed a fashionable Cleveland department store, proved to be the theater company's most profitable benefit to date. Forest City Enterprises, the building's new owner-developer, underwrote many of the expenses of the evening, which was an appealing blend of nostalgia and novelty.

While the developer worked tirelessly to bring the building back to its former glory, benefit volunteers recreated the store's ambiance in a series of displays called "vignettes," featuring period costumes, furs and furnishings. Store memorabilia was also put on display, and former elevator girls were recruited to assume their old posts, wearing authentically reproduced uniforms.

Elegance was the committee's watchword — from the formal invitations to the 30-inch tapers lighting each table. More than 1,000 guests in white or black tie explored the beautifully restored main floor before heading to a second-floor "ballroom" for a four-course dinner. Dancing to the strains of the Gene Donati Orchestra of Washington, D.C., began spontaneously before the meal was served, so festive was the mood of the crowd. An after-dinner mini-auction brought in an additional $22,000.

MOST VALUABLE LESSON LEARNED   "Printing deadlines for the invitations were changed on three occasions, necessitating contacting volunteers each time to rearrange schedules for addressing and stuffing invitations," says Marilyn Brentlinger. "To avoid major frustration, the person responsible for production must *personally* know at every step of the way the printer's timetable and build into that an additional element of time for unforeseen problems."

CLEVELAND'S SECOND ANNUAL WINE AUCTION

For the benefit of Cleveland Center for Economic Education, an organization dedicated to helping teachers and students increase their understanding of basic economic concepts. Held September 1986.

ATTENDANCE   250

NET PROFIT $49,000

CHAIRPERSONS   Linda Griffith and Margaret Mitchell

Held in a tent at Northfield Park thoroughbred racetrack, this black-tie evening was a gourmet's delight from beginning to end. Chefs from ten of the area's finest restaurants worked out of a makeshift kitchen, with neither refrigerator nor sinks and only a four-burner propane stove, to produce a flawless six-course dinner. And, unlike many benefit meals, this one was planned to incorporate trend-setting foods: veal tenderloin in filo with Madeira sauce; fresh linguini with tomato-basil sauce, mussels and clams; beef tenderloin in Pommery mustard sauce with vegetable frittata; radicchio and bibb lettuce salads with peach and walnut vinaigrette and a smorgasbord of tortes and cakes for dessert.

Twelve outstanding vintners, including Tom Burgess of Burgess Cellars, John Shafer of Shafer Vineyards, Henri Berthe of Brut d'Argent and Sandra and Bill MacIver of Matanzas Creek Winery, along with several local wine merchants, hosted tables where they poured their finest domestic and imported vintages for the guests who paid more than the $100 base ticket price to be seated with them. Tastings of new California sparkling wines, as well as new white and red offerings from France, accompanied hors d'oeuvres and the silent auction of items ranging from a Methuselah (six-bottle equivalent) of Brut d'Argent to a stunning, one-of-a-kind coffee table made of wooden case ends from well-known California wineries.

Following dinner, spirited bidding attended the oral auction of otherwise unavailable wines, collected from donors all over the country (many of which went for bids well over the value listed in the auction catalogue). Private winery tours to Europe and California and gourmet wine-tasting dinners offered especially for the occasion were also auctioned.

MOST VALUABLE LESSON LEARNED   "Expect that whatever can go wrong, will go wrong," Margaret Mitchell says. "However, the event will still be successful if it has been well planned. When things go awry, remind yourself of the purpose of the event — creating recognition and good will for the organization, as well as raising funds — and the minor problems will fall into perspective."

COUNTRY COOKOUT AT HICKORY LANE FARM   For the benefit of St. Thomas Medical Center of Akron, Ohio, a not-for-profit corporation founded in 1928. Held in September 1986.

ATTENDANCE   500 at $75 each

NET PROFIT $38,425

CHAIRPERSONS   Jackie Del Medico and Lena LaRose

Word of mouth is all the publicity needed to attract a crowd to the Country Cookout, held annually since 1977 at the William and Betty Zekan's Richfield, Ohio, farm. Patrons who have in previous years attended this elegantly relaxed affair—planned, executed and totally underwritten by the Zekans, a couple well known for their generosity to many causes in the Cleveland and Akron area—return with their friends the next time around.

While dress at the 1986 event was as casual as jeans or Western wear, guests weren't expected to rough it. Alighting at the Zekan's newly constructed showplace of a barn (complete with stained-glass windows), where the bar was set up, patrons enjoyed cool drinks while admiring the Arabian horses that the Zekans breed and raise and a nearby pond outfitted with a fountain. Later they piled onto a hay wagon for nearly a mile's trip up the hillside to a picnic site, where a gleaming white tent had been installed. A five-piece band played country and popular dance music while Akron's Tangier restaurant prepared perfect filets on an outdoor grill. Served buffet style, dinner featured an array of shrimp and crab-leg hors d'oeuvres, potatoes, beans and all the fixings and Betty Zekan's personal-recipe bread pudding for dessert.

Though the scenery was pastoral, the facilities were hardly rustic. The Zekans' full-time landscaping crew worked seven days a week before the event, manicuring the grounds and placing hundreds of blooming chrysanthemum plants around the picnic site. Even the permanent outhouses were decorated with antiques, flowers, fancy guest towels and washbowls. As patrons danced on until 11 p.m., glowing Coleman lanterns brightened the night.

MOST VALUABLE LESSON LEARNED   "This party is entirely the Zekans', and they just seem to have come up with a winning concept," says Lena LaRose. "It's such a friendly atmosphere, you could come without knowing anyone and have a great time—and people do, year after year. It started small and just grew. Maybe it's easy for people to come because the dress is so casual. The scenery is like something in a movie, and we've always had good weather. If it rained, though, it could be held inside the barn and it would still be fun."

DAZZLE—OPENING IN STYLE   For the benefit of the Kent State University Museum, the home of the Jerry Silverman-Shannon Rodgers collection of more than 3,000 period costumes, one of the country's largest and most comprehensive surveys of world fashion. Held in September 1985.

ATTENDANCE

185 Founders at $500 each
175 Patrons at $250 each
240 at $150 each

NET PROFIT $100,000

CHAIRPERSON   Lindsay Jordan Morgenthaler

Timed to celebrate the grand opening of the Kent State University Museum, DAZZLE was positioned as an extremely glittery and exclusive event. Attendance was limited to 600 guests (originally set at 500, demand was such that the limit was stretched).

The logistics of the evening proved to be more difficult than ticket sales. Cocktails were served at the museum, where guests were greeted by 40 Kent State students in pink ties and cummerbunds lined up at the door. After docent-led tours of the new galleries, in which university faculty members quietly played chamber music, the spectacularly gowned women and their black-tie-clad escorts were whisked by a "fashion express" down Kent's main street, which had been newly widened and festooned with flags and banners, to dinner in the university cafeteria, successfully disguised as a silvery wonderland thanks to thousands of ceiling-to-floor streamers. During the ten-minute trip student ambassadors entertained the riders with information about the school, while behind the scenes valet parkers conveyed the guests' cars from the museum to the cafeteria.

After dinner, actor Cliff Robertson (one of the few expected celebrity guests who actually showed up, the others having been grounded by Hurricane Gloria) introduced the main event of the evening, a fashion show of Hollywood designer Bob Mackie's stunning evening clothes that had been organized by the Higbee Company, one of Cleveland's department stores and a major corporate backer of the new museum. The costumer of such stars as Cher, Barbara Streisand and Raquel Welch, Mackie had sent along a sampling of his trademark show biz outfits (would you believe a bearded female model in a circus-motif gown?). The show was followed by coffee and dessert served outdoors to the accompaniment of fireworks.

MOST VALUABLE LESSON LEARNED   "Forget the cookies, forget the stars and the music," says Lindsay Morgenthaler. "Sales, sales, sales is the most important goal of the chairperson. I think a letter prior to the party enthusing about the concept creates a receptive state of mind, and with an invitation and a phone call from a table hostess you can have an early sellout. Most beginning chairpersons carefully do everything else and two weeks before the benefit discover that no one is coming. Then, too late, they start to call."

Dazzle
Opening In Style

FANTASY   For the benefit of the Cleveland Play House, the oldest resident professional theater in the country. Held in June 1986.

ATTENDANCE

6 The Phenomenals at $1,000 each

50 The Spectaculars at $500 each
259 The Fantastics at $250 each
399 The Fabulous at $125 each

NET PROFIT $110,000

CHAIRPERSONS   Marilyn Brentlinger, Barbara Meals and barb Richardson

Fantasy offered a refreshing new twist on the dinner-dance theme with entertainment by a hot young New York performing troupe called Le Masquerade Fantasy Players. Nineteen exotically costumed dancers circulated among the crowd all evening, performing to taped popular music ranging from Fifties rock and roll to the soundtrack from *2001: A Space Odyssey*. Descending from portable cylinders placed throughout the Play House complex, where the benefit was held, they encouraged guests to join in the fun. Many of the 700-plus party-goers wore elegant "fantastic" apparel to complement the decorations: silver mylar bows and streamers that created a truly sparkling scene.

Dinner—filet mignon with herbed baby new potatoes and a medley of summer vegetables—was punctuated by visits from Masqueraders dressed as a banana daiquiri, a telephone booth, a piano and a one-headed bride and groom, among other spectacular costumes. Create-your-own ice cream sundaes were served in the theater's lobbies in order to get guests on their feet again for dancing.

MOST VALUABLE LESSON LEARNED   "Don't think we didn't consider using less expensive local performers," says barb Richardson, reflecting on the $19,000 fee paid to Le Masquerade. "The Play House is fortunate to have a costume collection of over 200,000 pieces, but nothing to compete with Le Masquerade's spectacular show stoppers (some were worth $2,000 apiece). Also, their performers have magnetic personalities and wonderful repartee developed from years of practice working with crowds and interacting with guests. No local actor, no matter how talented, would have the pizazz of these unique performers. In short, you sometimes have to pay more to get something special."

Fantasy

A FESTIVAL IN VENICE   For the benefit of Christ Child Society, Cleveland Chapter, a charity serving needy and disabled children and the elderly. Held in December 1986.

ATTENDANCE   500 at $75 each

NET PROFIT $30,000

CHAIRPERSONS   Sarina Teta and Julie Paulus

Though they spent only $2,000 on decorations, benefit organizers managed to transform banquet halls in a downtown hotel into a Venetian street scene that those who attended the Society's 70th anniversary dinner dance are still raving about. In the center of an exhibit hall whose columns had been decorated with lattice work, cocktails were served on a "piazza" created by means of a fountain filled with water and surrounded by small tables and chairs. On one side of the piazza, works of art were displayed for strollers to view as they sipped their drinks.

Live della Robbia wreaths with fruit and nuts, which the decorating committee hand-assembled, festooned the ballroom, whose balcony and stairway had been decked in greenery. The bandstand became a bridge adorned with pilings, lampposts and miniature white lights. Norfolk pines and 100 poinsetta plants (which were sold afterwards) placed artfully around the room added the proper holiday touch. A slide show projecting photographs of Venice onto a large screen behind the bandstand added to the authenticity.

Besides dancing, benefit patrons enjoyed a gourmet Italian meal of tortellini San Marco, radicchio with champagne vinaigrette dressing, lemon sorbetto, veal alla Veneziana (served with an herbed sauce of fresh basil, Italian parsley, shallots and white wine topped with roasted pine nuts) and tiramisu made with marscapone cheese. Even in the detail of party favors—torrone, an Italian candy made by one of the benefit volunteers and wrapped in cellophane and red and green ribbons—A Festival in Venice was a perfectly realized theme benefit.

A Festival in Venice

MOST VALUABLE LESSON LEARNED "Julie and I worked very closely with the banquet chef to get an excellent meal," says Sarina Teta. "When working with hotels, one must be very firm about the quality expected, its preparation and presentation. We had several tastings and made many suggestions. The fact that we were so knowledgeable about a very different menu made the chef enthusiastic and more cooperative."

HOLIDAY FESTIVAL For the benefit of The Junior League of Cleveland, Inc., an organization of women committed to promoting volunteerism and to improving the community through the effective action and leadership of trained volunteers. Held in December 1986.

ATTENDANCE

1,100 patrons at the Gala Opening Night Party
28,000 visitors at the Festival

NET PROFIT $98,100

CHAIRPERSON Lin Bartel

Since 1979 The Junior League of Cleveland's major fund-raiser, the Holiday Festival has become a seasonal tradition that lures thousands of individuals and families downtown each year to oooh and aaaah over a hall full of beautifully decorated Christmas trees. With tickets priced to be affordable ($3 adults, $1 kids) and the preview party primarily a complimentary "thank you" to supporters, the festival meets its financial goals primarily through underwriting, mass attendance and the massive involvement of volunteers.

More than 500 Junior League members took part in the seventh annual show. The underwriting committee successfully solicited decorators and sponsors for 75 trees; sponsorships ranged from $300 to $1,500. Twenty-two corporations agreed to underwrite, at $3,000 and $5,000 apiece, the "galleries" in which the trees were displayed.

Despite the fact that 50 percent of its membership is employed, volunteers were found to staff the hall from 10 to 9 each day for the five days of the display and run the concession booths and three boutiques, where, among other things, they sold wreaths donated by area florists. There was a lineup of almost hourly special events that took months of planning and coordination and, for the young at heart, a Crystal Castle of games and other amusements.

MOST VALUABLE LESSON LEARNED   "One must remain flexible in dealing with people and developments in order to pull off a project of this size," says Lin Bartel. "Circumstances can change from the beginning to the end of the project. For example, when I accepted the chair of Holiday Festival, we were planning on being at the Terminal Tower location where it had been held previously. When the Tower City redevelopment project was approved for the Terminal Tower, preempting our space, we had to start searching for a new location! We *had* to be flexible."

32nd ANNUAL HUMANITARIAN AWARD DINNER   For the benefit of the National Conference of Christian and Jews, an association of individuals interested in promoting intergroup cooperation and understanding. Held in October 1986.

ATTENDANCE   975 persons at $150 each

NET PROFIT $146,000

CHAIRPERSONS   Edward B. Brandon and Samuel H. Miller

A general reception and a VIP gathering for those who had purchased tables of ten kicked off the evening at 6:30 p.m. at a downtown Cleveland hotel. After enjoying cocktails, cheese and fruit with the award winner, Cleveland mayor George V. Voinovich, the upper-level patrons adjourned to the ballroom for dinner with the other guests. Simple centerpieces of gerber daisies and a string quartet set a dignified mood befitting the presentation of an award previously bestowed on such humanitarians as Bob Hope and John Cardinal Krol. The overwhelming success of this benefit year after year can be credited to its low overhead, sensitive selection of honorees and its high-powered executive dinner committee (116 salespersons strong in 1986).

MOST VALUABLE LESSON LEARNED

"It is extremely important to establish a concise time frame for the events of the evening and to adhere to it," says Sandra Schwartz, executive director of the organization. "Those in attendance are anxious to have the evening conclude no later than 9:30 p.m. Ample time must be allowed for the movement of the attendees from the reception area to the dining area. A glockenspiel (the hotel's suggestion) is inadequate to alert a group of this size."

LIGHT OF DAY   For the benefit of Playhouse Square Center, the largest theater restoration project in the world, which over the course of the past 15-plus years has raised $37 million to save three historic vaudeville houses in downtown Cleveland; and the Spina Bifida Association of America. Held in February 1987.

ATTENDANCE

200 patrons at $225 each
660 patrons at $125 each
100 patrons at $25 each (film only)

NET PROFIT $50,000

CHAIRPERSON   Diann G. Scaravilli

Attended by its stars, Michael J. Fox and Joan Jett, director Paul Schrader and more than 900 Clevelanders, the world premiere of the movie *Light of Day* was pulled together in a single month, after the film producers, Tri-Star Pictures, decided that the occasion should benefit both the Spina Bifida Association (Fox's favorite charity) and a Cleveland not-for-profit, Playhouse Square Foundation. All tickets were sold within two weeks — even before the invitations went out. Never underestimate the pull of celebrity guests. The fact that the movie had been filmed, in part, in Cleveland also helped to generate interest.

The evening of the benefit, as a continuous stream of limousines (actually the same few cars making a circuit) carrying the governor, the mayor and other VIPs pulled up in front of Playhouse Square's State Theatre at the appointed cocktail hour of 5:30 p.m., party-goers crowded around carved ice foxes in the newly restored Ireland Lobby to down shrimp, scallops and oysters with their drinks. Nightbridge kept up a steady rock beat. The film, about the exploits of a Cleveland bar band, was shown at 7. Afterwards dinner ticket-holders were treated to grilled veal chops and fresh asparagus accompanied by more rock music — all paid for by Tri-Star.

MOST VALUABLE LESSON LEARNED

"When working with an out-of-town co-sponsor, always appear charming

LIGHT OF DAY

and understanding of its needs but still keep control," says Diann Scaravilli. "You know what will or will not work in your city, so market your ideas strategically but firmly."

UNA NOTTE SENSAZIONALE   For the benefit of Lyric Opera Cleveland, a summer festival presenting up-and-coming operatic talents in innovative, rarely performed works. Held in October 1986.

ATTENDANCE   450 at $150 each

NET PROFIT $70,000

CHAIRPERSONS   Gina Ciresi and Floreen Consolo

The first benefit to be held in The Standard Oil Company's new head-quarters in downtown Cleveland more than lived up to its spectacular setting. Party-goers, many of them prominent Clevelanders seldom seen at benefits, gathered at 6:30 in the skyscraper's marble atrium for cocktails while Chuck Fuller and his All-Star Sensations kept up a lively beat on the second-floor balcony. A juggler, a fire-eater and clowns bearing balloons added to the festive mood.

In what was to be a nonstop evening of wining and dining, the crowd first feasted on an array of Italian hors d'oeuvres so extensive that some had to make room for the three-course dinner of lobster bisque, grilled veal chops and salad. Then came the *piece de resistence*: a one-ton ice sculpture of the Cleveland skyline wheeled out (very carefully, because of its weight—if placed on an insecure platform it could have been dangerous) with the dessert of continental pastries and chocolate. A Las Vegas-style cabaret featuring the show band Force followed.

Perhaps the most remarkable thing about the evening was that this elegant affair was Lyric Opera Cleveland's first big-ticket benefit. Equally impressive was the fact that 90 percent of the evening's expenses were underwritten.

MOST VALUABLE LESSON LEARNED   "By choosing many committee members who had never been involved with our company before we were able to attract an unusual mix of regular benefit-goers and fresh faces," says Gina Ciresi. "New faces on a committee naturally bring new faces to your event.

"Such a success the first time out can be a tremendous burden, though. People always expect you to top your last event. You must be innovative and give your public something unique and exciting. This is difficult to do in a city that has so many benefits. We all run out of ideas sooner or later and need time off so we don't burn out."

UNA NOTTE
Sensazionale

LE PAPILLON 1986   For the benefit of Shaker Lakes Regional Nature Center, which has for more than 20 years provided Clevelanders, especially the young, with environmental education programs. Held in September 1986.

ATTENDANCE

80 Monarchs at $125 each
45 Viceroys at $100 each
126 Admirals at $75 each

NET PROFIT $32,540

CHAIRPERSONS   Phyllis Baker and Mary Marm Wilson

A more picturesque site for the cocktails that kicked off this evening of dining and dancing under the stars could hardly be imagined. The 250 guests exploring the center's All People's Trail (a wooden walkway winding through woods and marsh at the head of one of the man-made lakes created by the Shakers when they dammed up a creek to power their mills) could pause, if they chose, at one or all of ten hors d'oeuvres stations set up along the way. These tables featured an astounding array of goodies ranging from Chinese noodles to Cajun shrimp prepared by professional and amateur gourmet chefs, who also shared their recipes in a spiral-bound booklet presented to guests as a party favor.

Silk kites in the shape of butterflies decorated the party tent where dinner was served. The menu of cold salmon mousse with dill watercress sauce on hydroponic bibb lettuce, charcoal broiled filet of beef tenderloin, tomatoes filled with creamed spinach, basil and Italian herbs and Jamaica chiffon torte was complimented by a Night Harvest Cuvee sauvignon blanc and an R.H. Phillips cabernet sauvignon. After dinner, quiet piano music gave way to the spirited sounds of a jazz quintet.

This event was a small-scale reprise of the much-beloved Party in the Park, the center's very popular annual benefit that was abandoned in 1983 after 17 years, when its planners felt that it had run its course. Like its predecessor, Le Papillon demonstrated that food, glorious food is always excellent entertainment. With the beginning ticket price set at a reasonable $75, it also proved to be a real bargain.

MOST VALUABLE LESSON LEARNED   "Pick your committee with care," says Betsy Beckwith, the center's administrative assistant. "Several of our committee members personally came up with underwriting, which was a significant factor in the financial success of the benefit. In addition, since the center was celebrating its 20th anniversary, a special committee of trustees was formed to raise money to meet other expenses of the benefit. The result: Over $19,400 was raised in underwriting, thanks to the commitment of our volunteers."

PUTTIN' ON THE RITZ   For the benefit of Cleveland Ballet, co-founded in 1976 by artistic director Dennis Nahat, who has built a broad-based repertory that includes Balanchine, De Mille, Tudor and a full-length *Nutcracker* and *Swan Lake*. Held in May 1985.

ATTENDANCE

350 Emperors at $125 each
1,350 Rockhoppers at $20 each

NET PROFIT $49,080

CHAIRPERSONS   Marilyn K. Brown and Kay Cottone

Co-sponsored by Sea World of Ohio to promote the grand opening of its new penguin exhibit, this clever benefit won international publicity for Cleveland Ballet. The highlight of the evening was a 40-minute ballet choreographed by Nahat for ten dancers dressed as penguins, one whale and two dolphins — a brainstorm that was covered by such national newspapers as the *Wall St. Journal* and television stations as far away as China.

In order to win new friends for the ballet among the amusement park's mass audience, planners offered a very inexpensive ticket (named for a type of penguin) that included admission to all the festivities except dinner. Cocktails were served in an area near the new Penguin Encounter, allowing patrons a sneak preview of the realistic arctic environment. After dinner, guests watched black-and-white costumed members of Cleveland Ballet perform to the strains of Irving Berlin's "Puttin' on the Ritz" on a stage erected over a tank in which Shamu and the dolphins could be seen "dancing." At the end of the piece, two of the dancers leaped into the frigid tank — a climax that kept guests buzzing throughout the grand dessert and dancing that followed.

Sea World, whom the ballet had vigorously pursued after word leaked of its interest in hosting a benefit, underwrote the cost of invitations, publicity posters, stage construction and tents. The Aurora, Ohio, amusement park also provided stuffed penguins as favors and coffee and doughnuts before the drive home.

MOST VALUABLE LESSON LEARNED   "Be careful not to price your tickets too low," says Teri Levine, who was chairperson of the ballet's benefit advisory committee at the time. "The Rockhopper ticket was such a good deal that I now think the majority of people came to have a good time *on* the ballet instead of *for* the ballet. The gain of new supporters was marginal."

RED, WHITE AND BRAVO!   For the benefit of Ohio Ballet, the Akron-based company that serves as a showcase for the choreography of artistic director Heinz Poll. Held in April 1985.

ATTENDANCE

400 Champagne Dinner Dance patrons at $100 each

7,000 Grand Finale patrons at $5 each

NET PROFIT $90,000

CHAIRPERSON Helen Moss

Ohio Ballet celebrated its tenth anniversary with a bang! of a party that provides a detailed blueprint for those not-for-profits seeking to expand their base of support. The ballet turned what had been an exclusive black-tie patrons dinner, at which the troupe's annual Bravo award for leadership in cultural affairs was presented, into an all-day bash for the entire community. The day began with 2 and 5 p.m. performances of the Ohio Ballet that drew a crowd of 7,000. The $5 ticket (5,000 of which had been presold at all branches of Bank One, Acme-Click grocery stores and O'Neil's department stores) entitled one not only to see the ballet but to attend the Grand Finale Party.

 While the community at large enjoyed the performances, ballet patrons attended the traditional awards ceremony and dinner dance, which had been underwritten entirely by O'Neil's. Other major Akron corporations provided support for the Grand Finale: five different parties held simultaneously on five different levels of Akron's new Oliver F. Ocasek State Office Building. About 350 students, Boy Scouts and senior citizens had been recruited to set up tables and serve food donated by 30 local restaurants. With entertainment ranging from a street fair complete with jugglers, acrobats, clowns, fortunetellers and flower and balloon vendors to a cabaret with room for 400 to dance, the Grand Finale served double duty as the community's introduction to its newest downtown landmark. The fund-raising goal for the day, set at $60,000, was easily surpassed.

MOST VALUABLE LESSON LEARNED "Set lofty, but realistic, goals," says Helen Moss. "Be sure the party is planned carefully and fully. Once that is done, the chairperson must never doubt or lose confidence in the success of the event or the volunteer committee will sense it, and you will not meet your goals. If you keep your committees confident, excited and involved, they will guarantee you a great success."

RIBAFFAIRE '86 For the benefit of National Multiple Sclerosis Society, which supports research on the cause and cure of this crippling disease, and its northeast Ohio chapter. Held in August 1986.

ATTENDANCE 1,050

NET PROFIT $145,000

CHAIRPERSONS Gerrie R. King and Bruce Weiner

The preview party for Cleveland's annual National Rib Cook-Off, a competition to decide the best amateur and professional rib barbecuers in the country, Ribaffaire '86 took place in "the largest tent ever put up in Cleveland." Erected on the mall between city hall and the federal courthouse, it measured 80 by 160 feet, which was hardly large enough to contain the good spirits of the crowd. Patrons danced in the aisles and around the tables during and after dinner to the sounds of The Motion. Dress was casual chic, while the tent was adorned with twinkling lights and multitudes of multicolored paper flowers on tables and pillars.

The $100 base ticket entitled patrons to valet parking and a buffet rib feast with passed hors d'oeuvres, strolling musicians and an 80-foot cocktail bar. Seven National Rib Cook-Off award-winning restaurants from around the country provided 15,000 ribs (which worked out to 14 $\frac{1}{3}$ ribs per person). Side dishes of salads, corn on the cob, baked potatoes and relishes were prepared by Executive Caterers. More than $70,000 in underwriting was raised, which more than covered the $60,000 of expenses.

MOST VALUABLE LESSON LEARNED "Long speeches and tributes at a benefit are a definite turn-off," says Gerrie King. "People know why they are there and what their money went for."

Ribaffaire '86

SCHEHERAZADE For the benefit of The Cleveland Orchestra, under the musical direction of Christoph von Dohnanyi. Held in February 1986.

ATTENDANCE 700 at $100 each

NET PROFIT $283,214

CHAIRPERSONS Janet Neary and Nancy Goslee

Begun in 1970 and alternating every other year with a black-tie ball as the Cleveland Orchestra Women's Committee's major annual benefit, Scheherazade centers around an elaborate silent and oral auction of hundreds of items, many of them one of a kind. Cocktails and dinner (often held in new locations and partially underwritten by the May Company department store), elegant as they always are, are secondary to the evening's entertainment: watching patrons race to outbid each other for private performances by orchestra members, dinners for eight catered by some of Cleveland's most prominent citizens in their own homes and the most coveted prize of all — the chance to conduct the Cleveland Orchestra in concert!

Scheherazade 1986, the first benefit to be held in the Cleveland Clinic Foundation's new medical building, designed by internationally acclaimed architect Cesar Pelli, took a year to plan and 200-plus volunteers to organize. Party-goers were greeted at the door by the strains of a string quartet performing amidst a spring garden of hyacinths, primroses and tulips. Before the live auction at 9 p.m., they feasted on lobster bisque, filet, hearts of palm and artichoke vinaigrette and luxurious finger-food desserts (mousse in chocolate cups, mini creampuffs, dipped fruits) placed on each table for self-service as the auction began.

Expenses for the evening totalled nearly $75,000, including such easy-to-overlook line items as $3,700 for the auctioneer, $2,200 in expenses incurred in moving items from the orchestra's Severance Hall home to the display area at the Clinic and $1,175 for postage. Clearly, this is an ambitious undertaking that only an experienced and large volunteer group could successfully coordinate. Work involved soliciting and processing more than 600 different contracts covering 500 items for the silent auction and 77 items for the oral (many of them packages consisting of donated air fare, hotel accommodations, admission to attractions, etc.).

To whet appetites for bidding, descriptions of selected offerings had been included in the benefit's save the date card, invitation and ads in the program books of the orchestra's concerts; some items had been displayed in the Severance Hall Green Room and posters listing others set up on the box level during the two concert weekends preceding the event. The evening of the event enticing displays of oral auction items — a large-screen TV, paintings, a mini race car and a fur coat hanging beside a full-length mirror with an invitation to "try me" greeted patrons as they traversed the skyway from the parking garage to the new wing. During the oral auction, photos of all items were projected on TV screens around the room, so that every guest had a clear view of what was up for bid. The gratifying results of these herculean efforts: $101,815 raised by the silent auction and $134,854 by the oral.

MOST VALUABLE LESSON LEARNED   "With its long tradition and the widespread community support of the orchestra, Scheherazade has a built-in audience," Janet Neary and Nancy Goslee say. "But the downside of doing it over and over again is boredom, so the site becomes very important for variety. 'Unique sites' are rarely designed for this type of event, so chairpersons must face the challenge with ingenuity and flexibility. We flew in the auctioneer, whom we had lined up a year ahead, to judge how the Clinic building with all its large interior pillars would work and to pick his brains on popular auction items around the country.

"But the key to Scheherazade is the secretary we hire for six months to handle all record keeping. A card file of donors and solicitors is kept from auction to auction, and copies of correspondence are kept. Forms have been developed for every function; we use 37 different printed pieces altogether.

"We found kickoff parties to be useful in assembling our solicitation team. They are the best way to hand out forms, get spouses involved, build spirit and share techniques, ideas for items, sources and connections. We had a few pep talks on solicitation planted at our two kickoffs. It's a very individual matter whether to write, phone or call in person. Just provide materials for the solicitor to do it the way she's most comfortable.

"To share ideas we used yellow 4 x 6 cards noting: 'ski house in Alps,' 'Chinese cooking teacher,' 'inflatable boat' — and posted them at meetings for inspiration or to urge contact. We sent a weekly, one-page newsletter to all 185 solicitors with news of successful fellow solicitors, running totals of contracts in and descriptions of the interesting items we were getting and urging more effort and seeking specific items.

"We used the orchestra's computer to help determine the winning silent auction bidders the morning after the auction. All guests, their phone numbers and their bidding numbers had been entered during the two or three days before the event. On Sunday morning, the last three bidders' numbers and their dollar bids were entered. The computer then gave us one list of all the items and the names of the top three bidders and another list by person, telling which items they had won or came in second or third on. We could easily tell people their total dollars owed with the aid of the printouts. Since we have a fair number of items that are refused for a variety of reasons, the finance committee could easily move on to the second bidder. We will refine this system a little next time, but it showed us there's a good use for computerization.''

SCHEHERAZADE

A STERLING SPECTACULAR   For the benefit of Great Lakes Theater Festival, a Cleveland-based summer Equity company presenting Shakespeare and other classics. Held in February 1986.

ATTENDANCE

170 Sterling Patrons at $100 each
132 Special Friends at $55 each
597 Sparklers at $35 each

NET PROFIT $40,822

CHAIRPERSON   Mary Papandreas

Always a crowd-pleaser, the fashion show/luncheon has been a staple of the GLTF Women's Committee fund-raising repetoire since 1961. Underwritten in its 25th year by E.F. Hutton and Saks Fifth Avenue, which provided clothes, models and staff help, A Sterling Spectacular featured designer Mary McFadden's spring collection, with her trademark pleated outfits this season rendered in dramatic combinations of black and white and in colorful mosaics inspired by a trip to India. McFadden, whose participation had been kept a secret until the kickoff party for the benefit, mingled beforehand over cocktails and/or hot soups with those of the 881 guests who had purchased Sterling tickets. (Early purchasers of Sterling tickets were also treated to a luncheon at the home of the benefit chairperson.) After the show, salad in a tortilla basket and a lavish chocolate "top hat" dessert were served. Three guests won designer outfits from Saks drawn in a mini-raffle, and a patron at every table won a box of old-fashioned glasses inscribed with the GLTF logo and that of the donor, E.F. Hutton.

MOST VALUABLE LESSON LEARNED   "It is important to make everyone feel that his or her contribution is necessary and valued—no matter how large or small," says Mary Papandreas. "This means communicating on a one-on-one basis, sharing your enthusiasm not only with regular contributors but friends, business contacts, relatives, key members of all kinds of

organizations. Phoning, publicity and letters sent periodically to remind people of the occasion and its progress — even affairs such as luncheon and kickoff parties that are complimentary to patron supporters — all help to emphasize how important their involvement is to you."

VESTAX CLEVELAND POLO CLASSIC
For the benefit of the Boys and Girls Clubs of Greater Cleveland, which provide meeting places and educational and recreational programming for more than 3,500 inner-city children annually. Held in June 1986.

ATTENDANCE

240 Champagne Brunch patrons at $100 each
32 Tailgate ticket purchasers at $100 each
400 Dancing Under the Stars patrons at $40 each

NET PROFIT $20,000

CHAIRPERSONS   R. Eric Kennedy and Curtis Lee Smith, Sr.

A first-time event, the polo classic — a Sunday afternoon match-up of the top players from the Cleveland and Detroit Polo Clubs — was also the first-ever benefit for the Boys and Girls Clubs of Cleveland. Benefit organizers landed an impressive $23,500 in underwriting for the event itself from Vestax, an Akron, Ohio, financial planning group with an interest in gaining exposure in the Cleveland market, where it has a branch office.

The polo weekend kicked off with a black tie-optional dance held Friday night in a tent on the polo fields. The ticket price included beer, wine, snacks and a general admission to the match. Vestax also sponsored a party tent on Sunday, where those who had purchased a $100 box seat could enjoy champagne, hors d'oeuvres, chicken and ribs during breaks in the play. Tailgate tickets — a sideline parking spot plus ten general admissions — could also be had for $100 for those who preferred to bring their own picnics or feast on barbecued ribs offered at a volunteer-run concession. Volunteers also operated pony rides for the kids, but their biggest effort went into ticket sales.

As this was a first-time benefit, a mailing list had to be constructed from scratch from the membership lists of every country club, athletic club, eating club, social club and civic organization the benefit committee could find. Ten thousand invitations were ultimately mailed.

MOST VALUABLE LESSON LEARNED   "A large mailing list is a plus," says Eric Kennedy, "but the only way to sell a benefit is through personal contacts made by the board of trustees, all committee members, friends and family. We even had a telethon on two different evenings to contact persons with whom we were acquainted who had been sent invitations."

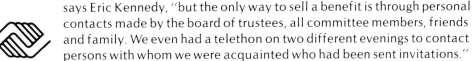

11th ANNUAL WESTERN RESERVE ANTIQUES SHOW
For the benefit of the Western Reserve Historical Society, a museum recreating, through period rooms and special exhibits of clothing, artifacts and memorabilia, life in northern Ohio from the Revolutionary era to the early 20th century. Held in October 1986.

ATTENDANCE

34 Benefactors at $800 each
112 Sponsors at $150 each
332 Patrons at $95 each

NET PROFIT $96,000

CHAIRPERSON   Mary Abbott

The WRHS Women's Advisory Council benefit is an outstanding example of how to maximize income generated by a single event, in this case a three-day antique show in which upwards of 40 dealers from across the country usually exhibit. Booth rentals do not generate any income, as the costs of readying the exhibit area are offsetting. But benefit organizers, assisted by only one paid consultant — a professional show manager — sell general admission tickets and prepare and serve a daily fixed-priced luncheon that made a profit the first year it was instituted. (Each day's luncheon requires its own subcommittee.)

Another subcommittee sells advertising and sponsored pages in the show catalogue, in 1986 a 112-page booklet of articles and exhibitors' listings. In addition, volunteers also host an annual preview party that most recently attracted nearly 600 antiques buffs to the museum for an advance peek at the show (see ticket breakdown above). The evening following the preview is "Collectors Night," which draws young marrieds to the museum for an informative lecture tour of the exhibit area and nibbles at a cost of $20 per person. One hundred fifty persons attended (at $18 a ticket) a Sunday lecture by the chief curator of Colonial Williamsburg, followed by brunch. Finally, organizers mount a silent auction of antiques, collectibles and artwork that all show visitors can participate in, with the winning bids announced in the show's final hours.

MOST VALUABLE LESSON LEARNED
"I would not consider publishing a catalogue unless it has interesting and informative articles that people will use as a reference," says Mary Abbott. "If the only thing needed is a directory of exhibitors, a small program would better serve the purpose. Your editorial chairperson should try to get the features free or at least underwritten by asking individuals or companies to sponsor a page in the catalogue. (Their name appears at the bottom of the page.)

"The cost of producing the 1986 catalogue was $l6,000 for 2,000 books. If the catalogue is free, more will have to be printed. If it is sold, the price should be between $2 and $4. Do not overprice it, as you want people to pick it up and read it so that your advertisers get their money's worth.

"An advertising chairperson and ten very hard-working salespeople could do an *excellent* job. Make sure they have a good cover letter, any printed pieces of information about the benefit and a very detailed contract that spells out all the requirements. Send complimentary general-admission tickets to all your advertisers and make sure they are on the mailing list for receiving invitations and flyers. Don't forget to send copies of their previous ads and a contract to all previous advertisers."

ZIPPITY ZOO DOO   For the benefit of Cleveland Metroparks Zoo, the fifth oldest zoo in the country. Held June 1986.

ATTENDANCE

22 Himalayan Pheasant Patrons at $500 each
27 Tibetan Pheasant Patrons at $250 each
105 Burmese Pheasant Patrons at $125 each
546 Sponsors at $80 each

NET PROFIT $75,000

CHAIRPERSONS   Cici Riley and Mary Susan Lyon

Held outdoors at the zoo every year since 1972, this casual affair to help support new construction is always sold out in advance. Regulars, often sporting clothes with wild animal prints, know they're in for an evening of just plain fun. At the most recent Doo, crowded zoo buses whizzed 700 revelers to scattered cocktail sites, giving everyone a chance to see what was new at the zoo. Dinner, featuring an always-popular soup bar, was served buffet style in picnic pavilions at Zoogate Commons. Because proceeds from the evening would help defray the costs of a new natural habitat for exotic pheasants, the tables were decorated with edible center-pieces of white cardboard pheasants guarding chocolate nests filled with frosted cake "eggs." After dinner there was dancing and an auction of a fanciful array of items ranging from gourmet birdseed to a trip, called "London, Zoo and Air Fare Too," featuring a week's lodging in a Mayfair flat and a VIP tour of the Regent Park Zoo. The auction alone netted $27,500. Patrons who purchased $500 tickets received special recognition on a permanent plaque placed at the new pheasant habitat.

MOST VALUABLE LESSON LEARNED   "The party is spread over 137 acres," says Cici Riley. "The process of getting people back to the pavilions for dinner must be addressed, as well as the timing. At the appointed dinner hour, the bars at outlying stations are closed and buses continue on their routes, picking up guests. Even so there are always stragglers in getting back to Zoogate Commons. Finally the main bar is closed—this forces everyone to get in the buffet line."

WESTERN RESERVE
Antiques Show

Zippity Zoo Doo!

JOB DESCRIPTIONS

BENEFIT CHAIRPERSON (Reports to president of the board or chairperson of the standing committee on benefits)

Responsible for planning, organizing and executing all details of a benefit: managing volunteers and coordinating work with staff members; collaborating with co-sponsor (if any); and meeting financial goal set by board. (Responsibilities may be divided among co-chairpersons.)

SPECIFIC TASKS
- Prepares and administers budget in order to meet financial goal.
- Secures board approval and support for general benefit plan and budget, including ticket prices and projected attendance.
- Recruits executive committee members and delegates responsibilities according to their experience, abilities and interests.
- Develops project time line and monitors progress of work.
- Chairs all meetings of the general benefit committee and executive committee (consisting of subcommittee chairpersons and co-sponsor's representatives).
- Is available throughout planning period (usually 6 to 12 months) to assist committee members with any and all specific tasks, answer questions and help solve problems, appointing someone to assume this responsibility in the event of temporary absence.
- Assists underwriting committee in development of prospect list and solicitation.
- Approves all expenditures and may cosign checks with treasurer.
- Approves copy for press releases, fact sheets, invitations, programs and all other printed materials.
- Helps to promote benefit through hosting press luncheon and/or kickoff party, giving media interviews, etc.
- Buys at least one table, preferably at the highest patron level, and encourages as many friends as possible to do likewise; assists patron committee with solicitation of board members and other potential high-level patrons.
- Keeps notebook or file of all agendas, minutes, contracts, budgets, publicity materials, etc.; after event, passes notebook to development department.
- Acknowledges both verbally and in writing all contributions of time, effort, money and materials by volunteers, staff, co-sponsor and major underwriters; hosts thank-you luncheon or tea for executive or entire committee after benefit.
- Chairs wrap-up meeting; submits final report and evaluation to board.

QUALIFICATIONS
- Has previously chaired or served as a subcommittee chairperson

for several successful benefits.
- Has a strong interest in and previous involvement with the organization; is preferably a board member.
- Understands finances; capable of developing and enforcing a realistic budget.
- Is an idea person who is also well organized and attentive to detail; a perfectionist who can also delegate responsibility to others.
- Has a wide network of contacts, is able to obtain cooperation from friends and highly placed business associates, inspires loyalty and dedication, is enthusiastic, personable and well liked.
- Has a professional image, is poised and articulate when speaking before groups or one-on-one, has a good relationship with local media.
- Is able to devote sufficient time to the project; is willing to contribute numerous personal expenses such as telephone, mileage, parking, entertaining committee members and prospective donors.

TIME COMMITMENT

6 to 12 months or longer; approximately 15 hours per week until last month before event, during which period commitment is full time (up to 60 hours per week).

COMPOSITION OF COMMITTEE

50 to 100 or more members including volunteers, co-sponsor's representatives, consultants and table hosts/hostesses, as well as organization's staff members. Executive committee consists of subcommittee chairs listed below.

ADDRESSING/MAILING CHAIRPERSON (Reports to benefit chairperson)

Assembles large committee for addressing, stuffing and sorting invitations and other mailings; supervises work sessions; arranges delivery of bagged mail to post office.

SPECIFIC TASKS
- Notifies volunteers of dates and locations of list collating/ updating and addressing/sorting sessions.
- Collates, corrects and updates mailing lists with assistance of her committee and staff.
- Arranges for spacious, easily accessible location to hold work sessions; sets up tables, boxes for sorting, mailing lists and supplies; provides coffee and snacks for volunteers.
- Week before mailing date, obtains supplies (rubber bands, bulk stickers and mailing bags) and up-to-date information on bulk-mailing requirements from post office; checks whether there is

enough money in organization's bulk mailing account to cover cost of benefit mailings.

- Supervises labeling, hand-addressing and sorting procedures so that finished mailing will conform to postal requirements.
- Arranges for delivery of bagged mail to post office bulk mailing department on appointed day and pays postage if not already in account.

QUALIFICATIONS

- Preferably is an active member of organization's volunteer support group; otherwise, someone who can assemble 10 to 20 friends (sometimes on short notice) for a day's work.
- Is well organized and efficient; previous experience in handling bulk mailings is desirable.

TIME COMMITMENT

1 to 5 full days at time of each mailing (for invitations, 10 weeks before benefit date so that they arrive 2 months in advance), depending on number of pieces and whether they are to be labeled or hand-addressed. If collating or updating lists, begin at least 8 weeks before first addressing/sorting date.

COMPOSITION OF COMMITTEE

20 to 30 people (assuming 6,000 pieces to be mailed) willing to put in a day of work. For each additional mailing (kickoff party, save the date, etc.) contemplated, another shift will be required of each volunteer. One volunteer with station wagon or van is desirable.

AUCTION CHAIRPERSON (Reports to benefit chairperson)

Runs auction component (if any) of benefit, assuming responsibility for acquisitions, compiling and printing catalogue, display of items, engaging auctioneer and collecting purchasers' payments.

SPECIFIC TASKS

- Recruits large acquisitions committee to solicit businesses and individuals for auctionable merchandise, services, art works, vacation packages, etc.
- Engages experienced auctioneer; recruits volunteer spotters, cashiers, models (for clothing and jewelry), etc.
- Compiles auction catalogue to be mailed to ticket-holders prior to benefit and to be used during event.
- Supervises the creation of displays and/or photos or slides to be used during auction.
- Arranges installation of podium, public-address system and special lighting as needed; meets with auctioneer on site day before benefit to test equipment and make any necessary adjustments.

- Establishes method of payment; provides receipts, certificates or other form of acknowledgement for winning bidders; assists treasurer in collecting and recording all payments on the spot.
- Acknowledges all donations in writing; notifies donors of winning bidders in order to arrange delivery.

QUALIFICATIONS
- Has experience attending and, preferably, working at auctions.
- Has numerous personal and business contacts.
- Is well organized, creative, resourceful, persuasive and persistent.
- Is an officer or active member of organization's volunteer support group or someone who can mobilize a large committee.

TIME COMMITMENT
Depends greatly on scope of auction: approximately 5 hours per week for 12 weeks if mini-auction, up to 40 hours per week for large-scale general offering; some follow-up required after benefit to coordinate delivery of purchased items.

COMPOSITION OF COMMITTEE
Recruiting an established support group is desirable, with other volunteers added as necessary; acquisitions committee should be as large as possible. Unless auction is limited to a specific category (e.g., fine art), members should represent a wide variety of interests, business contacts and geographic areas in order to provide "something for everyone" at a wide range of prices.

DECORATIONS CHAIRPERSON (Reports to benefit chairperson)

Coordinates design of the entire physical space to be occupied by the benefit.

SPECIFIC TASKS
- Works with volunteer committee, design professionals and suppliers to create a coherent visual theme and color scheme.
- Solicits donations of supplies and services or borrows items needed to carry out the visual theme.
- Clears all plans and proposed expenditures with the benefit chairperson.
- Works with printing coordinator or graphic designer to assure consistency of visual theme in invitations, program and other printed pieces.
- Supervises, coordinates and assists with installation and removal of all decorations.

QUALIFICATIONS
- Has experience, preferably professional, in decorating, interior design, theatrical design or similar field.
- Has network of contacts with design skills and access to materials

and services needed to create decor.

- Has ability to develop and execute master plan carried out by a variety of volunteers and paid workers on a strict timetable.
- Has ability to keep within budget and secure substantial contributions and/or discounts on materials and services.
- Enjoys entertaining, especially at large parties.

TIME COMMITMENT

Varies greatly depending on amount of decorating to be done. Count on devoting full time to project during last few days before and day after benefit.

COMPOSITION OF COMMITTEE

Depends on amount and complexity of work. Members should have skills similar to those of chairperson, but in complementary areas of design.

ENTERTAINMENT COORDINATOR (Reports to benefit chairperson)

Secures and coordinates all entertainment for benefit; responsible for entertainers' travel and performance arrangements; responsible for ensuring quality of sound and lighting equipment

SPECIFIC TASKS

- Auditions performers, researches fees and availability and chooses entertainment with approval of executive committee.
- Negotiates contracts with all performers, including date, time, fees, special requirements, cancellation and "no-show" clauses, and has appropriate representative of organization sign it.
- Arranges transportation, lodging and meals for performers if so specified in contract.
- Arranges for dressing rooms, set-up and rehearsal time on benefit site.
- Coordinates installation of sound and lighting equipment, piano moving and tuning, etc., and ensures their adequacy; works with union personnel and technicians as necessary.
- Develops alternate entertainment plan in case of cancellation or other unforeseen event.
- Serves as only liaison with all entertainers, to avoid confusion.
- Keeps abreast of committee plans affecting entertainment, e.g., timing of all activities, floor plan, stage decor, etc.; apprises performers of appropriate dress code and other expectations the executive committee may have.

QUALIFICATIONS

- Is a person who attends many live events (at home and when traveling) of the type sought for the benefit, has some knowledge of the art form or style (e.g., jazz, musical theater) and preferably

has contacts in the entertainment industry.
- Is able to negotiate with artists, agents and union personnel.
- Is flexible and resourceful in dealing with contingencies.
- Is a super salesperson, able to communicate excitement and uniqueness of entertainment to media and potential patrons.

TIME COMMITMENT

Approximately 5 hours per week during early planning stages, minimal once contracts have been signed, active again last week and during event.

COMPOSITION OF COMMITTEE

Usually 1 or 2 persons handle all arrangements.

FOOD AND BEVERAGE CHAIRPERSON (Reports to benefit chairperson)

Coordinates all arrangements with caterer and/or volunteer cooks.

SPECIFIC TASKS

- Obtains bids and sample menus from 2 or 3 caterers or recruits qualified volunteer cooks to provide food.
- Obtains prices and recommendations on quantity of liquor and wine needed.
- Determines whether temporary liquor license and/or health department certification is needed; if so, arranges for appropriate officer from the organization to complete applications; follows up to confirm approvals.
- Negotiates contract with caterer and has appropriate representative of organization sign it; writes letter to confirm all arrangements when standard contract is unavailable.
- Arranges to rent or borrow tables, chairs, linens, dishes, etc., if caterer does not provide these items.
- Chooses menu and wines in consultation with benefit chairperson or executive committee.
- May arrange tasting of complete meal as quality control device.
- Arranges for set-up and takedown of temporary kitchens, bars, waiters' stations, tables and chairs, etc.
- Hires or recruits all necessary servers (if not provided by caterer); assures that they are appropriately trained and dressed.
- In consultation with benefit chairperson, has caterer or skilled draftsman prepare a floor plan (showing not only all dining tables but server's stations, stage, registration desk, restrooms, coat check, etc.) to scale.

QUALIFICATIONS

- Is a person who entertains frequently, has worked with caterers before, understands the complexities of menu planning and

appreciates good food.
- Is able to negotiate contracts.
- If using volunteers, is someone who cooks well and knows many other qualified cooks, is enthusiastic, persuasive.
- Is well organized and able to arrange for the necessary cooking and serving facilities to accommodate benefit's needs.

TIME COMMITMENT
Approximately 3 to 4 hours per week if experienced caterer with sufficient equipment is used; extensive if coordinating volunteer chefs and cooking facilities.

COMPOSITION OF COMMITTEE
1 to 3 persons if caterer is used; more are needed if numerous cooks are involved.

HOSPITALITY CHAIRPERSON (Reports to benefit chairperson)

Recruits and trains a sufficient number of hosts and hostesses to greet the other guests and to assist them in finding their tables, bars and other facilities.

SPECIFIC TASKS
- Determines the number of volunteers needed to keep crowd moving from one area to another according to event agenda by assessing number of guests, size and configuration of facility, location of dangerous passages and number of times group must move from one area to another.
- Recruits required number from ranks of benefit committee members, staff and, if needed, benefit patrons.
- Prepares written instructions and floor plans, if necessary, for greeters.
- One or two days before event, meets with hospitality committee on site to review instructions, event agenda and floor plan; points out potential problem areas and assigns volunteers to monitor those areas.
- Prepares identification such as flowers or ribbon for hospitality committee members.

QUALIFICATIONS
- Is thoroughly familiar with benefit facility and plans.
- Knows enough committee members and patrons personally to recruit sufficient workers.
- Is personable, enthusiastic and able to give clear directions.

TIME COMMITMENT
Few hours to recruit subcommittee (this must happen before invitations are printed so that names can be included); 3 to 4 hours during final week to conduct subcommittee orientation and review floor plan.

Because responsibility is limited, chairperson may serve on other subcommittees as well.

COMPOSITION OF COMMITTEE
Benefit committee members and staff not previously assigned tasks during event and benefit patrons, preferably board members or others close to the organization; number to be determined by chairperson, as noted above.

PATRON CHAIRPERSON (Reports to benefit chairperson)

Coordinates solicitation of prospects for upper-level ticket sales.

SPECIFIC TASKS
- Selects corporate and individual prospects from invitation mailing list; contributes additional names and addresses from private club and business/professional association lists, making sure they also receive invitations.
- In consultation with development officer, writes and signs solicitation letter to be sent to all prospects prior to mailing of invitation, urging them to come and purchase tickets at higher price levels.
- Coordinates personal note-writing campaign to these prospects (notes may be added to above letter, substituted for same or written on invitation, at benefit and patron chairpersons' discretion).
- Coordinates telephone follow-up.

QUALIFICATIONS
- Is a representative of the board of trustees at the highest possible level, preferably a member of the executive committee or past president.
- Is willing to purchase own tickets at the same price level requested of prospects.
- Has personal acquaintance with many people in community who attend benefits and are able to make substantial contributions.
- Is persuasive salesperson.

TIME COMMITMENT
Approximately 10 to 20 hours per week for 3 to 4 weeks 3 months before the event.

COMPOSITION OF COMMITTEE
15 to 25 members, primarily trustees, ideally including president and individuals prominent in community.

PERSONNEL MANAGER (Reports to benefit chairperson)

Hires and supervises all paid workers, except caterer, auctioneer (if any) and entertainers, needed before, during and after benefit; i.e., security, maintenance, parking, restroom and check room attendants.

SPECIFIC TASKS
- Assesses personnel needs in consultation with executive committee and facility manager.
- Researches workers' rates, restrictions and requirements.
- Negotiates contracts where needed and has appropriate officer of organization sign them; writes letters to confirm all arrangements when standard contract unavailable.
- Meets and directs all paid workers or foremen when they arrive on the job; supervises their work, answers questions and provides assistance if necessary.
- Arranges for workers' meals, if specified in contract, and dressing rooms, if necessary.
- Arranges to provide any equipment or uniforms needed, but not provided by workers.
- Locates and sets up first aid station or provides first aid kit; arranges for voluntary medical assistance — doctor or paramedic — to be on call.
- Gives benefit treasurer list of people to be paid by check at close of event and the total amount of their wages, if known in advance.

QUALIFICATIONS
- Is an effective supervisor and preferably has previously worked with the kinds of workers needed. If using organization's own facility and hiring its workers, a staff member may be in best position to do this.
- Is able to negotiate contracts.
- Is sensitive to labor union issues and knowledgeable about union regulations.
- Is alert to potential problems; keeps a cool head and knows whom to call in case of emergency.

TIME COMMITMENT
Approximately 5 hours per week, beginning about 2 to 3 months before benefit; full time during last week before and day after benefit.

COMPOSITION OF COMMITTEE
Usually 1 or 2 persons handle all arrangements.

PRINTING COORDINATOR (Reports to benefit chairperson)

Coordinates writing, design and production of all printed pieces; secures approval of all copy and design by co-sponsor and staff development or public relations director before production begins.

SPECIFIC RESPONSIBILITIES
- Unless printing is being donated, obtains samples of work and

bids from 2 to 3 graphic designers and/or printers for all printed pieces needed, invitations, save the date cards, stationery, programs, seating assignment cards, catalogues (if any), tickets, signs, etc.
- If offer of donated printing is received, evaluates whether printer can deliver necessary quality and meet deadlines.
- Sets up master production timetable specifying when copy, design, typesetting, keylining and printing are to be completed in order to produce each piece on time.
- Writes and/or compiles copy; has benefit chairperson, development or public relations officer of the organization and co-sponsor (if any) approve wording and proofread and double-check listings of committee members, underwriters and patrons.
- Delivers clean final copy to designer/printer; follows up by phone to make sure there are no problems or delays in schedule.
- Has designs and printer's proofs approved by benefit chairperson, development or PR officer and co-sponsor.

QUALIFICATIONS
- Considerable experience in graphic design and production is desirable; some experience working with printers and basic understanding of production schedules needed.
- Is a good writer, accurate typist and eagle-eyed proofreader.
- Has ability to explain benefit concept and theme clearly so that designer can interpret them appropriately.
- Has ability to adhere to strict deadlines and get others to do likewise.
- Is available throughout benefit planning period to move each piece quickly through successive stages of production.

TIME COMMITMENT
Varies widely depending on number and complexity of printed pieces; as high as 20 hours during critical weeks.

COMPOSITION OF COMMITTEE
Usually a 1-person job but may be divided between a writer and a graphic designer; requires input from various executive committee and staff members, co-sponsor, etc. If extensive catalogue is needed for auction or exhibition, usually a separate editor and subcommittee are required.

PUBLICITY CHAIRPERSON (Reports to benefit chairperson)

Informs local and national (if appropriate) media about benefit and notifies them of newsworthy developments; coordinates effort with organization's public relations officer.

SPECIFIC TASKS
- Attends all meetings of benefit executive committee in order to

keep abreast of developments.

- Forms a plan and timetable for releasing information to newspapers, magazines, radio and TV stations so as to gain the best possible coverage before, during and after the benefit; works with organization's PR staff to avoid interfering with other planned media campaigns.
- Writes all press releases, fact sheets and public service announcements or works with the organization's PR department to prepare all necessary written information.
- Personally invites reporters and editors who may be interested in doing a story on the event to kickoff party; offers further information and arranges interviews as necessary.
- Identifies reporters who should receive complimentary invitations to the benefit; coordinates their seating with reservations chairperson.
- Prepares press kits containing fact sheets, guest list and seating chart for reporters who are attending kickoff and/or benefit (press kits may be mailed a few days in advance of the latter); greets reporters and photographers at door and introduces them to key people; is available to assist them throughout event.
- Hires a qualified photographer to take pictures for committee's and organization's own use.

QUALIFICATIONS
- Is a good oral and written communicator.
- Preferably has experience in public relations, is familiar with formats of press releases, PSAs, etc.; understands what makes an event newsworthy; and already enjoys good working relationship with members of local and, possibly, national media.
- Is enthusiastic and persistent; can be creative in finding new angles to familiar story.

TIME COMMITMENT
4 to 10 hours per week throughout benefit planning period.

COMPOSITION OF COMMITTEE
Ideally includes both members of PR staff and volunteers who are known and respected by local media. Number depends on the amount of contacts to be made.

RESERVATIONS/SEATING CHAIRPERSON (Reports to benefit chairperson)

Receives and records reservations, ticket payments and donations; gives checks to treasurer for deposit; pursues unpaid reservations; provides benefit chairperson with running tally of paid and unpaid reservations; makes table assignments and prepares seating chart.

SPECIFIC TASKS

- Allows her name and address to be printed on the return envelope of the invitation and her telephone number to be used in publicity about the event.
- Collects mail, posts daily receipts and files reservation reply cards, including seating requests.
- Acknowledges reservations with form letter, personalized if word processing is available, and sends tickets (if any) upon receipt of payment.
- Delivers checks promptly to treasurer; regularly double-checks her records against treasurer's to assure that all money and reservations are accounted for.
- Compiles table groupings from information provided by table hosts/hostesses and reservation reply cards.
- Assigns unpaired guests, VIPs and media representatives to unfilled tables with consent of hosts.
- Answers telephone inquiries about reservations; follows up by telephone all unpaid reservations and questions regarding seating requests.
- Frequently reports progress on and problems with reservations list to chairperson and development director.
- Provides head count to caterer by agreed-upon deadline (2 to 4 days in advance).
- In consultation with benefit chairperson and co-sponsor's representative, prepares seating chart according to dictates of established floor plan, taking care to honor seating requests and perks.
- Prepares alphabetized guest lists for use by chairperson, development officer, registration table workers and media.
- Fills out seating assignment cards to be presented to guests at benefit and coordinates their proper dissemination by registration table workers whom she has recruited.

QUALIFICATIONS

- Has experience in handling reservations and seating arrangements for previous benefits.
- Is well organized, precise, attentive to detail and able to maintain good humor under pressure of time and conflicting demands.
- Is able to keep accurate financial records.
- Is available by phone at predictable hours for 4 to 6 weeks preceding benefit.
- Is familiar with the organization's supporters and community benefit-goers, knows who's on friendly or non-speaking terms with whom, is sensitive to considerations of status, physical infirmities, etc.
- Is preferably a socially or civically prominent person who has a reputation as a gracious hostess.

TIME COMMITMENT

Approximately 10 hours per week, beginning 6 to 8 weeks before benefit; 20 to 30 hours per week during last 2 weeks and all day during last two days.

COMPOSITION OF COMMITTEE

3 to 4 people usually including the co-sponsor's representative and volunteers familiar with the organization's supporters.

TREASURER (Reports to benefit chairperson)

Responsible for financial record keeping and transactions.

SPECIFIC TASK

- Researches local banks for most favorable checking account rates; opens special checking account (preferably interest-earning) for benefit committee.
- Meets frequently with reservations chairperson to take receipt of checks; records and deposits all receipts from both ticket sales and contributions; double-checks books against reservations chairperson's records.
- Pays by check all expenses approved by benefit chairperson, who may also be required to sign checks.
- Supervises cash box and record keeping for raffle, auction or other income-producing activities at event itself.
- Provides monthly written reports and periodic updates of income and expenses to benefit executive committee; assists chairperson in preparing final financial report for board of trustees and development department.

QUALIFICATIONS

- Has ability to work with figures and some accounting or bookkeeping experience.

TIME COMMITMENT

Average 5 hours per week during 6 weeks before and 2 weeks after benefit.

COMPOSITION OF COMMITTEE

Usually a 1-person job.

UNDERWRITING CHAIRPERSON (Reports to benefit chairperson)

Secures funding and in-kind contributions from corporations and individuals for line items in budget

SPECIFIC TASKS

- Commits to underwriting goal as approved in budget.
- Compiles prospect list (individual and corporate) with help of

development director and assigns each subcommittee member
to call on prospects best known to him or her.
- Researches current names, addresses and phone numbers of
corporate CEOs or appropriate contact persons, if development
department does not provide this information.
- Researches appropriate timing of requests and proposals.
- Keeps accurate records of contacts made by each underwriting
committee member: acceptances, refusals, requests for additional
information or follow-up call.
- Coordinates or personally handles prompt follow-up on abovementioned requests.
- Acknowledges all donations promptly in writing.
- Reports all donations to benefit chairperson for inclusion in
printed program and to development office for records.

QUALIFICATIONS
- Has many personal or business contacts in position to make
contributions.
- Represents organization at a high level (is preferably a trustee)
and is familiar with its history.
- Is assertive but not pushy, well informed and able to make a
concise presentation, tenacious and positive in approach; in short,
a good salesperson.
- Has shown creativity in unearthing new funding sources.

TIME COMMITMENT
Approximately 10 hours per week during early planning period.

COMPOSITION OF COMMITTEE
8 to 10 members, mostly board members, ideally including president
and individuals prominent in community.

BENEFIT SECRETARY (Optional temporary paid position — reports to
benefit chairperson)

Assists benefit executive committee in clerical tasks relating specifically
to the event.

SPECIFIC TASKS
- Records, types and distributes minutes of all executive committee
and some subcommittee meetings, as needed; types and mails
meeting announcements and progress reports.
- Types committee lists, reservations/seating lists, correspondence,
publicity materials, copy for invitations, programs, etc., and final
report to trustees.
- Inputs or updates computer mailing list files, using information
provided by addressing/mailing committee; corrects mailing list
as undeliverable pieces return.

- Keeps records of contributions and ticket sales for underwriting and reservations/seating committees; turns over checks to treasurer; sends acknowledgement promptly to all ticket purchasers and donors; provides daily updated reservation list to benefit chairperson.
- Answers phone calls relating to benefit; provides basic information or referrals to appropriate executive committee members; relays messages to committee members.
- Makes and distributes photocopies of documents requested by executive committee.
- Provides further assistance to executive committee as requested.

QUALIFICATIONS
- Is a fast, accurate typist and has at least rudimentary bookkeeping skills; word processing experience is desirable.
- Is well organized, efficient, attentive to detail and able to work independently; has a pleasant, courteous manner, both in person and on the phone.
- Some experience working on benefits or with not-for-profit organizations is desirable.

HOURS
40 hours per week for 4 to 6 months prior to and 2 weeks after benefit.

ACCOUNTING AND TAX ADVICE

We are grateful to Thomas G. Stafford, CPA, partner of the Cleveland-based international accounting firm Ernst & Whinney and president of the Great Lakes Theater Festival board of trustees, and Donna Hartley, associate director of the Philanthropic Advisory Service of the Council of Better Business Bureaus based in Arlington, Virginia, for helping to answer some of the more common questions benefit committees and patrons have concerning tax-deductibility of benefit contributions. Each volunteer and patron should consult his or her tax advisor for specific information based on the current tax codes.

How do I know the organization sponsoring the benefit is a bona fide charity?
Incorporated not-for-profit organizations are designated tax exempt under Section 501 (c)(3) of the Internal Revenue Code (IRC). Contributions to such organizations are tax deductible by individuals for federal income tax purposes under Section 170. Most not-for-profit organizations make a statement in their annual reports or other publications to the effect that they qualify. When in doubt, ask an official of the organization whether it has applied for and been granted this status from the IRS. In addition, Publication 78 of the Internal Revenue Service, which lists all qualified charitable organizations, is available in many libraries or from the IRS.

How much of the benefit ticket price is tax deductible?

Only the amount given to the organization in excess of the fair market value of the privileges received qualifies as a tax-deductible contribution. Moreover, there must be evidence that the excess amount is intended as a gift. Though the burden of proof is on the taxpayer, benefit committees can help by providing the pertinent information on the invitation, ticket or receipt. For example, the reservation form might indicate: "$125 ticket ($75 tax deductible); $250 ticket ($200 tax deductible); $500 ticket ($450 tax deductible)." This means that the benefit committee has determined in advance that a fair market value for the event (one's prorated share of the food, drink, entertainment and so on) would be $50 and that the rest of the asking price is intended as a gift to the organization.

If the benefit's expenses are completely underwritten, does the entire ticket price count as a gift?

No, it makes no difference in the way the individual patron's deduction is calculated.

If a patron buys a ticket but doesn't attend the benefit, is the full amount tax deductible?

No, the same rules for determining the tax-deductible portion of the ticket price apply.

Can a patron deduct the amount paid for auction items or raffle tickets purchased at a benefit?

Not if the amount is less than or equal to the fair market value of the items offered, even though those items have been donated. Although raffle tickets often have the word "donation" printed next to the price, they don't qualify as deductions because they represent chances to win something of far greater value. Note also that raffle tickets may not be sold or sent through the U.S. mail.

Can one deduct personal expenses incurred while working on a benefit?

Volunteers may deduct mileage, telephone, postage and the cost of items such as decorations purchased and donated to the benefit. In addition, meals, travel and lodging are deductible in limited circumstances: if the taxpayer is away from home and if there is no significant element of personal pleasure, recreation or vacation in the travel. In other words, the deduction only applies if you travel expressly on benefit business, not if you happen to purchase decorations while on vacation.

Entertainment costs are deductible except to the extent that the individual receives personal benefit (the cost of a meal, for example, for the individual is not deductible but the cost of buying a meal for a potential benefit underwriter would be deductible). You may not take a deduction for time, however, even if you perform services for which you normally charge by the hour.

Can suppliers claim a deduction when donating their services?

Suppliers may deduct the cost of materials donated, but may not deduct wages of employees or themselves for time that they contribute to the benefit. The IRS will disallow a deduction for a contribution of services by an individual or firm that has made its own services available on a charitable basis (i.e., an airline contributing free airline tickets or a laundry contributing laundry services). However, a taxpayer can get a charitable deduction by contributing to charity the right to some other firm or person's services (i.e., a radio station donating the use of lodging and transportation acquired in exchange for radio advertising time).

What are the general guidelines for in-kind donations?

Individuals and corporations generally may deduct an amount equal to the fair market value of property donated to the charity. (Special rules for the contribution of appreciated ordinary income property such as the inventory of a corporation and capital-gain property may act to reduce the value of the gift in these circumstances.) The 1986 Tax Reform Act requires a qualified appraisal to support a deduction if the fair market value of the donated item is greater than $5,000. Gifts of appreciated property may generate a tax preference item for purposes of the alternative minimum tax. A corporation may not deduct gifts to fraternal associations. Property contributed by a corporation must be for personal, domestic use in order for the company to take a deduction.

Is there any limit to the amount that can be deducted in a given year?

Corporations may deduct donations of up to 10 percent of taxable income. Individuals' cash donations are limited to 50 percent of adjusted gross income. Non-cash contributions are limited to 30 percent of adjusted gross income, with certain elections available for capital-gain property. If the contribution is to a private foundation, it is further limited to 20 percent of adjusted gross income.

Is there a standard method to use in reporting income and expenses?

According to Stafford, "A specific, generally accepted method does not exist. Reporting in the overall budget of the organization should be as a component of 'contributed' or 'unearned' income depending on how the organization titles its revenues. The amount included should be the *net income* from the benefit."

"Net income" is defined as *gross income* (including all revenue from the event including ticket sale proceeds, cash contributions, raffle ticket sales, gross auction bids, admission fees and interest income on funds invested up to the date of the event), less expenses. Stafford asserts: "Gross income should also include the fair value of donated materials and facilities provided the organization has a clearly measurable and objective basis for determining the value." In other words, in-kind donations should be included as part of the benefit's gross income and subtracted as part of its expenses.

Index

BOOKS OF INTEREST FROM OCTAVIA PRESS

Photocopy this coupon to order additional copies of *The Ultimate Benefit Book* — or any of these other popular titles.

YES! Please send me:

Quantity

_____ *The Ultimate Benefit Book: How to Raise $50,000-Plus for Your Organization*, by Marilyn E. Brentlinger and Judith M. Weiss, $22.95 hardback

224 pages, including a variety of adaptable forms and planning aids

_____ *Superman at Fifty: The Persistence of a Legend*, edited by Dennis Dooley and Gary Engle, $16.95 hardback

192 pages, four 4-color plates

_____ *Halle's: Memoirs of a Family Department Store (1891-1982)*, by James M. Wood, Geranium Press, $29.95 hardback

224 pages, duotone photography and graphics

_____ *America's Soapbox: 75 Years of Free Speaking at Cleveland's City Club Forum*, by Mark Gottlieb and Diana Tittle, Citizens Press, $17.95 hardback

256 pages, illustrated; foreword by David S. Broder

Please add $1.50 postage and handling for one book, 50 cents for each additional book. Ohio residents add 6.5% sales tax. Deduct 10% on orders totalling $50 minimum before shipping and applicable sales tax.

_____ Payment enclosed _____ Please charge my: _____ MasterCard

_____ VISA _____ American Express

Account no. _____ Exp. date _____

Signature _____

Name _____

Address _____
(no P.O. Box numbers, please; we ship UPS)

City _____ State _____ Zip _____

Send form to: Octavia Press
3546 Edison Road
Cleveland, Ohio 44121